JOHN HICK'S THEOLOGY OF RELIGIONS

A Critical Evaluation

Gavin D'Costa

UNIVERSITY
PRESS OF
AMERICA

LANHAM • NEW YORK • LONDON

Copyright © 1987 by

University Press of America,® Inc.

4720 Boston Way
Lanham, MD 20706

3 Henrietta Street
London WC2E 8LU England

British Cataloging in Publication Information Available

Library of Congress Cataloging-in-Publication Data

D'Costa, Gavin, 1958-
John Hick's theology of religions.

Revision of thesis (Ph.D.)—University of Cambridge,
1986.
Bibliography: p.
Includes index.
1. Hick, John. 2. Christianity and other religions.
I. Title.
BL43.H53D37   1987   261.2'092'4   87-21569
ISBN 0-8191-6617-0 (alk. paper)
ISBN 0-8191-6618-9 (pbk. : alk. paper)

All University Press of America books are produced on acid-free
paper which exceeds the minimum standards set by the National
Historical Publication and Records Commission.

To: John Hick and Julius Lipner

-Teachers and friends-

ACKNOWLEDGEMENTS

This book is a version of my Ph.D thesis submitted to and accepted by the University of Cambridge in 1986. Many people, more than I could possibly mention, have supported, guided and stimulated me over the years of research. To them I am grateful. I especially wish to thank my research supervisor Dr Julius Lipner for his humane, astute and friendly guidance. Professor John Hick, an earlier teacher of mine, read and commented on many drafts during the writing of my thesis with generosity and penetration. To both these teachers and friends I owe a great deal. Throughout the writing of this book, the support and patience of Beryl Gladstone and my family has been (generally) unfailing.

I also wish to thank Professor John Hick and Professor Paul Knitter for use of copyright material.

CONTENTS

TECHNICAL NOTES

The following reference system will be used throughout the book to allow for brevity and clarity. All secondary sources, other than Hick's works, will be cited in the footnotes by means of an author-date system of reference. Full publication details will be found in the general bibliography which includes books, journal entries, and unpublished manuscripts.

There is a separate bibliography of Hick's published books and articles. The titles of his major works are abbreviated in the notes to reflect the title as clearly as possible. For example: J.Hick, God and the Universe of Faiths = GUF. A full list of abbreviations used is given below. All other works by Hick will be referred to by the author-date system.

The RSV Bible has been used for all biblical quotations. Diacritical marks have not been added to quotations when these have been omitted in the original text. The use of capital letters has also been left unchanged in cited material.

ABBREVIATIONS USED FOR HICK'S PRINCIPAL WORKS

Only the dates of editions cited in the thesis are given. Works edited by other authors with a contribution by Hick are also listed if the book is frequently cited. Full publication details can be found in the bibliography.

CC	Christianity at the Centre (1968)
DEL	Death and Eternal Life (1976)
EE	Encountering Evil, ed. S.Davis (1981)
EGL	Evil and the God of Love (1979)
FK1	Faith and Knowledge (Ist ed. – 1957)
FK2	Faith and Knowledge (2nd ed. – 1978)
GMN	God Has Many Names (1980)
GMNUS	God Has Many Names (US ed – 1982)
GUF	God and the Universe of Faiths (1977)
IM	Incarnation and Myth: The Debate Continued, ed. M.Goulder (1979)
MGI	The Myth of God Incarnate, ed. J.Hick (1977)
PR1	Philosophy of Religion (Ist ed. – 1964)
PR2	Philosophy of Religion (2nd ed. – 1973)
PR3	Philosophy of Religion (3rd ed. – 1983)
PRP	Problems of Religious Pluralism (1985)
SC	The Second Christianity (1983)
TCC	The Centre of Christianity (1977)
TD	Truth and Dialogue, ed. J.Hick (1974)
TEG	The Existence of God, ed. J.Hick (1964)
WBG	Why Believe in God?, with M.Goulder (1983)
WRT	The World's Religious Traditions: Current Perspectives

in Religious Studies. Essays in Honour of Wilfred Cantwell Smith, ed. F.Whaling (1984)

PREFACE

This book is an attempt to challenge the assumptions and directions of an increasingly influential approach by Christian theologians towards other religions. To this purpose, I concentrate on the theology of religions proposed by John Hick – probably the most influential representative of theological "pluralism". Loosely defined, the "pluralist" is concerned to maintain that all religions are equal and effective paths to the divine reality which Christians call "God". Hick is especially interesting because of the sophistication of his defence of pluralism. He has also developed his position over a number of years demonstrating, I believe, the logical outcome of theological pluralism. I offer a detailed outline and analysis of each stage of development. My questioning of pluralism is based on theological, philosophical and phenomenological considerations. However, my task is not entirely negative. In criticising Hick's theology of religions, (or more properly called in its later stages a philosophy of religions) I try and suggest an alternative and possibly more "traditional" approach and assessment of non-Christian religions in contrast to Hick.

The purpose of dividing the bibliographical section is to allow scholars interested in the theology of religions to have a useful bibliographical list for their students and themselves. The separation of Hick's entire bibliography will aid scholars in inspecting any aspect of Hick's thought and see the development of his intellectual interests. It is the most comprehensive bibliography of Hick's work to date.

While the book is addressed primarily to theologians and philosophers of religion, I hope that students of religious studies in general will find this work of use. If I have asked more questions than I have answered, my purpose will be achieved.

xi

CHAPTER 1: THE BACKGROUND TO JOHN HICK'S COPERNICAN REVOLUTION IN THE CHRISTIAN THEOLOGY OF RELIGIONS

(1.1).Introduction.

John Hick's proposals for a "new" approach in theological attitude towards non-Christian religions have sparked off debate in a number of countries.[1]   His work has been translated into Spanish, Dutch, Portuguese, Finnish, German, Japanese, Swedish, Korean, Hindi, Arabic and Chinese. His proposals have also stimulated a Jewish rabbi and a Muslim theologian to suggest[2] similar shifts within their own religious traditions.   Paul Knitter, an American theologian, has proclaimed that "Hick is the most radical, the best known, and therefore the most controversial of the proponents of a theocentric model for Christian approaches to other religions."[3]

In this book I wish to outline and critically examine John Hick's proposal for what he has called a "Copernican revolution" in the Christian theology of religions.   I use the term "Christian theology of religions" to designate what Cornelius Ernst has expressed so succinctly:

> By 'theology', in this context...I mean the activity of self-understanding...the explanatory, continually renewed effort within the Christian tradition to examine the implications of that tradition where it is continually being interrogated by the conjectures of historical change; the diversification of human experience by factors which are not themselves at the very least explicitly given in that tradition. The entrance of world religions into the course of European history forms one series of such factors of diversification.[4]

---

[1]. For example: Wickremesinghe 1979, from Indonesia; Das Gupta 1978, from India; Knitter 1985 pp.146-52, 175-76, from the United States; Forrester 1976 and Lipner 1976, from Europe; Almond 1983, from Australia.
[2]. Within Judaism: Sherbok 1984; within Islam: Askari 1982 ch.4, 1985. Askari & Hick 1985 contains essays from "like-minded" thinkers from within Judaism, Hinduism, Islam, Christianity and Buddhism on religious pluralism.
[3]. Knitter 1985 p.147
[4]. Ernst 1979 p.30. In Hick's early Copernican writings this is
(Footnote continued)

1

With the unavoidable consciousness that Christianity exists in a world of religious plurality, Christian attitudes to other religions are a pressing issue on today's theological agenda. The minutes resulting from such theological reflection will affect a number of practical issues. For example: how should religious education be taught; what kind of social and political cooperation is permissible with people of other faiths; is it proper to use Buddhist meditational techniques for prayer or Hindu scriptures in the liturgy? On a less institutional level, those mixing daily with people from other religions are faced with more personally pressing questions: is the Hindu really damned because he or she is not a Christian? How can one appropriately maintain a Christian witness in a shared house with three Sikh students? These issues primarily confront Christians who are being interrogated by the changing historical circumstances. However, it should be noted that the questions that are raised can be traced back to the very beginnings of the Christian tradition - primarily in relation to Christian apostates, Judaism, the Hellenistic religions, and later in relation to Islam.[5] Through its subsequent history, Christianity has eventually come into contact with all the major world religions. It is also possible that these questions, or at the very least their answers, may be of interest to non-Christians.[6]

The central theological question that arises in a Christian theology of religions is whether salvation is possible outside Christianity.[7] Hick expresses this succinctly in his first seminal essay on this topic: "Do we regard the christian way as the only way, so that salvation is not to be found outside it; or do we regard the other great religions of mankind as other ways of life and salvation?"[8] In addressing this problem I will examine a host of intrinsically related theological issues and

---

[4](continued)
also his understanding of the term (GUF pp.121-22), although recently he sometimes speaks of a "philosophy" of other religions, rather than a "Christian theology" of other religions
[5] see GMNUS ch.6. See 5.5.1 below.
. See ed. Sanders 1980, (et al) 1981, (& Meyer) 1982; Sandmel 1978; Brown 1967-1970; Cash 1937; Bühlmann 1982 ch.5 gives an overall view of "The Church's Associates in History".
[6]. The phrase "non-Christian" designates, within a single umbrella term, the variety of different beliefs and ways of life other than Christian. It is not pejorative.
[7]. The question of salvation within traditionally understood "non-religious" movements, such as Marxism, is implicitly addressed in dealing with the question of salvation outside Christianity.
[8]. GUF p.120.

tentatively answer some of the preceding practical questions. Very briefly, let us look at some of the theologial questions ahead.

The issues can be conveniently focused in relation to two traditionally held Christian axioms. The first axiom states that salvation is through Jesus Christ alone. If salvation is through Christ alone (Jn. 14:6, Acts 4:12) and there is no salvation outside Christianity, can the Christian still believe in a God who desires the salvation of all humankind (Acts 14:17, I Tim. 2:4, Rom. 2:6-7)? Could a loving God consign the majority of humankind to perdition because they did not know Jesus, often through no fault of their own? What also of the experience of "holiness" which one may encounter in a Buddhist friend or within the Muslim religion? Are these experiences deceptive? Related to this, one may ask what form missionary activity should take? Furthermore, is there anything of worth to be learned from other religions, or are they "properly" characterised as sinful grasping after idols?

Alternatively, if the stress falls on the second axiom that God desires the salvation of all humankind, is this salvation gained through or despite the non-Christian religions? If, on the one hand, salvation occurs through these religions is there any need for mission? And what of Jesus' claim that he alone is "the way, and the truth, and the life" and Christianity's claim to absoluteness? What of those within certain religions who do not even believe in a God, such as the Theravādin Buddhist or Advaitin Hindu? And what exactly is the status and worth of non-Christian scriptures, practices, beliefs and cultures? Are they all of equal value and if not, by what criteria should one decide?

However, if salvation can be found outside Christianity but only despite, and not through, the various religions, then how precisely does this happen? Will it occur through death-bed confrontation, or special interior revelation, or perhaps a rational assent to God? Do these explanatory theories do justice to the social and historical nature of men and women and the communitarian character of religion? And what of those non-Christians who seem to reflect the "presence of God" in their lives before they are on their death-beds? Will the attendant understanding of the nature and purpose of mission differ from those who believe that no salvation is possible outside Christianity? Within this perspective what is the perceived value of non-Christian scriptures, practices, beliefs and cultures?

A host of complicated and intriguing theological questions present themselves. These questions are related to central

---

[9]. See Percy 1961 p.9; Lindsell 1970; Sadgrove & Wright 1977.

theological issues concerning the nature of God, the human person, Christ, the Church and its mission, creation and history. In other words, what is the impact and challenge of the world religions upon Christology, ecclesiology and missiology?

Hick argues that a number of theological, philosophical and phenomenological considerations provide good grounds for adopting his "Copernican" approach. I shall outline his various arguments in chapter two. Negatively, they are aimed at rival theological approaches. In this respect, Hick's proposals must be viewed in the context of twentieth-century reflections on other religions if his position and its significance are to be fully appreciated. Positively, his arguments present a cumulative case for his own alternative approach.

In this chapter I will undertake two basic tasks to situate Hick's work in its historical and theological context. I shall present a biography of Hick's life, tracing significant and formative intellectual influences, while at the same time chronologically detailing his different theological interests and major publications. Then I shall offer an overview of some twentieth-century theologians who have undertaken the task of formulating a Christian theology of religions. This latter section should aid the reader in a number of ways. The survey will focus on some central issues which determine a Christian response to other religions. In subsequent chapters many of these issues will be examined in greater depth in relation to Hick's thesis. Hick often criticises or critically develops the positions of a number of theologians whom I shall discuss below. The survey will also help to situate Hick's theology of religions in its twentieth-century context, allowing us to gauge his relation with like-minded theologians. While my survey is not exclusively confined to theologians cited by Hick, I hope that it will provide a sense of the vitality, complexity and urgency of the questions with which I shall be dealing in this book.

Chapter one acts as an introduction to the historical and theological context of Hick's "Copernican revolution". It is mainly descriptive, but is unique in placing Hick's contribution in such a perspective. Although there have been various surveys of Christian attitudes to other religions which deal with Hick, none deals primarily with Hick's theology of religions, relating[10] this to other theological positions as I shall be doing. Understandably, journal articles on Hick's theology of religions have not attempted to place Hick within such an extensive historical and theological context.[11] Chapter one is also

---

[10]. See Warren 1976; Cragg 1977; Sadgrove & Wright 1977; Newbigin 1978; Toon 1978; Howard 1981; Cobb 1982; Race 1983; Anderson 1984; Coward 1985; Knitter 1985; Cracknell 1986.

unique in presenting the most comphrensive single biographical guide to Hick's life and works. It is rivalled only by a brief, but now outdated autobiographical essay written in 1979, [12], and an autobiographical essay written in 1983 which only adds to the previous one in relation to Hick's controversy with the Presbyterian Church regarding his beliefs in the 1960's on the virgin birth. [13] Chapter one also acts as a preparation to a detailed exposition of Hick's Copernican revolution (chapter 2), followed by a critical evaluation of Hick's proposals (chapter 3 and 4), up until some later radical developments in 1980. Finally, I deal with these later developments which constitute a minor revolution within the Copernican revolution itself (chapter 5).

(1.2). John Hick: A brief biography.

(1.2.1). First phase· 1922-1956: Early life, education and influences:

John Harwood Hick was born in Scarborough, Yorkshire on 20 January 1922 to Mark Day and Mary Aileen (Hirst) Hick. As a child he was taken to the "local Anglican parish church; and the services", he remembers, "were a matter of infinite boredom." [14] Despite this, after leaving Bootham School in York to read law at University College, Hull, Hick retained a "strong sense of the reality of God as the personal and loving Lord of the universe, and of life as having a meaning within God's purpose." [15] It is interesting to note that the eighteen-year-old Hick, later to be a champion of what I shall call religious "pluralism", recalls reading The Principles of Theosophy. Although initially impressed by its "comprehensive and coherent interpretation of life", he later "rejected it as being too tidy and impersonal." [16] One can see, even in this early stage, Hick's critical attraction towards total explanatory systems of thought.

In his first year at Hull, Hick "underwent a spiritual conversion in which the whole of Christian belief and experience came vividly to life." [17] For a theologian who was always travelling "forward" in his ideas, the young Hick's conversion took place appropriately "on the top deck of a bus". He

---

[11]. See for instance, Lipner 1975, 1976, 1977; Forrester 1976; Russell 1977; Wickremesinghe 1979; Byrne 1982; Almond 1983; Griffiths & Lewis 1983; Trigg 1983; Hughes 1984.
[12]. GMN ch.1.
[13]. PRP ch.1.
[14]. GMN p.1.
[15]. GMN pp.1-2.
[16]. GMN p.12.
[17]. GMN p.2.

continues, in a moving and humorous style:

> As everyone will be conscious who can
> themselves remember such a moment, all
> descriptions are inadequate. But it was
> as though the skies opened up and light
> poured down and filled me with a sense of
> overflowing joy in response to an immense
> transcendent goodness and love. I
> remember that I couldn't help smiling
> broadly - smiling back, as it were, at
> God - though if any of the other
> passengers were looking they must have
> thought that I was a lunatic, grinning at
> nothing.[18]

This was not the moment of conversion itself, which was spread
over several days, but just one particular incident within those
days. Mainly due to friendships with Inter-Varsity Fellowship
students (a conservative evangelical group), Hick "became a
Christian of a strongly evangelical and indeed fundamentalist
kind."[19]   Consequently, by 1940, Hick accepted wholeheartedly,

> the entire evangelical package of
> theology - the verbal inspiration of the
> Bible; creation and the fall; Jesus as
> God the Son incarnate, born of a virgin,
> conscious of his divine nature and
> performing miracles of divine power;
> redemption by his blood from sin and
> guilt; his bodily resurrection and
> ascension and future return in glory;
> heaven and hell.[20]

Hick would later come to question, reject or reinterpret
nearly all these beliefs,[21], and the form in which they were
initially held is therefore significant. What influences caused
the young Hick, who now wished to be ordained, to undergo such a
radical change of theological outlook?

Undoubtedly, many factors coalesced in Hick's development, but
three in particular may be usefully isolated. The first lies in
Hick's intellectual openness - his desire to take seriously
contemporary developments in the fields of theology, science,
sociology and later the study of the different world religions.
He aimed through this encounter with contemporary knowledge to

---

18. WBG pp.40-1.
19. GMN p.2.
20. GMN p.2.
21. See GUF ch.7, SC p.74.

6

expound a credible and rationally intelligible theology - a second factor. A third, which can be viewed negatively or positively, is his primarily philosophical, rather than theological, approach. Negatively, this is reflected in his lack of attention to tradition, ecclesiology and biblical theology. Positively, it denotes his fruitful dialogue with and response to some current philosophical trends - mainly limited to the Anglo-Saxon analytical tradition. [22]

In 1940 Hick entered the Presbyterian Church of England and enrolled at Edinburgh Univeristy to study philosophy. His evangelical leanings continued: "At Edinburgh I was a keen member of the Christian Union, attending virtually all its Bible studies, prayer meetings and talks." [23] However, he was also greatly "influenced by the teachings of Norman Kemp Smith, in the idealist tradition", who was the resident Professor of Logic and Metaphysics and a major Kantian scholar. [24] Hick became increasingly dissatisfied with his fellow evangelicals' "narrowness and...lack of sympathy with questioning thought." [25] Here we can dimly recognise Hick's later distinction and characterisation of the "two Christianities" within Christianity. [26] The "conservative evangelicals", the first Christianity, are characterised as devotionally strong, with a "simplistic conceptuality...which is upset or confused by theological and political experimentation." [27] The "second Christianity" seems to consist of liberal Christians, who are truth seekers rather than confessional proclaimers, [28] ', 29 involved in more "experimental forms of Christianity." [29] It is interesting to note that Hans Küng and Edward Schillebeeckx are seen as members of the "second Christianity", whereas by default, other Roman Catholic theologians such as Hans von Balthasar, Karl Rahner, Henri de Lubac, Cornelius Ernst, Yves Congar and Bernard Lonergan are presumably equated with "conservative evangelicals", or perhaps "conservative non-evangelicals" who nevertheless still

---

22. Hick neglects continental trends such as existentialism, transcendental analysis, or the hermeneutical tradition. M.Heidegger and J.P.Satre receive brief attention in DEL pp.97-104. K.Rahner is given some consideration: see GUF pp.127f, 1984a. There is a brief review of Ricoeur, The Symbolism of Evil, (1968g). Hick's dialogue partners are primarily Anglo-Saxon positivists and analytical philosophers such as B.Russell, A.J.Ayer, L.Wittgenstein's disciple D.Z.Phillips, R.B.Braithwaite, J.H.Randall, N.Malcolm and J.Wisdom.
23. GMN p.3.
24. FK2 p.v.
25. GMN p.3.
26. SC p.74.
27. SC p.74.
28. GMN pp.80-1.
29. SC p.84.

belong to the first Christianity. [30]   This is not a polemical
point. I wish to indicate Hick's range of sympathies. He writes,
I "can still enter imaginatively into the conservative
evangelical thought world", which for him is equated with
"established orthodoxy". [31]   The other thought world which Hick
in fact inhabits is that of modern liberal Christianity. For
Hick, these seem to be the main available options. [32]   Hick's
imaginative sympathies are relevant in regard to his evaluation
and schematization of the different approaches to non-Christian
religions - as outlined below.

The outbreak of the Second World War interrupted Hick's
studies. As a conscientious objector he joined the Friends
Ambulance Unit. [33]   In 1944, at the age of twenty two, Hick
recalls being on a "troop ship that was being attacked by
submarines just outside the Straits of Gibraltar". [34]   In
slightly more reflective moments during the Italian winter that
same year, Hick wrote a sketch for what would later be his first
book, Faith and Knowledge. [35]   This diligence and
single-mindedness characterise Hick's career in taking up
particular problems: faith and cognition, theodicy, the cognitive
status of religious language, eschatology, and the theology of
religions - and constantly applying himself to these issues.

After the war Hick returned to Edinburgh, graduating with
first class honours in 1948. With the aid of a Campbell-Fraser
scholarship, he began research at Oriel College, Oxford "under
the benign but penetratingly critical supervision of H.H.Price"
who was then Wykham Professor of Logic. [36]   Price's influence
on Hick is implicit, but undeniable. [37]   In his doctoral thesis,

---

[30]. Hick May 1984 (private letter) describes these theologians as
belonging to a "conservative non-evangelical" first Christianity.
[31]. GMN p.3.
[32]. This is the case in his debate with Goulder in WBG, where the
options available, for both, seem to be either "red-blooded
fundamentalist theology" (p.68) or Hick's form of liberal
Christianity - which is obviously too liberal for Goulder (p.27).
[33]. Hick 1954a, GMN p.3.
[34]. TCC p.110.
[35]. FK2 p.v.
[36]. FK2 p.v.
[37]. Price (1953a) was interested in problems of perception and
thinking. Hick refers to this book in FK2 p.122. Price (1938 p.6)
also criticised Braithwaite for misunderstanding the "realist"
intention of theistic language. Hick's criticism of Braithwaite,
some years later (PRP pp.90-3), reiterates Price's objections.
Price (1938 p.18), like Hick (PR2 p.30), was sceptical about
proofs for the existence of God and thought that science, while
not disproving theism did not support it either. Price turned to
(Footnote continued)

8

The Relationship Between Faith and Belief, Hick developed the idea of faith as an "interpretative element within religious experience, arising from an act of cognitive choice." [38] He stressed the subject's interpretation of events in a world which is essentially ambiguous and capable of various interpretations. Consequently, for Hick, the veracity of religious experience depends on verification in the next life. Hick's epistemological presuppositions, which have a decidedly Kantian pedigree, affect his entire corpus. Hick says of Faith and Knowledge, (which was a re-working of his doctoral thesis):

> If one wanted to set this in a tradition one would have to refer to Kant as the thinker whose philosophical revolution made possible theories in which the subjective contribution to knowledge is given a key role. [39]

Hick also acknowledges the influence of John Oman's, The Natural and the Supernatural, thereby indicating indebtedness to a tradition leading back to Schleiermacher – and a strong emphasis on religious experience. [40] This emphasis on religious experience, rather than "discrete arguments or even proof" as the basis for belief, inevitably led Hick seriously to consider non-Christian religious experience. [41] If one's own experience is treated seriously, Hick later argued, then the golden rule requires that the experience of others is treated with equal seriousness. [42]

Having completed his doctoral thesis in 1950, Hick went on to

---

[37] (continued)
parapsychology and psychical research for the answers. Hick turned to religious experience and included, in his later writings, parapsychological evidence. In DEL pp.256-70, Hick shows sympathy with Price's (1953b) post-mortem, mind-dependent world.
[38]. FK2 p.v.
[39]. FK2 p.viii. See also Mathis 1985 pp.6-7; Brakenheilm 1975 ch.3; and 5.2.and 5.5 below.
[40]. Hick's debt to Oman is evident in FK1 pp.xix,130,166,173,182. Hick sees his own work as developing "Oman's basic standpoint in relation to the very different world of contemporary philosophy." (FK2 p.7). Oman argued that religious consciousness is an immediate, self-authenticating awareness of the supernatural. Oman's main concern was to show that religious experience was not isolated from, but continuous with, other spheres of experience. Hick inherited both these concerns. Oman, deeply influenced by Schleiermacher, was also the first English translator of Reden uber die Religion in 1893. Significantly, Schleiermacher tried to
(Footnote continued)

9

Westminster Theological College, Cambridge to train for the ministry. He had intended entering the ministry for a number of years. For three years he undertook his first formal study of theology. Hick's courses consisted of Old and New Testament studies, Christian Doctrine and Church History. During this period he was deeply influenced by Herbert Farmer, lecturer in Christian Doctrine at Cambridge University. Farmer was himself taught by Oman, his "revered teacher and friend".[43] Farmer also considered Christianity's relation to other religions,[44] and was involved in the Tambaram Missionary Conference in 1938.[45] Hick recalls Farmer as one of the two best preachers he has heard, the other being Reinhold Niebuhr. He remembers enjoying all the courses at Cambridge with the exception of Church History.[46]

Hick married (Joan) Hazel Bowers,[47] and moved north to Belford Presbyterian (now United Reformed) Church, Northumberland, to his only parish appointment. During these years, 1953-1956, he wrote the manuscript for his first book, Faith and Knowledge, and dedicated it to the "kindness of the congregation and the office bearers" of the Belford Church.[48]

(1.2.2). Second phase: 1956-1967: Early teaching career and "orthodox" period:

Faith and Knowledge was published by Cornell University Press when Hick was appointed Assistant Professor of Philosophy at Cornell University (1956-1959). His next appointment was to the Stuart Professorship of Christian Philosophy, Princeton Theological Seminary (1959-1964). In 1961-1962 Hick was involved

---

[40](continued)
navigate a course between contemporary German rationalism and the dominant formalist orthodoxy and argued that the essence of religion was not to be sought exclusively in the will or in dogma (compare Hick's Scylla and Charybdis: William James' voluntarism, and Aquinas' intellectualist propositional notion of faith - see FK2 chs. 1-2). The essence of religion was to be found in the inner feelings and intuitions of the divine. Schleiermacher, with his interest in all forms of religious experience, prefigured Hick's attention to non-Christian religious experience - see Sykes 1971 pp.47-9. Schleiermacher defines religion as the "feeling of absolute dependence" which is universally experienced in the world religions, and most clearly in Christianity (1928 pp.17, 383ff). This feeling of dependence was exemplified in Jesus' special relationship to the Father. Hick's later Christology introduces Schleiermacher's phrase, "God-consciousness", without acknowledging the term's ancestry. This historical background is missing from Brakenhielm's study of Hick's epistemology (1975 ch.3).
[41]. FK2 p.18.

in contesting the validity of his ministry with the United
Presbyterian Church because of his beliefs regarding the virgin
birth. [49]   Inklings of his later liberal leanings were present.
During this period he developed three major concerns. First,
arguments about the necessary existence of God. [50]   Second, a
topic which continually preoccupied Hick - a defence against
logical positivist criticisms of theistic language. [51]   Hick
accepted the basic empiricist insight that to "exist" is to make
an in-principle observable difference, thereby accepting an
empiricist notion of verification and falsification as being
applicable both to the natural sciences and theology. The third
concern, also a life-time preoccupation, was with the problem of
evil.

Since 1962 Hick had been writing <u>Evil</u> <u>and</u>   <u>the</u> <u>God</u> <u>of</u> <u>Love</u>.
After thinking that <u>Faith</u> <u>and</u> <u>Knowledge</u> would be his only book,
he became increasingly absorbed with the "theodicy issue, the
question whether the reality of suffering and wickedness are
compatible with the reality of a loving God." [52]   His theodicy
was "built upon the epistemology developed in <u>Faith</u> <u>and</u>
<u>Knowledge</u>, particularly the notions of 'epistemic distance' and
of faith as a fundamental expression of human freedom." [53]   Hick
felt that theism must stand or fall upon the resolution of this
issue and his "Irenaean" theodicy was to be a determinative
influence on both his later theology of religions and his
eschatological speculations. [54]

In 1963 Hick took up the S.A.Cook Bye-Fellowship at Gonville
and Caius College, Cambridge. Hick gained a Cambridge Ph.D by
incorporation. He returned to Princeton seminary for one semester

---

42. <u>GMNUS</u> p.24.
43. <u>Farmer</u> 1954 p.x.
44. Farmer 1954.
45. Farmer 1939.
46. Hick July 1984 (private letter).
47. Hick had four children, one of whom died in 1985.
48. <u>FK</u> p.vi.
49. See <u>PRP</u> pp.1-4.
50. Hick 1960j,k; 1961c.
51. The debate was initiated in eds. Flew & MacIntyre 1955. The
positivist movement has English roots in Hume and Locke, and in
Wittgenstein which influenced the Vienna Circle - see Magee 1982
pp.76-93. Hick responded to the empiricist challenge in 1960e,
and reprinted this essay along with other important contributions
to the debate in <u>TEG</u>.
52. <u>GMN</u> p.4.
53. <u>GMN</u> p.4, <u>FK2</u> p.vi.
54. By Irenaean, rather than Augustinian, Hick intends and
proposes the view of a gradual development, in response to the
(Footnote continued)

and then took up the post of Lecturer in Divinity at Cambridge University (1964-1967). During this period he published Evil and the God of Love (1966), numerous articles and reviews, and a notable Christological contribution in a Festschrift for H.H.Farmer. [55] This latter essay gathered scattered reflections from previous years, [56], and marked his last close identification with what he termed the "full orthodox faith" before he began a gradual [57] and ultimately radical shift of theological perspective. Fifteen years later, Hick noticed that he held a position which he had previously criticised in the above cited Christological essay. [58]

(1.2.3). Third phase: 1967-1986: The beginnings of the Copernican revolution to recent times:

Hick's theological shift began after he left Cambridge in 1967 to occupy the H.G.Wood Professorship in Birmingham University's Theology Department. Three inter-connected problems coincidentally confronted Hick, resulting in his Copernican theology of religions. The first arose as an implication of his Irenaean theodicy:

> I had concluded that any viable Christian theodicy must affirm the ultimate salvation of all God's creatures. How then to reconcile the notion of there being one, and only one, true religion with a belief in God's universal saving activity? [59]

Although Hick only briefly mentioned this problem in his Christological essay, [60], a year later he made some prophetic remarks on a possible resolution of this issue. [61]

---

[54] (continued)

challenges of life, of men and women into children of God (see EGL) - a development which he later saw as extending over many lives in many worlds (see DEL). See Mathis 1985 ch.4 - who argue that eschatological verification is unnecessary to affirm the cognitive value of religious language.

[55]. Hick 1966e.

[56]. Hick 1958a, 1959a,g; 1960d,g.

[57]. GMN p.3.

[58]. Hick GMN p.3. It is all the more surprising that Hick juxtaposes this "orthodox" essay (1966e) with his "unorthodox" suggestions in GUF chs.11,12 respectively.

[59]. GMN pp.4-5.

[60]. Hick 1966e p.16.

[61]. CC pp.80-1.

12

His Copernican theology was also precipitated by his "move...to Birmingham, with its large Muslim, Sikh and Hindu communities, as well as its older Jewish communities," which made this issue "a live and immediate one" for him.[62] His involvement in race and community relations work brought him into even closer contact with people from other faiths.[63] A third factor contributing to Hick's Copernican shift was his plan to write a major work on eschatology based on eschatological thought in Hinduism, Buddhism, Christianity and Humanism. This began in 1970 and was published six years later as Death and Eternal Life. Coinciding with Hick's theological and practical interests, he travelled to India (1974 and 1975-1976) and to Sri Lanka (1974), ostensibly to learn about "indian conceptions of reincarnation" for this book.[64] Death and Eternal Life is also Hick's main contribution to the programme of "global theology". That is, "the construction of theologies (in the plural) based upon the full range of man's religious awareness", and not exclusively upon one religious tradition.[65]

Cumulatively these factors, combined with Hick's increasingly liberal theological leanings, resulted in Hick gently dipping his theological toes into new waters before taking the plunge in his controversial God and the Universe of Faiths.[66] In this book, Hick argued that the incarnation should be understood metaphorically or mythically, not literally as had apparently been the case for most of Christian history. A literal understanding was untenable in the light of modern biblical and philosophical thought. Most importantly, this new mythological understanding allowed for a viable theology of religions whereby Christ would not be seen as the sole means of salvation, but that God should instead inhabit the centre of the universe of faiths

---

62. GMN p.5.
63. Hick held the following positions - 1969-1974: Chairman of the Religious and Cultural Panel, Birmingham Community Relations Committee; 1971-1974: Chairman of the Co-ordinating Working Party, Statuatory Conference for Revision of Agreed Syllabus of Religious Education; 1972-1974: Co-founder and President of All Faiths for One Race; 1972-1973, 1978-1980: Chairman of Birmingham Interfaiths Council. See PRP pp.4-15.
64. DEL p.16. In India, Hick was visiting Professor at Banaras Hindu University, Visva Bharati University, the Punjabi University, and attended the International Seminar on World Philosophy at the University of Madras. In Sri Lanka he was British Academy Overseas Visiting Fellow at the University of Ceylon (sic).
65. GUF p.103.
66. Hick tried his ideas out in various lectures, seminars and articles (see GUF pp.xi-xii) before collecting them together in GUF. As early as 1970 he had given some attention to the problems of a theology of religions, see TD pp.164ff.

and salvation. Hick uses an astronomical analogy. Ptolemaic astronomers saw the earth at the centre of the universe and explained the movements of planets (which did not conform to the theory) by postulating "epicycles". The growing number of epicycles rendered the Ptolemaic view less and less plausible. Finally the Copernican view, in its simple explanation of the facts by the theory that the sun, rather than the earth, was at the centre of the universe, replaced it. [67] In an analogous manner, Hick thinks that the old Ptolemaic theology (which he characterises as completely denying salvation to non-Christians) and its more recent epicycles (whereby non-Christians are regarded, for example, as hidden or anonymous Christians) props up an increasingly implausible system with the Church/Christianity/Christ at the centre of the universe of faiths. Instead, God should be at the centre. Consequently, he proposes a Copernican revolution in theology whereby Christians "shift from the dogma that Christianity is at the centre to the realisation that it is God who is at the centre and that all religions...including our own, serve and revolve around him." [68] Hick's Copernican attitude was to characterise and shape his future thinking, and God and the Universe of Faiths acts as a landmark for the beginning of Hick's radical theological developments.

By taking on this Copernican mantle in theology, Hick indirectly aligned himself with the Copernican revolution in philosophy initiated by Immanuel Kant. We have already noted Kant's influence on Hick. Kant thought he had initiated a "Copernican revolution" in philosophy by his turning away from the object of perception, to the knowing subject. [69] Ironically, Copernicus removed the earth and humankind from the centre of the universe and Kant, with his attention to the knowing subject, put them back again!

For three years after the publication of God and the Universe of Faiths, Hick was preoccupied with completing his eschatological magnum opus, Death and Eternal Life. Despite this massive task and other involvements, Hick still attended to questions he had raised concerning the Christian theology of religions and its Christological implications. [70]

---

[67]. For an account of the Copernican revolution, see Kuhn 1957. Incidentally, Copernicus' theory eventually needed more epicycles than did Peurbach's revision of Ptolemy's system in order to maintain its plausibility!
[68]. GUF p.131.
[69]. Kant 1933 p.28. Gilson (1963 pp.440) implies that Kant's attention to the subject created a substantial rift in philosophical thinking and a move away from realism towards solipsism. Some of the criticisms that I shall later direct at Hick were also similarly directed at Kant - see 5.3 below.

After Death and Eternal Life was published in 1976, Hick returned more vigorously to his Copernican theology. 1977 marked another important milestone with his editorship of the controversial book, The Myth of God Incarnate. Hick argued that biblical criticism (and here he relied heavily on his co-contributors) and the evidence from other religions required a mythological, rather than literal, understanding of incarnational language. His contribution reiterated the thesis of God and the Universe of Faiths (ch.12). For some years a theological debate ensued over the Christological issues raised by The Myth of God Incarnate, highlighted by a conference (in 1978) which resulted in the publication of Incarnation and Myth: The Debate Continued (1979).[71]

Hick also continued to attend to other problems raised by his Copernican revolution.[72] For instance, while on a lecture tour in South Africa and as Visiting Professor at the Department of Divinity at the University of Natal, Hick was the major guest at a conference entitled "Cross Currents in Contemporary Christology".[73] Besides Christological and other implications, the Copernican shift inevitably involved philosophical problems which Hick began to tackle in the 1980's.[74]

Attention to these philosophical problems coincided with Hick's move, in 1982, to the Department of Religion, Claremont Graduate School, California, as Danforth Professor of the Philosophy of Religion. He had been part-time Professor at Claremont since 1979, travelling between Claremont and Birmingham for three years. Some of his writings since 1980, and certainly since 1982 seem to reflect a significant "epicycle" within Hick's own Copernican position. His theological reflections on the issues of religious pluralism were carried out in a multi-faith academic environment. The distinguished Buddhist scholar, Masao Abe, and the process theologian John Cobb were useful and stimulating colleagues to Hick.[75] In 1983 Hick also became Director of the Blaisdell Programs in World Religions and

---

[70]. Hick 1973j, 1974a,b; 1975a,b,c,d,e,h,i.
[71]. See also ed. Green 1977; Newlands 1980; ed. Harvey 1981, and IM pp.1-15.
[72]. Hick 1977g,h; 1978b, 1979d, and the significant re-editing and re-naming of CC to TCC.
[73]. Hick 1981d; and 1980d for his observations on apartheid.
[74]. GMNUS ch.6, originally published in 1980, was the first of many essays dealing with a variety of philosophical problems, collected together in PRP.
[75]. Abe 1980, argues for the end of religions, an even more radical position than Hick's. See also Abe 1985. Cobb (1975, 1982) offers a process perspective on other religions.

15

Cultures. [76]   While working mainly on his theology of religions, and updating previous publications, Hick has also maintained his wider theological interests in theodicy, epistemology and eschatology. [77]   In 1986 Hick delivered the Gifford Lectures in Edinburgh - which are to be published in 1988.

My book will deal with Hick's work up to and including December 1986. A critic may argue that my comments have a tentative status, for Hick could further refine and develop his position. However, this is unavoidable in any examination of a contemporary theologian and I believe that this possible shortcoming is adequately compensated for the following reasons. Hick has shown a constant and somewhat logical development in his theology of religions [78] it is unlikely that he will shift from his present direction.   Hence, my analysis of his position, its genesis and development, will be pertinent both in regard to a study of Hick specifically and also, more generally, to the problems involved in a theology of religions. Consequently, a constructive dialogue with and criticism of Hick's position up to 1986 will further the overall intention of my book: to discern the proper theological principles involved in formulating a Christian theology of religions. This will help point towards a "third Christianity" (extending Hick's metaphor) which may offer a viable theology of religions. However, fully examining and developing this "third Christianity" would be a project for future investigation. [79]

(1.3). <u>Some</u> <u>twentieth-century</u> <u>views</u> <u>on</u> <u>Christianity's</u> <u>relation</u> <u>to</u> <u>other</u> <u>religions.</u> <u>A</u> <u>background</u> <u>and</u> <u>context</u> <u>to</u> <u>John</u> <u>Hick's</u> <u>Copernican</u> <u>revolution.</u>

Hick argues that there are three main approaches adopted by Christians towards other religions. [80]   The first, he terms

---

[76]. He has organised a number of conferences and lectures, most notably on Gandhi (book forthcoming) and "Religious Pluralism" (book forthcoming) and a lecture by Smith - see Smith 1985.
[77]. This can be seen in Hick's constant (although not always consistent) updating of PR (1963, 1973, 1983), and CC to TCC, and then to SC. An example of inconsistency is seen in his retaining the title (used in CC pt.4): "The ultimate unity of mankind before God", in the updated version of SC. Elsehwere, in these two versions, Hick often replaces the term "God" with the neutral term of "Eternal One", but he does not carry out this procedure consistently. This is also reflected in the odd title of the US edition of GMN where the argument of the book demands the title The Eternal One Has Many Names.
[78]. This consideration is justified in my exposition in ch.2.
[79]. See D'Costa 1986a.

16

<u>exclusivism</u>. This position, he argues,

> relates salvation/liberation exclusively
> to one particular tradition, so that it
> is an article of faith that salvation is
> restricted to this one group; the rest of
> mankind being either left out of account
> or explicitly excluded from the sphere of
> salvation. [81]

The second paradigm, or approach, he calls <u>inclusivism</u> which in various ways affirms that "God's forgiveness and acceptance of humanity have been made possible by Christ's death, but that the benefits of this sacrifice are not confined to those who respond to it with an explicit act of faith." [82] Compared to the exclusivists approach, this second option still retains, according to Hick, the Ptolemaic world view, for it still "assumes without question that salvation is only in Christ and through incorporation into his mystical body, the church." [83] Hence, inclusivist theologies are Ptolemaic theological "epicycles". The third approach, or paradigm, is labelled <u>pluralism</u>, whereby the great religions are seen as equally valid and different ways of salvation: "In Christian theological terms, there is a plurality of divine revelations, making possible a plurality of forms of saving response." [84] It is within this third option that Hick places his own work.

Although such a typology may be in danger of neglecting differences within each approach, it is heuristically useful in isolating the different paradigms underlying the various Christian attitudes. In what follows, I will try to flesh out Hick's distinctions focusing on some seminal theologians and their underlying presuppositions. In doing this, I will attempt to locate Hick within a twentieth-century historical and theological tradition of religious "pluralism" in relation to other currents of opinion. This will provide a proper context for understanding the novelty or otherwise of Hick's proposals, and the positions and assumptions that he attacks. Although I am in basic agreement with Hick's classification, I have chosen to call these three approaches <u>paradigms</u> in a sense analogous to that proposed by Thomas Kuhn - as a whole set of methods and procedures dictated by a central problem-solving model. [85]

---

80. This typology has been adopted by a number of theologians - see for example, Race 1983; Cracknell 1986.
81. <u>WRT</u> p.150.
82. <u>WRT</u> p.152.
83. <u>GUF</u> p.126.
84. <u>WRT</u> p.153.
85. Kuhn 1970, 1974. See Bernstein 1983 pt.II, for a perceptive defence of Kuhn from the charge of paradigm incommensurability.

Practitioners within one paradigm tend to share a number of basic presuppositions dictating their attitudes and approaches to solving problems. If the problem is the relation of Christianity to other religions, then the paradigmatic presuppositions will be certain theological tenets which dictate the various answers. Such a model also usefully accommodates diversity within a paradigm, while facilitating inspection of the key issues determining each paradigm.

To set the scene I shall selectively consider Protestant and Roman Catholic thought on our subject during the first half, and then in the latter part, of this century.[86] I have employed these subdivisions so that the material may be clearly assimilated and also because there are certain themes and concerns often related to theologians in particular traditions. For instance, the importance of ecclesiology is more often, although not exclusively, a concern for Catholic theologians. Furthermore, Hick's own analysis distinguishes between Catholic and Protestant responses to religious plurality. As Hick does not mention the Eastern Churches' contribution to the debate, I have not considered Eastern theologians.[87]

(1.4). The background: 1900-1950.

(1.4.1). Protestant theology: 1900-1950:

During this period heated and creative discussions took place in missionary circles. Three distinctive paths can be discerned in the theological landscape. In 1913, John Farquhar's The Crown of Hinduism gave forceful and clear expression to the view that Christ (and not Christianity) was the fulfilment and crown of Hinduism, analogous to Christ's fulfilment of the law and prophets of Judaism. He argued that his thesis was not an imposition of Christian categories on to something entirely alien, but was substantiated by a historical encounter and detailed study of the dynamics of Hinduism.[88] For Farquhar, missionary activity sought not to destroy but to fulfil the potential in Hinduism which only Christ could bring to fruition.[89] Missionary activity was important, although not primarily to

---

86. Subsequently "Catholic" will be used for "Roman Catholic".
87. The exception is Hick's reference to Khodr 1974. This reference is in relation to Khodr's tracing what Hick interprets as a pluralist strand, "though only a slender one, within the total Christian tradition." - GUF p.174. However, Khodr is clearly an inclusivist as noted by Knitter 1985 p.136; see also Verghese 1974, another Eastern Orthodox theologian.
88. Nevertheless, Farquhar was criticised on both historical and theological grounds: see Hogg 1914; Sharpe 1977 p.29, 1971 ch.4.
89. For like-minded theologians of this period and further discussion of Farquhar, see Sharpe 1962, 1965.

18

bring Hindus into the Christian Church, but to bring them to Christ. Hence, in his view Hinduism is understood as incipiently[90] included within the Christian plan of salvation.

Although Farquhar's work is well known as representing the beginnings of twentieth-century Protestant inclusivism, he is by no means the first exponent of such a view in the twentieth[91] century. This inclusivist note was echoed in later theology, especially in Catholic circles, fulfilling Farquhar's position, so to speak, with an emphasis on the fulfilment taking place through the Christian Church and not in Christ alone. A general difference in emphasis between Catholic and Protestant theology is in terms of the Catholic stress on the indivisible relation between Christ and, in Hick's terms, "his mystical body, the church."[92]

If Farquhar represented the emergence of modern inclusivism, the later works of Ernst Troeltsch and the work of William Hocking exemplified the seeds of Protestant "pluralism". Hick has not referred to Hocking's work, which I shall turn to in a moment, but has referred to Troeltsch as a precursor of his own[93] Copernican pluralism. Troeltsch developed his position from that initially taken in 1911 in his later book, Christian Thought. Its History and Application. Earlier Troeltsch had argued that Christianity was the absolute religion for all humankind in as much as its specialness lies in developing "the personalistic religious idea and its liberating power to its maximum clarity and strength."[94] However, this absoluteness was in principle surpassable, although Troeltsch considered it unlikely that any new revelatory event would be comparable. Hence, the earlier work of Troeltsch represented a type of inclusivism, for all that is good and true finds its culmination and fulfilment in Christianity. He wrote of the Christian revelation, that it "must be understood not only as the culmination point but also as the convergence point of all the[95] developmental tendencies that can be discerned in religion."

---

90. Farquhar 1930 pp.457-58.
91. Dewick (1953 p.120) notes that this approach "can be traced, almost (though perhaps not quite) continuously throughout the history of the Church". Hick does not refer to Farquhar's work. For some important Protestant inclusivist theologies before Farquhar, see Maurice 1866; Slater 1903.
92. GUF p.126. See Schineller 1976, for a nuanced analysis of the differences within modern Catholic theologies of the Church, and also the diversity within other Christian denominations, which qualifies this generalisation.
93. GUF p.174.
94. Troeltsch 1972 p.125.
95. Troeltsch 1972 p.114.

19

However, Troeltsch's position underwent a substantital shift. In an unpublished paper, Hick notes that Troeltsch's later work represents a "paradigm shift from" a "'pre-Copernican' or 'Ptolemaic' view" to "a 'post-Copernican' view of the relation[96] between Christianity and the other world religions." Troeltsch's sociological and historical studies eventually led him to conclude that Christianity could not viably claim special status or superiority among the world religions, but should be seen as one among many paths of salvation which takes its distinctive shape due to its cultural milieu. For Troeltsch, Christianity must now be regarded as a "purely historical, individual, relative phenomenon, which could, as we actually find it, only have arisen in the territory of the classical cultures, and among the Latin and Germanic races."[97] Troeltsch regarded the comparision of whole cultures and civilisations (and therefore religions)[98] as an impossible task, reserved exclusively for "God Himself". Consequently, one could only legitimately claim the validity and truth of Christianity for oneself - as one experienced it within western culture. To claim, for instance, that it was more valid than another religion, or that it invalidated other religions, would be to claim the inadmissible, and would only reflect a western cultural superiority.[99] Hick twice cites a seminal passage from Troeltsch's later work showing Troeltsch to be the father of twentieth-century pluralism. Troeltsch writes that Christianity is a manifestation of Divine Life in the west (note also the Schleiermachieran emphasis on experience):

> The evidence we have for this remains essentially the same, whatever may be our theory concerning absolute validity - it is the evidence of a profound inner experience. This experience is undoubtedly the criterion of its validity, but, be it noted, only of its validity <u>for</u> <u>us</u>. It is God's countenance as revealed to us; it is the way in which, being what we are, we receive, and react to, the revelation of God. It is binding upon us, and brings us deliverance. It is final and unconditional for us, because we have nothing else, and because in what we have

---

96. Hick 1978m p.2.
97. Troeltsch 1923 p.22.
98. Troeltsch 1923 p.27.
99. See Pye's (1976) criticism of Troeltsch for this type of cultural relativism. See also Adams 1961/62; Santmire 1973 pp.365-99; Coakley 1979; Race 1983 pp.78ff; Knitter 1985 pp.23-36.

> the possibility that other racial groups,
> living under entirely different cultural
> conditions, may experience their contact
> with the Divine Life in a quite different
> way, and may themselves also possess a
> religion which has grown up with them,
> and from which they cannot sever
> themselves so long as they remain what
> they are.[100]

It is interesting to note that many of the criticisms aimed at Hick have previously been directed at Troeltsch.[101] This is hardly surprising as Hick seems to support Troeltsch's position when he writes:

> Nevertheless (minor) shortcomings do not
> vitiate Troeltsch's central insight that
> each of the great world religions is
> 'absolute' in its own estimation, but
> that we have to recognise a plurality of
> such 'absolutes'.[102]

Troeltsch, like Hick, tended to view the various religions as legitimate and different revelations of God's activity and precluded the idea of a common world religion.[103] In this respect, they both envisaged that ultimate unity "will be an eschatological unity".[104]

Hocking, on the other hand, argued that there was a future common essence to the world religions which could only eventually emerge through the critical interaction between the different religions in history. Hocking, in the idealist tradition, regarded all the world religions to be moving towards the future "spiritual unity of all men and races."[105] Hocking was

---

[100]. Troeltsch 1923 p.26. Cited by Hick in GUF p.174; 1978m pp.2-3.

[101]. Coakley 1979 pp.243ff notes their similarities and differences.

[102]. Hick 1978m p.5. The two shortcomings that Hick refers to concern Troeltsch's alleged equation of religions with races rather than cultures – although Troeltsch does not in fact do this. Hick's second criticism is that Troeltsch failed to see the many "positive possibilities of inter-faith dialogue" – (p.5). While this is true to some extent, Troeltsch (1923 p.30) allows for an important "measure of agreement and mutual understanding" through inter-religious dialogue.

[103]. Troeltsch 1923 pp.28ff; Hick GUF p.147.

[104]. Hick GUF p.147; Troeltsch 1972 p.123.

severely criticised for his lack of historical knowledge of the
world religions as well as his extreme theological liberalism.
[106] Hocking went so far as to suggest the future emergence of a
world faith. As the various religions reconceived themselves in
the light of truths from other religions, they would slowly
recognise a common essence and would one day eventually unite
together in a world faith, rid of their irreconcilable
differences. Nevertheless, Hocking thought that the world
religions would and should retain their different identities. He
writes:

> In proportion as any religion grows in
> self-understanding through grasping its
> own essence, it grasps the essence of all
> religion, and gains in power to interpret
> its various forms.[107]

Although Hocking's notion of a common essence existing within the
world religions has led a number of recent theologians to
classify him as a pluralist,[108] it should be noted that
Hocking equated this common essence with Christianity in "its
ideal character...(which) is the 'anticipation of the essence' of
all religion, and contains potentially all that any religion
has."[109]

Hocking paid scant attention to ecclesiology and his notion
of a common essence led to definite implications for missiology.
He argued that mission must now be adapted not for teaching but
"learning", "conversation and conference", and "give and take
with the thought and feeling of a nation and a world."[110]
Hocking shared with Troeltsch an aversion to any form of cultural
superiority. They also shared the pluralist conviction that the
various religions are different but nevertheless valid paths to
the "Divine Life". However, Hocking, unlike Troeltsch, argued
that mutual interaction and dialogue between the religions was
the key to growth and a new form of world religion. Although Hick
criticises Troeltsch for underplaying the value of dialogue,[111]
he does not have the same ambitions as Hocking, but he does have,
as I shall show in chapter two, substantial expectations from
future dialogue and interaction.

Hendrik Kraemer, deeply influenced by Karl Barth and Emil
Brunner, forcefully challenged the position of Farquhar,

---

105. Hocking 1932 p.77.
106. See Speer 1933.
107. Hocking 1932 p.198.
108. Race 1983 pp.74-6; Knitter 1985 p.44.
109. Hocking 1932 p.249. His position is admittedly ambiguous.
110. Hocking 1940 p.205.
111. Hick 1978m p.5.

Troeltsch and Hocking in the late 1930's and onwards. Kraemer propounded a dialectical theology which stressed Christ's relationship to the religions as one of discontinuity and judgement, rather than fulfilment (Farquhar) and mutual appreciation and co-existence (Hocking and Troeltsch). Although Kraemer was critical of Christianity as a religion, he thought that its special relationship to Christ gave it unique status among the world religions. Kraemer criticised the reduction of evangelism to social service and mutual enrichment. He also insisted that conversion to Christ and his cross could not be minimised in inter-religious encounter. The missionary's sole aim was "to persuade the non-Christian world to surrender to Christ as the sole Lord of Life".[112] Hick notes that exclusivism, "derives in recent theology from the massive dogmatic work of Karl Barth...and the detailed application of this to the world religions by the great Dutch missionary scholar Hendrik Kraemer".[113]

Hick's statement requires a number of qualifications. Hick is correct in noting Barth's influence on the exclusivist position.[114] However, he is incorrect in suggesting that Kraemer simply applied Barth's early theology, with only more of a historical knowledge of the non-Christian religions. Kraemer's independence of mind and critical distance from Barth have been noticed by a number of scholars.[115] Kraemer was dissatisfied with Barth's undialectical (!) "theological maxims, made into self contained entities" and his insensitivity to the dynamics of history.[116] Strictly speaking, neither Barth nor Kraemer thought that their exclusivist theologies actually entailed that all those who did not confess Jesus as Lord suffered eternal perdition.[117] The main thrust of both these theologians was to maintain the priority and "necessity" of confession and surrender to Jesus as Lord.

This exclusivist approach characterised the three great International Missionary Conferences held at Edinburgh (1910), Jerusalem (1928) and Tambaram (1938).[118] This approach also

---

112. Kraemer 1938 p.444.
113. GMN p.81.
114. See Barth's seminal essay 1970 pp.280-362. His influence can be seen in Berkouwer 1958; Bloesch 1968; the Lausanne Statement 1975; Kantzer 1975; Scott 1978; Bolich 1980; Ramm 1983. This is just a sample.
115. See Neill 1960 ch.8; Hallencreutz 1966 pp.14ff & notes, ch.7; Newbigin 1969 ch.5, pp.77ff; Davis 1970 p.46.
116. Kraemer 1956 pp.192-93.
117. See my discussion of this tension in D'Costa 1986a ch.3, 1986d.
118. See International Missionary Council Texts 1910, 1928, 1939.
(Footnote continued)

23

dominated the World Council of Churches under the Directorship of Willem Visser't Hooft until his retirement in 1966.[119] Visser't Hooft wrote that "the attitude of the Christian Church to the religions can...only be the attitude of the witness who points to the one Lord Jesus Christ as Lord of all men."[120]

Variations of these three paradigms (inclusivist, pluralist and exclusivist) characterise the discussion which continued in the next half of the century.[121]

(1.4.2). Roman Catholic theology: 1900-1950:

The majority of Catholic theologians concerned with the theological question of other religions in this period were European scholastics. Consequently, much of the discussion followed Thomist lines. Phillipe Glorieux developed Aquinas early remarks that God would "reveal by internal inspiration what (the good infidel following the dictates of conscience) has to believe".[122] Glorieux argued that a special death-bed illumination would be granted, thereby allowing an assent of faith necessary for salvation.[123] Riccardo Lombardi followed the later thought of Aquinas, which stressed the assent to God by means of natural reason.[124] Lombardi also developed Aquinas's argument that this rational assent contained an implicit desire for baptism into the Church. Implicit desire entails that a situation must be viewed in terms of its potentiality. Lombardi gives an example. If a Communist in Russia comes to a belief in God, by means of reason, yet does not know about the Church, then it is argued that if that person was confronted with the Church, they would have no hesitation in joining it through baptism. However, such a person cannot be blamed for their visible exclusion from the Church, so the notion of implicit desire accommodates this difficulty, by viewing the person as implicitly related to the Church and salvation. The notion can also be applied, as it was, to the situation of a person in a state of invincible (or non-culpable) ignorance of God. The same logic is entailed, although in this situation the

---

[118](continued)
On the complex background to these conferences see Hallencreutz 1966; Hogg 1952 chs.3-6; Sharpe 1977 ch.3.
[119]. Hick is in agreement with this assessment - see GMN p.81.
[120]. Visser't Hooft 1963 p.116.
[121]. Good theological and historical surveys of this period, not already mentioned, are Jathanna 1981; Warren's (1967) study of the social, economic and religious factors in mission history; and Neill 1964 esp. chs.10-13, and his extensive bibliography.
[122]. Aquinas 1975 14:11, my brackets.
[123]. Glorieux 1932, 1933; Thurston 1935 collates evidence from drowning people's memories to supplement this thesis.
[124]. Aquinas 1968 1a, q.89, art.6; 1969 1a2ae, q.1, art.2.

person has no explicit knowledge of God.

Hick cites the teaching of the Holy Office in 1949 in the dispute about salvation outside the Church, caused by Leonard Feeney's defence of a literalist understanding of the no salvation outside the Church teaching. The 1949 document made the official Catholic position clear:

> To gain eternal salvation it is not always required that a person be incorporated in fact as a member of the Church, but it is required that he belongs to it at least in desire and longing. It is not always necessary that this desire be explicit...When a man is invincibly ignorant, God also accepts an implicit desire, so called because it is contained in the good disposition of the soul by which a man wants to be conformed to God's will. [125]

Hick deems this position a "Ptolemaic epicycle", as he would no doubt view Lombardi's analysis. [126]

One other early Catholic theory worth mentioning was that put forward by Cardinal Billot. Disturbed by his (degenerate - as he thought) French contemporaries' inability to arrive at theism through the use of reason, Billot argued that infidels possessed the moral level of infants, thereby declaring them morally inculpable and destined to limbo - as were infants. [127] Although Hick does not consider this position, he takes it for granted that the idea of "limbo" has been "under increasing criticism among Roman Catholic thinkers." [128]

Most of these theologians mentioned above laboured under the often rigidly interpreted Catholic axiom, extra ecclesiam nulla salus (no salvation outside the Church). [129] A difference between the Catholic axiom and Protestant forms of exclusivism was the Catholic stress on the Church, rather than the Protestant stress on Christ alone. [130]

---

125. Denzinger 1957 pp.274-5, my emphases. Cited in Hick GUF p.124.
126. GUF p.124.
127. Billot 1919-1923.
128. DEL p.237.
129. Denzinger 1957 p.165. From now on the axiom will be abbreviated extra ecclesiam.
130. Eminyan 1960 contains a scholarly survey and comprehensive bibliography of European Catholic theology in this period, as does the two volume work of Capéran 1934.

It should be noted that a progressive group of mainly French and Belgian Catholics in India propounded a form of inclusivism in the light of their studies of, and encounters with, the Hindu tradition of Advaita Vedānta.[131] Following in the tracks of Pierre Johanns and George Dandoy, in 1950, Jules Monchanin and Henri le Saux (later called Swami Abhishiktananda), founded an Indian-Christian ashram on the banks of the Kavery River at Kulitalai in Tamil Nadu, South India. Hick briefly refers to Abhishktananda's work, and to that of his successor, Bede Griffiths.[132] The ashram was named Saccidānanda, after the Hindu characterisation of divine reality, interpreted by Abhishiktananda as Sat (being), Cit (Logos), Ānanda (Bliss of Love and Beauty). At Saccidānanda, Abhishiktananda and Monchanin meshed together Hindu spirituality and a Benedictine monasticism to forge what they perceived as a totally Indian, totally Christian lifestyle. This included using the Vedas for meditative readings and chanting Sanskrit prayers in the liturgy. The motivation for their work was clearly inclusivist - "we must grasp the authentic Hindu search for God in order to Christianize it",[133] - although their ashram would no doubt have been encouraged by pluralists like Hocking.[134]

However, such inclusivists were exceptions to the otherwise prevailing negative attitude to other religions within Catholicism during this period.

(1.5). The foreground: 1950 - present.

After two world wars, the disintegration of empires and the upsurge of new theological movements, the three main paths outlined above took on varying contours in the changing historical and theological terrain. It was increasingly felt that mission must be separated from religious imperialism, while social service and proclamation came to be seen as inseparably connected.[135] The understanding of the Church took on a sacramental and social, rather than institutional, character especially in Catholic circles. Furthermore, many Christians had become deeply impressed by various religions and less confident

---

[131]. See D'Costa 1986a pp.10-11. See Mattam 1975 for a lucid survey of Catholic attitudes to Hinduism during this era.
[132]. Hick GMN p.80.
[133]. Cited in ed. Weber 1977 p.6.
[134]. See Hocking 1940 pp.206ff where he recognises the special potential of the Catholic missions.
[135]. Hoekstra 1979, argues that the notion of evangelical mission in the WCC has become largely eclipsed by a one-sided stress on social and political liberation. From a different perspective, but with similar criticisms, see Norman 1979.

about their own previous claims. However, the issues of
Christology, missiology, creation and the nature of God still
remained central to the theological debate, as did the importance
of empirical knowledge and a sympathetic understanding of the
non-Christian religions.

(1.5.1). Protestant theology: 1950 - present:

In the late 1960s, under the direction of Stanley Samartha, the
World Council of Churches' Programme on Dialogue with People of
Living Faiths and Ideologies forged a path between a weakened
form of inclusivist theology and a strong version of pluralist
practice. Two consultations edited by Samartha reflect this new
mood: Living Faiths and Ultimate Goals and Towards World
Community: Resources and Responsibilities for Living Together.
The first title indicates the strong respect, without compromise
on beliefs in ultimate goals, towards the lives and beliefs of
people from other faiths. Marxism was also represented in the
first consultation. The second title stresses the urgency of the
social tasks which now preoccupied mission thinking. Samartha
also presided over the compilation of the important document
issued by the World Council of Churches in 1972, Guidelines for
Inter-Religious Dialogue, which reflects a form of inclusivist
theology. Although Hick, when referring to this document,
suggests that it reflects a pluralist theology in his comment
that it is "truth seeking" rather than confessional, he seems to
qualify this almost immediately. [136]   Hick also commends the
commitment to a mutual searching for truth in dialogue, rather
than a "superficial consensus or a dilution of convictions", and
the commitment to "concrete action together for world peace." [137]

    Samartha's own views reflect this variation of inclusivism. He
affirms the decisive, but not exclusively unique, revelation of
God in Christ. He also reports that the fulfilment approach is
often "regarded as patronizing by our neighbors" whose religions [138]
he sees as "alternative ways of salvation".   Samartha
characteristically adds that demanding acceptance of Christ prior
to "sharing with our neighbors the love of God...is unhelpful."

---

[136]. GMN p.89. After citing World Council of Churches 1979 pt.II,
he adds that while confessional, it acknowledges truth in other
religions and is thereby confessional "within the context of
religious pluralism."
[137]. GMN pp.89,96.
[138]. eds. Anderson & Stransky 1975 pp.35-36.
[139]. eds. Anderson & Stransky 1975 p.55. Samartha's ambivalence
about the necessity of Christianity or Christ for salvation has
(Footnote continued)

Among Protestant theologians inclusivism is becoming popular. However, this tendency is increasingly marked by a reticence towards any evangelical form of mission demanded by exclusivists such as Kraemer, and a tacit theological encouragement of religious pluralism. One reason for this is reflected in the title of John Robinson's book Truth is Two-Eyed. Rather than stress the fulfilment of Hinduism in its encounter with Christ, Robinson argued that Christianity itself is fulfilled in its encounter with Hinduism! [140] Two eyes on the truth are better than one, although the focus for both lenses, so to speak, is Christ. Like Samartha, he holds to the definitiveness of the revelation of God in Christ[141] without denying that God has revealed Himself elsewhere. Hick makes no reference to Robinson's work.

Earlier, across the Atlantic, this same thrust was apparent in Paul Tillich's stimulating attempt to mediate between the pluralism of Troeltsch and the exclusivism of Barth and Kraemer. Starting from a somewhat different approach from Robinson, Tillich acknowledges the experience of the "Holy" in all religions and affirms, like Robinson, that the crucified Jesus is the most valuable criterion for discerning God's activity within the history of religions. Robinson said that in the criterion of Jesus "as embodying, fleshing out, the saving disclosure and act of God", one holds "the conviction, always to be clarified, completed and corrected in dialogue, that it is this (criterion)[142] which offers the profoundest clue to all the rest." Tillich, in a similar vein, writes that in the image of the crucified Christ, "the criteria are given under which Christianity must judge itself and, by judging itself, judge also the other religions and the quasi-religions."[143]

Tillich and Robinson neglect the implications of their positions for mission and ecclesiology, but their Christological criterion for evaluating other religions places them firmly in the inclusivist paradigm but with less stress on a one-way

---

[139](continued)
caused Knitter (1985 pp.157-59) to interpret his work as pluralist. Cracknell (1986), also propounds a similar position, and calls himself an "inclusivist pluralist". Hick is aware of Cracknell's work and invited him to contribute an appendix to the British edition of GMN (pp.98-106).
[140]. Camps (1983 pt.III) a Dutch Catholic missiologist, has charted the impact of various religions on Christian communities in different parts of the world.
[141]. Robinson 1979 p.129.
[142]. Robinson 1979 pp.119,129, my brackets.
[143]. Tillich 1963 p.82.

fulfilment. Tillich's words characterise this form of inclusivism: "Not conversion, but dialogue. It would be a tremendous step forward if Christianity were to accept this." [144]

Implicitly within this inclusivist tradition is John Cobb, a colleague of Hick's at Claremont. [145] Cobb offers a vision of transformation that is similar to Hocking's, without the assumption of a common future essence. His thrust is akin to Robinson's, although he goes so far as to suggest to Buddhists certain transformations that could occur within their own tradition, such as the idea that "Amida is Christ" - or expressive of the "Logos which Christians know as incarnate in Jesus." [146] Cobb represents a process theology form of inclusivism. [147]

In Europe, Tillich's work has been a source of stimulation for Wolfhart Pannenberg. Stressing the importance of the history of religions, combined with his own futurist eschatological perspective, Pannenberg remains within the inclusivist tradition: "the history of religions even beyond the time of the public ministry of Jesus presents itself as the history of the appearance of the God who revealed himself through Jesus." [148] Hick, curiously, does not refer to this essay of Pannenberg's when he briefly discusses an ambiguous passage in Pannenberg's, Jesus - God and Man. [149] The latter passage draws upon the "symbolic language of Jesus' descent into hell", [150], and it is not clear whether Pannenberg intends a post-mortem encounter with Christ by non-Christians in another life. In relation to this ambiguity, Hick notes that the idea of a post-mortem encounter as an inclusivist or exclusivist epicycle,

> is available to the liberal Protestant
> who finds acceptable the idea of a
> 'second chance' after death; although it
> is not available to the traditionally

---

[144]. Tillich 1963 p.95.
[145]. Although Hick has not discussed the work of Cobb, Cobb criticises Hick in Cobb 1982 pp.41-46.
[146]. Cobb 1982 pp.123-128.
[147]. See two other process theologians who keep Christ at the centre of their solutions - Ogden 1963 pp.164-87; Pittenger 1981 pp.23-32. Hick has not discussed their theology of religions, but has discussed their Christologies: Hick 1984f on Ogden; 1960g, PRP p.35 on Pittenger.
[148].
[149]. Pannenberg 1971 p.115.
[150]. Pannenberg 1971 was published in English two years before GUF. Pannenberg's work is not mentioned in the bibliographical guide on Christianity and other religions in eds. Hebblethwaite & Hick 1980.
[150]. Pannenberg 1967 p.272.

> orthodox Protestant or to the Roman
> Catholic, both of whom regard death as
> ending our period of freedom to respond
> to God in faith.[151]

Hick writes that he has heard of this post-mortem view "in discussion" but has "not seen it in the published literature of missiology or of the theology of world religions".[152] Since Hick wrote the sentences above, one such view has been defended by Origen Jathanna. Jathanna suggests that the notion of an encounter with Christ in another life (through rebirth) is the only way in which Christians can tackle the problem of those who do not know Christ through no fault of their own.[153] Other writers suggest a post-mortem encounter, but are reluctant to place this in the context of rebirth.[154] The important point to note about these theories is the underlying insistence and conviction that only confession and surrender to Jesus Christ as Lord can be effective for salvation. The underlying Christocentricism of such positions is paramount.

Jürgen Moltmann, like Kraemer, strongly relativises the Church and Christianity. This reflects his Barthian heritage. However, fulfilment for him is not in terms of the Church or Christ explicitly, but in the creation of hope. This is yet another novel development within the basic inclusivist paradigm. He writes that a major aim of mission should be to "'infect' people, whatever their religion, with the spirit of hope, love and responsibility for the world."[155] But, for Moltmann, ultimately, Christ is the original source of all hope, love and responsibility: "Outside Christ no salvation. Christ has come and was sacrificed for the reconciliation of the whole world. No one is excluded."[156]

This multi-faceted inclusivist development has come under fire from opposite theological wings, often repeating, but also furthering, the discussion that took place in the first half of the century. Many pluralists, developing the impetus of Troeltsch and to a lesser extent Hocking, have argued that Christ's decisiveness should be understood as a personal confession without objective or universally binding status. This

---

151. GUF p.130.
152. GUF p.129.
153. Jathanna 1981 pp.470-81. Jathanna makes a number of criticisms of Hick, with whom he is in strict disagreement - pp.4,5,248,467.
154. Boros 1965 p.4; and see Braaten 1977 p.117; Lindbeck 1984 pp.59ff.
155. Moltmann 1977 p.152.
156. Moltmann 1977 p.153. Clearly Moltmann is echoing the extra ecclesiam teaching!

30

follows Troeltsch's "only...for us" emphasis - drawing heavily on the Kantian tradition. Consequently many pluralists argue that Christians should not evaluate other religions through Christological spectacles and must re-think issues in the light of data from all the religions, developing a sort of world or global theology. A major proponent of this view is the subject of this study, John Hick. Hick places much emphasis upon the universal salvific will of God:

> Can we then accept the conclusion that the God of love who seeks to save all mankind has nevertheless ordained that men must be saved in such a way that only a small minority can in fact receive this salvation? [157]

Hick's answer is "No" as we have already seen and will do so in greater detail in the next chapter.

Another major pluralist is the historically, but less theologically minded Wilfred Cantwell Smith. Since 1970, Hick has shown much interest in Smith's thought. [158] Smith attacks the very concept of "religions" as mutually exclusive ideological communities. He argues that with the exception of Islam, it was not until the seventeenth century that such a concept of religion took shape and was especially nourished in the Christian west. This process came about for a variety of complex reasons and generally dominated over the prevalent view up until then, of "religion" as a way of life, faith, obedience and so on, rather than religion as a communally embodied system of beliefs. [159] Such an abstract and unhelpful "reification" of the notion of religion, argues Smith, encourages an "us-them" mentality. Smith proposes that the religious life of humankind should be distinguished not as different and competing religions, but in terms of "faith" and the various "cumulative traditions." [160] He argues for a common religious unity in "faith" which is expressive of the personal attitude of awe, surrender, trust, love and wonder in relation to the "transcendent". [161] Smith's use of these distinctions is not always logically consistent and has been criticised accordingly. [162] "Cumulative traditions" represent the historical accumulation of the observable manifestation of religions ("temples, scriptures, theological systems, dance patterns, legal and other social institutions, convention, moral codes, myths") within which one comes to know

---

157. GUF p.122.
158. See TD pp.140-48, GUF p.101, Hick 1978d, 1985b.
159. Smith 1978 chs.1-3.
160. Smith 1978 chs.6-7.
161. Smith 1978 pp.141,170-71,191 and fn 21,325,342.
162. Hick 1978d p.xvi ; Wainwright 1984; Cobb 1985; Meynell 1985.

the transcendent. [163]

Smith argues that the differences between elements of various cumulative traditions should not be minimised. In this, he differs from the pluralist historian Arnold Toynbee, who views these differences as historical accretions and non-essentials. [164] Rather, for Smith, a common unity is to be found in the personal, subjective and pragmatic appropriation of the "transcendent" within the attitude of "faith". [165]

While Smith leaves a number of theological questions unanswered, he has developed some of the implications of this pluralist view. Evangelization is clearly inappropriate. Rather like Hocking, he argues for a critical and corporate search for religious truth. [166] Smith is most radical in his suggestion for a global theology whereby the intelligibility of any theology is determined by its acceptability and coherence to theologians from all the various cumulative traditions. [167] As we shall see, Hick shares much in common with Smith, although he has criticised Smith's neglect of genuinely conflicting truth claims that can be given propositional articulation and Smith's [168] apparently subjectivist, pragmatist truth criterion.

Smith's influence has been considerable. [169] A significant point about Smith's pluralism is its theocentricism, rather than Christocentricism. While still affirming, like Troeltsch, that Christians may find God in Christ, Smith is adamant that the "transcendent" is to be found in "faith" and its respective appropriation in the different cumulative traditions. One other significant factor, which Smith shares with Hick and many other modern day pluralists, is his emphasis on an all-loving God which he argues runs against the exclusivist strain that implies that [170] only a small minority can come to know and worship God.

---

163. Smith 1978 p.157.
164. See Toynbee 1957, 1965. Hick does not mention Toynbee's work (except Toynbee 1968 in another context - DEL pp.13, 148-49), while Smith is aware of it - see Smith 1978 pp.122,259.
165. Smith 1978 p.192. Admittedly, Smith explicitly leaves the theological issues to the theologians - Smith 1978 p.325.
166. Smith 1980, 1967.
167. Smith 1972 p.123, 1980.
168. TD p.140ff.
169. See WRT. Race acknowledges his indebtedness to Smith and Hick, the latter being supervisor to Race's MA at Birmingham University, out of which developed his book: Race 1983 pp.vii, xiii, chs.4, 6. Hunter acknowledges his debt to Race - Hunter 1985 p.166. Knitter, a leading Catholic pluralist, also acknowledges a debt to Hick and Smith, although he is more critical than Race of both, as well as of Race - see Knitter 1985 pp.17-18, 44-47, 146-52, 175-6, 219ff, 269.

In part, these pluralists mentioned above, including Hick, represent the liberal reaction against harsh versions of exclusivist theology, such as propounded at the Congress on World Mission at Chicago in 1960. The Congress announced that:

> In the years since the war, more than one billion souls have passed into eternity and more than half of these went to the torment of hell fire without even hearing of Jesus Christ, who He was, or why He died on the cross of Calvary. [171]

Ten years later, the 'Frankfurt Declaration', composed mainly by German Lutherans who felt dissatisfied with the approach of the World Council of Churches and other Christian bodies, clearly refuted any idea of fulfilment or compromise on mission. The one and only priority was the "proclamation of the Gospel which aims at conversion." [172]

For both Hick and Smith, like the previous group of inclusivists, there is an acceptance of religious plurality. But Hick and Smith add a positive and explicit encouragement of, and theological justification for, such pluralism. They stress, like Hocking and Troeltsch their predecessors, the learning and growth that takes place through encounter. While both tend to neglect ecclesiological questions, Hick has dwelt upon the related Christological issues. This neglect of ecclesiology may reflect their dissenting backgrounds. These pluralist developments have not been without their critics whose main dissatisfactions centre around the allegedly vague and obscure understanding of God and the relativising of religious truth. [173]

Equally opposed to the various inclusivist approaches and the developed pluralism of Hick and Smith, are neo-Barthians such as Stephen Neill, Lesslie Newbigin and Norman Anderson. [174] While all three acknowledge that God operates outside ecclesial Christianity, Anderson characteristically denies that "other religions" may be viewed as "saving structures". [175] While all three unequivocally criticise Hick's position, Hick only notes

---

170. See Smith 1972 p.138, 1980 p.171; GUF p.131; Race 1983 ch.4; Knitter 1985 p.140.
171. ed. Percy 1961 p.9; cited by Hick in GUF p.121. He also cites the Wheaton Declaration of 1966 - see ed. Lindsell 1966.
172. Frankfurt Declaration 1970 p.846.
173. See chs.3-5 for such criticisms.
174. See Newbigin 1969, 1977a, 1977b, 1978; Neill 1970, 1984a; Anderson 1971, 1984.
175. ed. Anderson 1975 p.236. See also Lindbeck's (1984 ch.3) exclusivist approach from a socio-linguistic perspective.

the work of Newbigin, whom he characterises as neo-Barthian. He notes that Newbigin's theology represents an advance in its acknowledgement that dialogue is important, rather than the previous "confessional rejection of dialogue".[176] Nevertheless, Hick criticises Newbigin because such a confessional stance can eventually "only result either in conversion or in hardening of differences - occasionally the former but more often the latter."[177] These exclusivists emphasise the proclamation of the Word. However, they also stress a social involvement with, and a deep appreciation of non-Christian religions. They maintain that the gospel is compromised in the inclusivist and pluralist approaches, and that ecclesiology, missiology and Christology are thereby neglected.

Nuances within the exclusivist approach are evident. These modern exclusivists have been criticised as to the authority of their biblical foundations, their minimising of revelation outside Christianity and even in some cases, their alleged triumphalism and racism.[178]

(1.5.2). Roman Catholic theology: 1950 - present:

After the relatively quiet period before Vatican II's important Declaration on the Relation of the Church to Non-Christian Religions (1965), Catholic theology now blossomed into fruitful discussion. The document on non-Christian religions, which had originally been intended as a statement on the Jews, formalised a[179] shift of emphasis on the extra ecclesiam teaching. For the full implications of this emphasis, it must be read in conjunction with other Conciliar documents - as Hick clearly recognises.[180] Not only do the documents reiterate the "implicit desire" and "invincible ignorance" teaching (although without using these formal terms),[181], they went further in affirming that goodness, truth and holiness were to be found in the "ways of conduct and of life" and "rules and teachings" within other religions.[182] It is acknowledged that salvation can be found outside the visible Church.[183] The document also

---

[176]. GMN pp.81-2 - he only refers to Newbigin 1977b, rather than to his more substantial contributions: Newbigin 1969, 1978.
[177]. GMN p.85.
[178]. eds. Anderson & Stransky 1975 p.76.
[179]. For the background and intention of the document see Hastings 1968 ch.6; ed. Vorgrimler 1969 pp.90ff; Kunnumpuram 1971; D'Costa 1984a, 1985e,f,g.
[180]. GUF pp.125-27, where he cites Vatican II 1964 and 1965a, but fails to mention Vatican II 1965b which further clarifies the official teaching on this subject.
[181]. See Vatican II 1964 para.16.
[182]. Vatican II 1965a para.10.

notes the special relationship of the Christian Church to Judaism and Islam, and has specific, although brief sections on Hinduism[184] and Buddhism and implicitly deals with African religions. There were many questions left unanswered, but a number of statements from the Vatican, including Pope John Paul II's, reiterate this inclusivist teaching.[185]

Hick refers to the encyclical Redemptor Hominis as evidence of John Paul II's inclusivist position.[186] Hick acknowledges that in comparision to earlier statements, the "Vatican II[187] pronouncements are magnificently open and charitable." However, he feels that the Council failed to "make the Copernican revolution that was called for", as it "still assumes without question that salvation is only in Christ and through[188] incorporation into his mystical body, the church." This incorporation is through "implicit faith" as Cardinal Bea pointed out, a comment that Hick quotes in order to establish his critical objection.[189]

After Vatican II the floodgates for discussion had been opened and the debate mainly moved along the fulfilment and exclusivist paths, with a tendency to view pluralism as a species of indifferentism.[190]

An influential figure who dominated Catholic debate was the late Karl Rahner. Rahner coined the term "anonymous Christian". This term refers to a non-Christian who gains salvation through faith, hope and love by the grace of Christ, mediated however imperfectly through his or her own religion, which thereby points towards its historical fulfilment in Christ and his Church. For Rahner, grace, Christology and ecclesiology are inseparable. He tries to hold two axioms together: "God desires the salvation of everyone. And this salvation willed by God is the salvation won by Christ".[191] In this way many Catholic theologians are able

---

183. Vatican II 1964 para.16.
184. Laurentin & Neuner 1966, note the Council's intention to refer to African religions, although not by name.
185. Rosanno, then Secretary to the Committee for Non-Christian Religions, propounds such a view in eds. Stransky & Anderson 1981a ch.4; see also Pope John Paul II 1979 para.14; (Vatican) Secretariat for non-Christians (subsequently referred to as SNC) 1984.
186. WRT p.152.
187. GUF p.126.
188. GUF pp.125-26.
189. GUF p.127; Bea's remarks reported in ed. Neuner 1967 p.7.
190. Indifferentism (according equal value to all religions) has been formally condemned - see eds. Neuner & Dupuis 1983 pp.224, 259ff, 274.

to develop the _extra ecclesiam_ axiom, aided by a more sacramental
understanding of the Church initiated by Vatican II. [192]   Hick
has paid much attention to Rahner's work, and has constantly
criticised   it   for   its   imperialist[193]offensiveness   and   for
perpetuating a stalemate in dialogue.

If   Robinson   and   Tillich   represent   the   liberal   wing   of
inclusivism,   Rahner,   while   firmly   planted   within   the   same
tradition, occupies a more conservative position. While Robinson
and Tillich, in the tradition of Farquhar, emphasise Christ
alone, Rahner emphasises both Christ and his Church.

The Catholic discussion may be profitably charted in relation
to Rahner's version of inclusivism. [194]   On the one hand,
exclusivist theologians attacked Rahner for minimising mission,
dissolving   the   character   of   the   Church   and   Christian
discipleship, and compromising the cross and proclamation of
Christ. [195]   On the other hand, liberal Catholics like the Swiss
Hans Küng joined pluralists like Hick in criticising Rahner's
ecclesiocentricism. [196]   However, Küng is himself criticised by
Hick for his eventual Christocentricism.[197]   This is because
Küng allows other religions only a provisional salvific value and
suggests an "existential confrontation" with Christ after death
(interestingly echoing Glorieux's theory). [198]   In The Wider
Ecumenism, Eugene Hillman   discusses the important inclusivist
contributions   of   Catholic   theologians   such   as   Edward
Schillebeekx, Heinz Schlette, Yves Congar and Henri de Lubac.
Variations within this inclusivist tradition are clearly evident.

However, a small number of influential American Catholics have
argued for pluralism, criticising even liberal inclusivists like
Küng. Paul Knitter exemplifies this position, as do Rosemary[199]
Ruether and to a lesser extent, Gregory Baum.   Knitter

191
192. Rahner 1966b p.122.
192. Kunnumpuram 1971 highlights and extensively discusses this
point.
193. See GMNUS pp.27,68 and 2.2. below.
194. See Pedley 1984 pp.340-41; D'Costa 1985a p.146, n.1 for
citation of criticisms of Rahner.
195. Straelen 1966 ch.4; Balthasar 1969; Hacker 1980 ch.3.
196. Küng 1976 pp.97-8.
197. GUF pp.128ff. Hick sees Küng's position as the"boldest so
far" within Roman Catholic inclusivist theology - see GUF p.128;
GMNUS pp.68-9. Hick also notes Küng 1976 pp.89-166, and rightly
argues that this section represents no substantial change on
Küng's earlier position in Küng 1967 - a text on which Hick's
criticism of Küng depends. He also argues that Küng's position is
similar to Schlette 1966.
198. Küng 1967 p.52.

applauds the move away from ecclesiocentricism and Christocentricism, to a new theocentricism. Much of his contribution to the debate is in meeting the criticism that such a "Copernican" shift apparently violates

> the understanding of Christ maintained by the New Testament and by the tradition, and debilitates both personal commitment to Jesus Christ and a distinctively Christian contribution to the needs of the world. [200]

In dealing with this problem, Knitter attempts to circumvent the problems arising from certain aspects of Troeltsch's "historical relativism". [201] He does this by arguing that Christians could and should affirm the universal significance of Jesus, so that Christian truth claims can be "presented as universally relevant" rather than as "definitively and normatively relevant." [202] Hence, while remaining faithful to the Christian faith, Christians can discard the Aristotelian heritage of viewing truth claims as matters of "either-or", and adopt a "both-and" approach; the different religions being "more complementary than contradictory". [203]

Knitter thinks that this non-normative theocentric approach overcomes some major obstacles to dialogue: the imperative of conversion (exclusivism), and an implicit or explicit superiority by the Christian partner in dialogue (inclusivism). [204] Furthermore, Knitter joins hands with Smith and Hick, among others, in proposing a "global theology", where fundamental assumptions must be questioned by the presuppositions of other religions and systematic theology must take into consideration the data and experience of these religions. [205] Hick has not published anything on Knitter's work, but supports his position with enthusiasm and is planning to co-edit a volume of essays with Knitter on religious pluralism.

Catholics in India, as before, have been especially creative. However, as Hick only briefly mentions the work of Bede

---

[199]. Knitter 1985 also contains a masterly survey of literature on this topic; Baum 1966; Ruether 1972.
[200]. Knitter 1985 p.167.
[201]. Knitter 1985 p.36; he also thinks that Race ends up with the "'wretched historicism' and relativism that he warned against in his analysis of Troeltsch." - Knitter 1985 p.255, fn.33.
[202]. Knitter 1985 p.142.
[203]. Knitter 1985 p.220.
[204]. Knitter's position seems to be undergoing revision - see Knitter 1986a,b, and 5.5.2 below.
[205]. See D'Costa 1985h, 1986b for further discussion of Knitter.

Griffiths, [206] I would refer the reader elsewhere to my [207] discussion of modern Indian Catholic developments. [208] Following the pioneering work of Raimundo Panikkar, although less conceptual and more concerned with spirituality, is Abhishiktananda's successor, the Benedictine Bede Griffiths. He has attempted to concretise the process whereby Christianity is also fulfilled in its encounter with Hinduism. Like Robinson, he remains an inclusivist. Griffith's most important works are Return to the Centre and The Marriage of East and West. Many Indian Catholics have also sought to relate the spirituality of the ashram movement to social service. [209]

My observations have tended to concentrate upon individual theologians. Although I have discussed some major institutional documents from the World Council of Churches, Roman Catholic Church, and some evangelical declarations, a useful study of institutional developments can be found in Marcus Braybrooke, Inter-Faith Organizations, 1893-1979: A Historical Directory, and Walbert Bühlmann's journalistic, All Have the Same God.

(1.6). Conclusion.

In this brief survey I have tried to isolate the different paradigms underlying Christian attitudes to other religions in keeping with Hick's distinctions: pluralism, exclusivism and inclusivism. I have also tried to highlight some of the issues concerning the nature of God, the person of Christ, the Church, and the nature of mission. The variety of emphases within each paradigm should be acknowledged. It also appears that two underlying theological axioms are implicitly determinative of the various approaches: the universal salvific will of God and the claim that it is only in Christ (or his Church) that men and women can be saved.

The survey above has been far from exhaustive, although I have dealt with every twentieth-century Christian theologian that Hick discusses in his writings on the theology of religions - and others. Hick's work can clearly be located within the pluralist tradition, although, as I shall show in the following chapters, he has developed this position further than any of the pluralists I have mentioned. [210] Having placed Hick's work in its

---

[206]. See GMN p.80.
[207]. See D'Costa 1983, 1985a pp.139-46, 1986a p.17.
[208]. See Panikkar 1964, 1973, 1978, 1979 and D'Costa 1985a pp.139-46. Panikkar's own fulfilment-inclusivist position is undergoing change - see Panikkar 1981.
[209]. See Vandana 1982; ed. Dhavamony 1972. The many sides of the Catholic debate are well summarised by Knitter 1985 ch.7.
[210]. With the possible exception of Knitter. See 5.5.2 below.

historical and theological context, as well as highlighting some of the major theological issues at stake in the debate, I shall now turn to a critical systematic and detailed account of the arguments employed by Hick for his Copernican revolution.

CHAPTER 2: THE ARGUMENTS EMPLOYED IN FAVOUR OF THE COPERNICAN
REVOLUTION

(2.1). Introduction.

Having outlined Hick's career and his relation to other thinkers
dealing with a theology of religions, I now wish to focus upon
the arguments for his Copernican theology of religions. I isolate
seven arguments contained in Hick's proposals, noting
elaborations and modifications during Hick's subsequent
development. It is difficult and perhaps artificial to isolate
separate arguments as they are often interrelated. However, I
believe that such a procedure will greatly facilitate examination
of Hick's thought and will aid clarity, both in exposition and
analysis. I have at all times tried to relate arguments. If one
argument is seriously challenged, a "domino effect" may result in
the weakening of others. On the other hand, since some arguments
are not related, the "Alamo affect" may result: not until the
last argument is "breached" can the Copernican theology be
properly dismissed. [1]

(2.2). Argument 1: The argument from the untenable Ptolemaic
theology of religions.

Hick characterises most of the Christian tradition as
"Ptolemaic", which he defines as a theology "whose fixed point is
the principle that outside the church, or outside Christianity,
there is no salvation." [2] The distinction between outside the
Church and outside Christianity may be presumed to denote the
respective differences in emphasis between Catholic and
Protestant theologies. [3] Hick argues that both traditions, by
implication, consign most human beings to eternal perdition. Hick
recalls his own attitude as an evangelical as an example of the
ease with which one can ignore the horrific consequences of
cherished beliefs:

> I believed that God has made himself
> known to mankind with unique fullness and
> saving power in Christ, and has ordained
> that all men must come to him through

---

[1]. Although the concern of this study is Hick, the analysis of
his presuppositions will affect the estimation of other
pluralists, who often share the same assumptions. For a detailed
treatment of three other pluralists - Knitter, Smith, and Race -
who share many of Hick's assumptions, see D'Costa 1986b.
[2]. GUF p.125.
[3]. For these differences of emphasis see GUF pp.121-22, Hick
1984a p.198.

Christ. And although it follows from this
that those who do not become Christ's
disciples have missed the way to
salvation yet I did not explicitly apply
this conclusion to the hundreds of
millions of inhabitants of the globe. I
believed by implication that the majority
of human beings are eternally lost... [4]

Hick argues that this position and its consequences can be
traced through the past fifteen centuries of Christian history.
Within the Catholic tradition this attitude is epitomised in the
dogma - extra ecclesiam nulla salus. This dogma, Hick tells us,
was propounded by Boniface VIII in 1302 and formally crystallised
in the Decree of the Council of Florence in 1438-1445, which
affirmed that:

No one remaining outside the Catholic
Church, not just pagans, but also Jews
and heretics or schismatics, can become
partakers of eternal life; but they will
go to the "everlasting fire which was
prepared for the devil and his angels",
unless before the end of life they are
joined to the Church. [5]

This position is characterised by Hick as the "first phase - the
phase of total rejection" which is "as arrogant as it is cruel." [6]

Hick sees the official Catholic restatement of this position,
from Pius IX in 1854 up until Vatican II in 1965, as slowly
coming to terms with the wider religious life of humankind but in
a "characteristically Catholic way...continuing to pay allegiance
to the original dogma but at the same time adding an epicycle of
subsidiary theory to change its practical effects." [7]

Hick outlines and criticises, in turn, the various Catholic
epicycles since 1854. He protests that Pius IX's Allocution,
stating that those in "invincible ignorance" of the Catholic
faith may be saved outside the Church, is hopelessly vague for
"only God himself knows to whom this doctrine applies." [8] He
criticises the doctrine of "implicit desire" and "baptism by
desire" as a sleight of hand rendering those who are "consciously
outside the church" as "nevertheless unconsciously within it." [9]

---

4. GUF p.122.
5. GUF p.120; citing Denzinger 1957 714.
6. GMNUS p.29.
7. GUF p.123.
8. GUF p.123; citing Denzinger 1957 1647.

Furthermore, since "presumably only theists can have a sincere desire to do God's will, the doctrine of implicit desire does not extend to adherents of the non-theistic faiths, such as Buddhism and an important part of Hinduism."[10] While acknowledging Vatican II's Declaration on the Relationship of the Church to the Non-Christian Religions as "magnificently open and charitable", Hick complains that it still "assumes without question that salvation is only in Christ and through incorporation into his mystical body, the church."[11] Consequently, Vatican II does not undertake "the Copernican revolution that is needed in the christian attitude to other faiths."[12] These apparently later developments within the Catholic tradition are characterised by Hick as the "second phase...the phase of the early epicycles."[13]

Besides examining Catholic official pronouncements Hick also deals in slightly greater detail with two post-conciliar theologies of religion propounded by Küng and Rahner, both of whose works were noted in 1.5.2. above. This third phase is one of "later epicycles".[14] Here, according to Hick, "theological ingenuity goes to its limits to hold together the two propositions that outside Christianity there is no salvation, and that outside Christianity there is salvation."[15] Hick succintly summarises Rahner's thesis thus: "the non-Christian may be a Christian without knowing it, in that he is within the sphere of divine grace although he does not yet know the source of that grace as the God and Father of our Lord Jesus Christ."[16] Besides employing the same objections to the earlier epicycles, Hick further argues that this theory can be easily turned on its head and creates a stalemate in dialogue, for the "Vedantist", for example, can equally claim that a "Christian, and Jew, and the Muslim, and so on, can be said to be a Vedantist without knowing it."[17] In effect, "an honorary status (is) granted unilaterally to people who have not expressed any desire for it."[18] Hick argues that Rahner is limited to this position because of "his adherence to the Chalcedonian Christology[19] despite existing new insights which seem to point beyond it."[19]

Küng, at first sight, seems to achieve a greater "honesty and realism" in acknowledging the world religions as means of

9. GUF p.123.
10. GUF p.124.
11. GUF p.126.
12. GUF p.126.
13. GMNUS p.31.
14. GMNUS p.33.
15. GMNUS pp.33-4.
16. GUF p.127.
17. GUF p.131.
18. GMN p.50, my brackets.
19. Hick 1984a p.205.

salvation although as "ordinary" ways of salvation compared to Christianity, the "very special and extraordinary" salvific path.[20] But, Hick argues, what Küng gives away with one hand he takes back with the other in requiring that non-Christians eventually need to become Christians, "but in the meantime they are not condemned, for the gospel has not yet reached them in such a way as to overcome their hitherto invincible ignorance of its truth."[21] Hick clearly views the main options within modern Catholic theology of religions as variations on a theme: an attempt to acknowledge that salvation takes place outside Christianity while at the same time refusing to face the theological consequences of such a recognition.

Protestant theology differs from the Catholic positions and its epicycles only in that Christ rather than the Church is the fixed point outside of which there is no salvation. Hick never clearly defines what he intends by the distinction between Christianity and the Church which he so often uses. Nevertheless, according to Hick, this Ptolemaic view was generally held implicitly rather than explicitly, with exceptions such as the Congress on World Missions in Chicago and the Wheaton Declaration.[22] These latter positions parallel the Catholic first stage. Hick humorously adds that the main difference is that Catholics defined Christians as those "owing obedience to the pope, the latter (evangelical Christianity) is inclined to doubt whether the pope and his followers are Christians at all!"[23] Like the original Catholic dogma, the Protestant first stage is "entertained by few today" according to Hick.[24] In 1973 Hick believed that there was little published discussion on this issue in modern Protestant circles. While he discusses Pannenberg, who touches upon this subject, Pannenberg's reflections are not without a certain ambiguity - as was noted in 1.5.1. above. Although, more recently, Hick has become aware of further Protestant discussions, unfortunately, he has not devoted much space to them, presumably because he feels that they reiterate the basic Catholic position and can therefore be similarly criticised.

It should be noted that Hick pays little attention to Christian reflection upon this issue in the Bible or within the first five centuries of Christian thought. This may be because Hick considers that:

> neither Old nor New Testament writers
> knew of any of the great world faiths

20. GUF p.128; citing Küng 1967 p.53.
21. GUF p.129.
22. GUF p.121.
23. GMNUS p.30, my brackets.
24. GMN p.49.

beyond Judaism and Christianity. And
therefore no application of biblical
statements to Islam, Hinduism, Buddhism,
etc. can possibly claim to represent the
original meanings of the text. [25]

Consequently, Hick believes he is dealing with issues "which did
not and could not come within the purview of the prophets and
apostles of old." [26]

To summarise: Hick's first argument is to criticise the
tenuous nature of Ptolemaic theology which characterises nearly
fifteen centuries of Christian history. Ptolemaic theology,
according to Hick, ironically contradicts the very doctrine of
"God which it presupposes." [27]   Hick seriously wonders whether
one can accept its "conclusions that the God of love who seeks to
save all mankind has nevertheless ordained that men must be saved
in such a way that only a small minority can in fact receive this
salvation." [28]   When, in the later second and third phases,
Ptolemaic Christians came to acknowledge that salvation was
possible outside Christianity they still, by means of epicycles,
held to the underlying Ptolemaic principle of the first phase:
"outside the church, or outside Christianity, there is no
salvation." [29]   The very doctrine of God which the first phase
presupposes is, as we shall see, also the third and major
argument which Hick employs.

(2.3).   Argument 2: The argument from encountering saintly and
holy people within the non-Christian religions.

Hick appeals to the increasingly common experience (in the west)
of "new religious communities and new cultural influences in many
of our large cities." [30]   Hick writes that the problems of
religious plurality "did not particularly force themselves upon
my attention", [31]   till moving from Cambridge to Birmingham "with
its large Muslim, Sikh and Hindu communities, as well as its
older Jewish community." [32]   Through his involvement with race
and community relations work, Hick met individual saintly and
holy people from non-Christian religions. He also found within
their religious communities, "human beings opening their minds to
a higher divine Reality, known as personal and good and as

---

25. SC p.77.
26. SC p.77.
27. GMNUS p.31.
28. GUF p.125.
29. GUF p.125.
30. GMN p.28.
31. GUF p.122.
32. GMN p.5.

45

demanding righteousness and love between man and man." [33]   His
travels to India and Sri Lanka further convinced him of the
"immense spiritual depth and power" within the religious
traditions of Hinduism and Buddhism. [34]   The Copernican takes
cognisance of these experiences and formulates their theological
reflections accordingly.

Hick also observes that in the humane and loving treatment of
non-Christian "immigrants" in Britain by theologically Ptolemaic
Christians, practice had preceded theory. For instance, Ptolemaic
Christians helped Muslims to find places for worship, indicating
that the theological problems posed by non-Christian religions
had already "been solved, not in theory but in practice, by
allowing human needs to take precedence over the implications of
the accepted theological language." [35]   Hick's argument is that
Copernican practices require Copernican theologies. Ptolemaic
Christians will find that their practical attitudes are best
explained by a Copernican theology.

(2.4). <u>Argument</u> <u>3:</u> <u>The</u> <u>argument</u> <u>from</u> <u>an</u> <u>all-loving</u> <u>God.</u>

In 1966 Hick argued that a doctrine of hell would be
"incompatible either with God's sovereignty or with His perfect
goodness" because any notion of the everlasting suffering of the
damned in hell implies the eternity of sin and evil. [36]
Furthermore, such a doctrine also implies that "God does not
desire to save all His human creatures." [37]   Hell would thus
compromise the doctrine of God's sovereignty because it would
mean God's "purpose has finally failed in the case of some." [38]
Hick also dismisses the view of evil as privation as he believes
that it leads to the "divine annihilation or the dwindling out of
existence of the finally lost". [39]   Even if privation overcomes
the hurdle of "eternally useless and unredeemed suffering", it
fails to convince Hick, for it implies the failure of God's
purpose concerning "those souls whose fate is extinction." [40]

These considerations led Hick to suggest the <u>practical</u>
<u>certainty,</u> as opposed to the <u>logical possibility,</u> of universal

---

33. GMN p.5.
34. GMN p.5.
35. GMN p.41.
36. EGL p.378.
37. EGL p.378.
38. EGL p.378.
39. EGL p.378. The privation tradition is discussed and traced by
Hick in EGL pp.53ff, 183ff, 377ff. It is not appropriate to judge
the correctness of Hick's reading of this tradition, but see
Trethowan 1967.
40. EGL p.378.

salvation. In theological language, according to Hick, "this practical certainty is an aspect of Christian hope." [41]   Even in 1966 Hick implicitly foresaw his next major project, Death and Eternal Life, for the completion of God's purpose must "take place through a continued development within some further environment in which God places us", for our perfection as persons, he argues, is rarely complete at death. [42]   On moral grounds Hick rejects the possiblility that this completion is effected through instant divine fiat - as the freedom and integrity of the finite moral agent would be compromised. [43] Universalism is thus the inevitable consequence because it seems:

> morally (although still not logically) impossible that the infinite resourcefulness of infinite love working in unlimited time should be eternally frustrated, and the creature rejects its own good, presented to it in an endless range of ways. [44]

This strongly emphasised doctrine of a God of love seeking the salvation of all humankind, with its apparent universalist implications, is used by Hick as a critical weapon to attack centuries of Christian teaching - which according to him, implied the very opposite (see argument 1 above). The traditional Christian view presents a "paradox of gigantic proportions". [45] Hick goes so far as to suggest that the traditional Ptolemaic solution is actually

> ruled out by the christian understanding of God. For does not the divine love for all mankind...exclude the idea that salvation occurs only in one strand of human history, which is limited in time to the last nineteen centuries and in space virtually to the western hemisphere? [46]

This perceived paradox is crucial in identifying and understanding the genesis of Hick's Copernican revolution. A gigantic paradigm shift is required to solve an equally gigantic paradox. Christianity must shift from an "ecclesiocentric" or/and "Christocentric" paradigm to a "theocentric" paradigm initiated by the Copernican revolution. [47]

---

41. EGL p.381.
42. EGL p.383.
43. EGL p.383.
44. EGL p.380.
45. GUF p.122.
46. GUF pp.100-01.

No longer can one argue that Christianity or Christ is the sole means of salvation since it is evident that many outside Christianity, and outside the influence of the historical Jesus, are in fact saved (see argument 2 above). This is so, because if

> God's love is universal in scope, he cannot thus have restricted his saving encounter with humanity. If God is the God of the whole world, we must presume that the whole religious life of mankind is part of a continuous and universal human relationship with him.[48]

This Copernican shift involves a radical new attitude to the wider religious life of humankind (see arguments 5 and 6 below). However, the more immediate problem was the justification and implications of a theocentric, rather than an ecclesio- or Christocentric theology. Hick foresaw the possible objection that before "adopting the new picture a Christian must be satisfied that his devotion to Jesus as his personal Lord and Saviour is[49] not thereby brought into question or its validity denied." It is to this argument concerning the traditional understanding of Jesus to which I now turn.

(2.5). Argument 4: The argument from a proper understanding of Jesus.

This is a major controversial area in Hick's thought and before outlining his post-Ptolemaic understanding of Jesus, I wish to attend to the decisive problem addressed by Hick in regard to Christology and the world religions. In failing to appreciate the precise questions faced by Hick, the appropriateness or otherwise of his answers will be obscured.

The problem of "traditional" Christology, Hick argues, is in its literal understanding of the incarnation which inevitably involves the pernicious extra ecclesiam doctrine (see argument 3 above). The chain of reasoning is as follows:

> There is a direct line of logical entailment from the premise that Jesus was God, in the sense that he was God the Son, the Second Person of the Divine Trinity, living in a human life, to the conclusion that Christianity, and

---

[47]. GUF p.131.
[48]. GUF p.101.
[49]. GUF p.148.

Christianity alone, was founded by God in
person; and from this to the further
conclusion that God must want all his
human children to be related to him
through this religion which he has
himself founded for us; and then to the
final conclusion, drawn in the Roman
Catholic dogma "Outside the Church, no
salvation" and its Protestant missionary
equivalent "Outside Christianity, no
salvation.".[50]

According to Hick this unacceptable conclusion is avoided only
if we work "back up the chain of inference and
eventually...question the original premise" - that is,
"traditional" Christology.[51] However, Hick's Christological
suggestions are more widely determined: "This ("traditional"
Christology) has indeed in any case to be reconsidered in the
light of modern biblical scholarship" and the difficulties
inherited through Greek philosophical categories.[52]

Cumulatively, these three problematic areas (the world
religions, philosophical difficulties, and biblical criticism)
led Hick to occupy a position in <u>God</u> <u>and</u> <u>the</u> <u>Universe</u> <u>of</u> <u>Faiths</u>
which he had criticised seven years earlier.[53] In turn, I
shall examine the problems for Christology arising within each
area and Hick's response to them.

(2.5.1). The <u>world</u> <u>religions</u>:

We saw that for Hick a "traditional" Christology generates
"implications that would make impossible any viable theology of
religions" for it logically entails that no one can be saved
outside Christianity or/and the Church or/and Christ.[54]
Arguments 2 and 3 above also counter this allegedly traditional
Christian position thereby suggesting the inadequacy of
"traditional" Christology.

Another consideration from the world religions bearing upon
the necessity of re-interpreting Christology is a tendency
apparently found in Mahāyāna Buddhism specifically, and more
generally in the religious mind. This apparently <u>natural</u>

---

50. <u>GMNUS</u> p.58.
51. <u>GMNUS</u> p.58.
52. <u>GMNUS</u> p.58.
53. <u>GMN</u> p.3, where Hick acknowledges this, referring to 1958a,
1959a, 1966e.
54. <u>GUF</u> p.179.

49

religious tendency exalts founders of religions from a human to an elevated divine status. [55] The exaltation of Gautama in terms of the distinctive Mahāyānist doctrine of the Three Bodies (Trikāya), although different from the incarnation doctrine, is similar in two ways. In "each case it led the developing tradition to speak of him in terms of a complex belief which was only gradually formed by later generations of his followers." [56] Second, Hick also recognises a Feuerbachian note underpinning the phenomena outlined above: "Feuerbach's account of the idea of God as a projection of human ideals has a certain application here." [57] Hick is pointing to the projection of the Christian's "spiritual needs" upon Jesus (or the Buddhist's upon Gautama), a tendency he calls "subjective intentionality". [58] Hence, the question arises as to "what extent is the exaltation in Christian faith of the man of Nazareth into the divine Christ...a supreme example of this projection upon Jesus of ideals to answer our spiritual needs?" [59]

Another point related to this "subjective intentionality" is, according to Hick, the strong and understandable tendency to transpose psychological absolutes into ontologically exclusive absolutes. Due to the believer's momentous experience of encountering salvation, this "quality of psychological absoluteness" is transposed into a "doctrine of the exclusive validity of the believer's own experience". [60] A similar tendency is discovered in "non-religious" cases of being in love and experiencing intellectual illumination. A Copernican can see

> that it is possible for people genuinely
> to be in love with other than one's own
> beloved, genuinely to have the experience
> of intellectual insight in relation to
> different truths...We do not suppose that
> because our own love or insight or
> loyalty has the unqualified character
> that it has, other people's love, insight
> and loyalty must be less authentic...and
> (consequently) we can be sure of the
> authenticity of our own experience

---

[55]. MGI pp.168-70. This tendency can also be seen in relation to Mithras, Rāma, Krishna, Durga and Kālī - see GUF p.172,178. Although Hick does not cite modern-day examples, this same tendency seems to be exhibited in relation to Rāmakrishna, Rajneesh and certain African nationalist leaders.
[56]. MGI p.170.
[57]. MGI p.168.
[58]. MGI p.167.
[59]. MGI p.168.
[60]. GUF p.173.

without supposing that we thereby impugn
that of others.[61]

Hick therefore suggests that we should analogously realise that
the "experience of saving encounter with God does not in itself
entail that there are not, outside Christianity, other encounters
with God exhibiting the same quality of psychological intimacy
and finding expression in their own religious mythology."[62]
The claim that Jesus is God incarnate expresses the religious
significance and importance of Jesus to Christians, nothing more
and nothing less.

This element of "subjective intentionality" amounts to yet
another strand in Hick's argument against "traditional"
Christology. He begins by taking Christian religious experience
seriously. He then applies this principle of treating religious
experience as veracious to non-Christian religious experience -
and offers the Copernican revolution to harmonise the
consequences and application of this principle (see argument 2).
This subjective intentionality explains how Christians transposed
Christology from the language of myth (in one sense, the feeling
of psychological absoluteness) into the language of theory (an
exclusive absolute claim). In an age of religious plurality this
distinction, for so long unnoticed according to Hick, is crucial
for its Christological implications.

The final argument used by Hick is intimately connected with
argument 3 above and argument 5 below. Hick argues that
traditional incarnational language tells us more about the
culture of the time than the real status of Jesus. Consider an
eastern Christ. According to Hick, had Christianity expanded
eastwards, a rather different "christian orthodoxy...would have
resulted."[63]   For instance, "Jesus' religious significance
would probably have been expressed by hailing him within Hindu
culture as a divine Avatar and within the Mahāyāṇa Buddhism which
was then developing in India as a Bodhisattva".[64]   As with some
previous points, examples from the world religions serve to
highlight criticisms that could be made independently of these
examples - as is the case in pointing to the cultural relativity
of language. The considerations evinced from inspecting the
non-Christian religions, cumulatively undermine, according to

---

61. GUF p.173, my brackets.
62. GUF p.174. Hick cites Troeltsch's psychological and cultural
arguments to support his view in GUF p.174. See Troeltsch 1923
ch.1.
63. GUF p.117.
64. MGI p.176. However, in GUF p.115, Hick says that Jesus in a
Hindu culture would have been called a "jivanmukti" (sic). It is
not clear which Hick means, although Avatar is more in keeping
with his argument.

51

Hick, "traditional" Christology.

(2.5.2). Philosophical criticisms:

Hick employs a philosophical distinction to buttress his
arguments from other religions. In God and the Universe of
Faiths, Hick devotes chapter 12 to "Incarnation and Mythology".
He addresses a single question: "What sort of language are we
speaking when we affirm divine incarnation in Jesus of Nazareth?
What is the logical character of such a proclamation?" [65]   To
appreciate the intention of Hick's distinction between myth and
theory (the categories used to answer the question), it should be
remembered that Hick's "orthodox" Christological essay written
seven years earlier had concluded: "what I have been exploring is
not a way of explaining (Christianity's) central claim about
Jesus but only of indicating what this claim is." [66]   Bearing
this in mind, Hick suggests that the logical status of
incarnational language is mythological rather than theoretical or
literal.

A theory, he writes, "whether theological or scientific,
starts with some puzzling phenomenon and offers a hypothetical
description of a wider situation - wider spatially or temporally
or both - such that, seen within this wider context, the
phenomenon is no longer puzzling." [67]   For example in science,
Mendel's law of inheritance explained the distribution of plant
characteristics. Similarly, in theology, theodicy explains the
puzzling presence of evil in a world created by an unlimitedly
good and powerful God. [68]   Theories in science or theology are
also, in principle, capable of verification or falsification and
may consequently be either true or false, or partly true or
false. [69]   Hence, theories and hypotheses used for solving
puzzles and problems must be capable of verification or
falsification to qualify for cognitive status. Hick's acceptance
of positivist criteria also result in his consequent assimilation
of theology to science.

Hick defined myth as a story or image which is not literally
true or false. Myth operates symbolically, poetically or
metaphorically and is applied to something or someone, inviting a
particular attitude in its hearers. [70]   If the attitude to the
object or person is "appropriate", the myth may be deemed true.
This is a kind of mythical or "practical truth" as opposed to a
theoretical or literal truth. [71]   Hick gives an example:

---

65. GUF p.165.
66. GUF p.165.
67. GUF p.166.
68. GUF p.166.
69. GUF p.166.
70. GUF p.166, GMN p.70.

> I may say of a certain happening that it
> is the work of the devil. If this is not
> literally true, the statement is mythic
> in character, and it is a true statement
> in so far as the attitude which it tends
> to evoke is appropriate to the actual
> character of the event in question. [72]

From this it may be deduced that false and inappropriate myths
are possible. Although Hick does not give any examples, the
proposition that "Nero was the saviour of the Christians" may be
a candidate. I use such a tasteless example as it is so obviously
inappropriate to the actual character of the events in question.

Some other aspects of myth are also worth noticing. Besides
being practically true rather than literally true, myths also
lack, unlike theory, an explanatory function. Through myth, Hick
writes, we "relate ourselves to the (problematic) phenomenon
situation in question without being able to explain it." [73]
Furthermore, when myth is understood literally or theoretically,
innumerable and unnecessary difficulties are introduced. Hick's
example of the lover proclaiming that Helen is the "sweetest girl
in the world" supports this point:

> Logically, there can only be one sweetest
> girl in the world; but if we treat the
> lover's words literally and infer from
> the claim that every other girl in the
> world is less sweet than Helen, we shall
> not be doing justice to the kind of
> language he is using. [74]

The subjective intentionality argument explains why people use
this sort of language. The present argument explains its logical
status.

The use of the mythic/literal distinction is applied to the
incarnation through an analogous understanding of the fall of
Adam and Eve in Genesis. [75]   If the fall is taken literally as
positing two ancestors in a paradisal state who introduced
corruption and sin into the human race by disobeying God, Hick
retorts that there is "no evidence to support" such a view and
"much that conflicts with it." [76]   Hick thinks that scientific

---

71.
72. GUF p.167.
73. GUF p.167.
74. GUF p.166.
75. TCC p.32.
76. GUF pp.167-68. Wiles 1978, uses a similar argument.
  . GUF p.168.

evidence provides good grounds for questioning the status of the[77] fall as a "literal" account of the beginnings of humankind. The correct status of the fall as narrative myth, and not as literal theory, serves to remind us of the profound insight that there "is a sense in which our 'true' nature is good even though our actual state is bad, and may prompt us to realise our 'true' moral nature. Thus the myth <u>functions</u> in a way close to that of[78] <u>moral</u> <u>exhortation</u>". According to Hick, language about incarnation should be viewed analogously to that about the fall.

For a variety of reasons Hick argues that incarnational language should not be literally interpreted. Besides the arguments outlined above (and below), Hick also argues that philosophical analysis of the <u>actual</u> <u>character</u> <u>of</u> <u>incarnational</u> <u>language</u> suggests this conclusion. Because incarnational language professes and expresses rather than explains and elucidates, its mythical character becomes evident. Myth, like poetry, according to Hick, is expressive not explanatory. In fact, Hick at first believed Christian history to support this idea. He lists incarnational theories (Arian, Eutychian, Nestorian and Appollinarian - and more recently D.M.Baillie's "paradox of grace" Christology) which have attempted to explain the concept of the incarnation and concludes:

> Every attempt to specify further the idea
> that Jesus was both God and man has
> broken down. It seems impossible to take
> the thought of the God-Man beyond the
> phrase "God-Man" and find any definite[79]
> meaning or content to it.

The reason why these theories were deemed heretical,[80] was because they made the mistake of treating mythical language as theoretical and literal language. Even Nicaea and Chalcedon seem to testify to the mythical character of the incarnation for they

---

[77]. SC pp.102-08.
[78]. GUF p.168, my emphases. This functional and pragmatic notion of myth is similar to Braithwaite's understanding of religious language as ethical, although Hick's distinction between true and false myth steers away from Braithwaite's ethical emotivism - see Braithwaite 1955. There is also some similarity here with Bultmann's translation of myth into existentialist anthropological statements - see Bultmann 1953. However, Hick clearly distinguishes his own understanding of myth from that of Bultmann (GUF p.166), although in 1984 he seems to imply that his own understanding of myth is similar to that of Bultmann's - Hick 1984f p.368.
[79]. GUF p.170.
[80]. Baillie received judgement at the hands of the orthodox Hick in 1958a.

"simply reaffirmed the mystery in its full paradoxical character, without explicating it, whilst the heretical theories...explicated it, but only at the cost of denying one or other of the paradoxical aspects of God-Manhood."[81]

It should be noted that Hick's attitude to "orthodoxy" (in the form of Nicaea and Chalcedon) is ambiguous. It is not clear whether Hick thinks that:
a) The Councils believed that they were intentionally propounding myth (in Hick's sense) - and their teachings would therefore be consistent with, and supportive of, Hick's thesis.[82]
b) The Councils unintentionally understood incarnational language literally. However, they cannot be blamed for this as they did not, according to Hick, have our "sharply posed...modern distinctions" between mythic and literal language.[83]
c) The Councils meant incarnational language to be understood literally and this was their explicit teaching. This seems to be Hick's understanding of the Councils in his earliest writings where he argued that Chalcedon emphasised Jesus' agapé to be numerically identical, "actually and literally" with God's agapé.[84]

Post-1973, option (c) is dominant in Hick's understanding of the Councils. For instance, in 1977 he writes: "the Nicene formula was undoubtedly intended to be understood literally. It asserts that Jesus was literally (not merely metaphorically) divine and also literally (and not merely metaphorically) human."[85] Since then Hick has not changed his mind.[86] For example, in 1984 he writes of the Chalcedonian formula that it has "now become little more than a mysterious formula which is obediently repeated but no longer bears any intrinsic meaningfulness."[87]

If option (c) reflects Hick's attitude post-1973, the arguments above would still operate - but not with the support of "orthodoxy" and tradition, but still with the support of the early disciples whose statements, like that of the lovers, were in the language of poetry and myth according to Hick. This poetic/mythic language was transformed into prose and metaphysics (theory) mainly because "the language of divine sonship floated loose from the original ground of Jewish thought and developed new meaning as it took root again in Graeco-Roman culture."[88]

---

81. GUF p.175.
82. GUF ch.12.
83. MGI p.175.
84. GUF p.154. Insufficient editing explains Hick's inclusion of this paragraph in GUF p.154, 17 pages before he affirms the very opposite.
85. MGI p.177.
86. SC p.31.
87. Hick 1984a p.207.

Echoing Harnack and the liberal Protestant tradition, Hick potrays Greek philosophy as introducing a "wrong turn" into Christian history with its predominantly static metaphysical categories. [89] Greek metaphysics offered an "all-or-nothing model...for something either is or is not composed of a given substance." [90] Forced into this rigid framework, the confessional language of poetry "hardened into prose and escalated from a metaphorical son of God to a metaphysical God the Son." [91]

The reason why literal interpretations of incarnational language fail, as is witnessed in the history of heresy, is because "the Incarnation is not a theological theory but a religious myth." [92] It cannot reconcile irreconcilable characteristics:

> how one person can be both eternal and
> yet born in time; omnipotent and yet with
> the limited capacity of a human being;
> omniscient and yet with finite human
> knowledge; omnipresent and yet confined
> to one region of space at a time; how, in
> short, the same person can have the full
> attributes of both God and man...seems
> indeed to be on a par with the statement
> that a figure drawn on paper has the
> attributes of both a circle and square. [93]

If the incarnation is akin to a square-circle, one may ask does Jesus lose his central significance for Christianity? Hick's unequivocal answer is "No"!

Hick argues that the doctrine of the incarnation can be seen as an appropriate myth to express the "religious significance of Jesus in a way that has proved effective for nearly two millennia." [94] It evokes the appropriate response to Jesus as Saviour: "For it is through Jesus that we have encountered God as our heavenly Father and have entered into the new life which has its ultimate centre in God." [95] Or again: "in following him (Jesus) we find salvation, in believing as he believed we are believing rightly concerning God and man, and in living in his

88. GUF p.116.
89. See ed. Reardon 1968.
90. GUF p.116.
91. MGI p.176.
92. GUF p.170.
93. TCC p.31.
94. GUF p.172.
95. GUF p.172.

fellowship we participate in the life eternal." [96]

Hick then responds to the question as to whether it is appropriate to worship a man who is not literally God incarnate. Hick suggests that finite anthropomorphic "images" or "pictures" are needed by humans to direct their minds towards the "infinite divine reality that exceeds all human thought." [97] According to Hick, it would be idolatry to regard Jesus as the infinite, but he is, to be sure, "the christian image of God through whom our worship is focused, and the idea of the Incarnation is an effective mythic expression of the appropriate attitude to him." [98]

(2.5.3). Biblical criticism:

In Hick's earliest Christological writings little attention is paid to historical biblical criticism. [99] In those writings, Hick had attempted to give contemporary philosophical expression to the teachings of Nicaea and Chalcedon - indicating orthodox claims, not explaining them. He had noticed how the semi-divine "title of Messiah and the semi-divine title of the world of mystery cults, κύριος" soars to the "ultimate heights of the Johannine theology with its proclamation" of John 3.16. [100] This biblical theology is taken for granted.

In Hick's first sustained attack upon "traditional" incarnational theology, there is little use of modern biblical criticism to sustain his arguments. [101] This tends to suggest Hick's supplementary use of biblical criticism, for the first two arguments (2.5.1. and 2.5.2.) are decisive whatever the results of biblical criticism. For instance, if it were shown that the New Testament really did imply the type of Christology that Hick came to reject, the argument from the transposing of psychological into ontologically exclusive absolutes could be deployed, as well as the argument concerning philosophical intelligibility. It might be said that Hick's use of biblical criticism is something of an afterthought.

However in The Myth of God Incarnate, with its band of biblical exegetes arguing for a somewhat similar thesis to that propounded by Hick in God and the Universe of Faiths, Hick employs biblical criticism to sustain his earlier arguments. [102]

---

96. GUF p.176.
97. GUF p.178.
98. GUF p.179.
99. For example, FK1 pt.4 and 1966e.
100. Hick 1966e p.202.
101. GUF chs.7,8,11,12.
102. See Rodwell 1979, who charts the differences and similarities between the mythographers.

57

He pursues two interdependent lines of attack. The first is critical and the second is constructive.

Echoing the "historical scepticism" initiated by Bultmann and others in the late nineteenth and early twentieth century,[103] Hick tells us that "New Testament scholarship has shown how fragmentary and ambiguous are the data available to us as we try to look back across over nineteen and a half centuries" – to the extent that Hick calls Jesus the "largely unknown man of Nazareth."[104] Consequently, it is difficult to ground a literal "traditional" Christology upon this shadowy figure, especially as we come to "acknowledge our ignorance of his inner life and thoughts."[105] However, Hick does not escape from the problem through a Bultmannian exit but goes on to spell out the implications of this partial scepticism.

First, he argues that it is highly unlikely from the little we do know that "Jesus thought of himself, or that his first disciples thought of him, as God incarnate."[106] Hick suggests that the titles ascribed to Jesus cannot carry the weight of later "traditional" interpretation. The meaning of the "mysterious title Son of Man remains to this day uncertain."[107] Even the title of Messiah would evoke in Jesus' contemporaries a "political and military leader, an annointed son of David who would come to institute God's rule over and through his chosen people."[108] Clearly this does not go as far as Nicaea and Chalcedon. Similarly, tracing the title "Son of God" to its Old Testament context, Hick argues that it echoes the coronation ceremony of the earthly king and certainly does not "imply the trinitarian notion of God the Son as this was to be developed in the theology of the church."[109] The Trinitarian theology of the New Testament and St John's high Christology are recognised by the bulk of New Testament scholars, according to Hick, to be a "profound theological meditation, expressing the Christian interpretation of Jesus which was formed fairly late in the first century."[110] Consequently, we cannot "properly attribute its great christological sayings – 'I and the Father are one','He who has seen me has seen the Father' – to Jesus himself."[111]

[103]. Some of the major landmarks are Schweitzer 1954 and Bultmann 1972. For an alternative critical tradition within New Testament studies see Cullmann 1963 pp.1-10; Moule 1967 pp.43-81; Guthrie 1970 pp.220-36. For an overall account of important trends see Hunter 1951; Wood 1960 pp.62-151,169-86.
[104]. MGI pp.177-78.
[105]. GUF p.114.
[106]. GUF p.114.
[107]. GUF p.114.
[108]. GUF p.114.
[109]. GUF p.114.
[110]. GUF pp.115-16.
[111]. MGI p.171.

The aim of this argument is in keeping with Hick's liberal Protestant sympathies: to distinguish the "Christ event" and the subsequent history of the Church which, it is thought, had become somewhat contaminated by Greek metaphysical thinking. Therefore, regarding Jesus' deification, Hick reminds us that "this crucial first step was part of the process whereby the church sought to interpret to itself the meaning of the Christ-event, and (was) not part of that event itself."[112] Assuming that Jesus did not view himself, nor did the early Church, as God incarnate, the Second Person of the Trinity, and also that the bulk of these interpretations appeared a century later, Hick writes:

> What seems to have happened during the hundred years or so following Jesus' death was that the language of divine sonship floated loose from the original ground of Jewish thought and developed a new meaning as it took root again in Graeco-Roman culture.[113]

The subjective intentionality argument is introduced to explain this development as is the argument concerning imposed Greek categories.[114] Both these factors resulted in the Nicene affirmation that Jesus was the "only-begotten Son of God, begotten of the Father before all ages, Light of Light, true God of true God, begotten not made, of one substance with the Father, through whom all things were made."[115]

Cumulatively, these arguments form a single attack upon what Hick takes to be "traditional" Christology. Although Hick acknowledges other influences affecting his Christological shift, it is evident that the main reason lay in his perception of "traditional" Christology as inevitably resulting in the extra ecclesiam doctrine. By removing an obstacle which generates "implications that would make impossible any viable theology of religions" Hick has further paved the way for his Copernican revolution.[116]

The four arguments outlined in this chapter so far demand that we understand anew the nature of religion and religious history. This new understanding, however, is not purely the result of the Copernican shift, but is itself yet another cause for such a shift. Therefore, the nature of religion and religious history

111. GUF p.171.
112. GUF p.114, my emphasis and brackets.
113. GUF p.116.
114. GUF pp.116-17.
115. GUF p.116.
116. GUF p.179.

constitutes a separate argument.

(2.6). Argument 5: The argument from the nature of religion and religious history.

Hick is deeply indebted to Smith's The Meaning and End of Religion. He alerts us to this "important and illuminating book", [117], "already a modern classic of religious studies" which demands our rethinking the concept of religion. [118] As I have outlined Smith's thesis earlier (1.5.1), I will only indicate how Hick utilises Smith's thesis for his Copernican revolution.

Hick argues that Smith challenges our notion of "religions" as "mutually exclusive entities with their own characteristics and histories." [119] From the time of the Enlightenment, with Christianity on the defensive, the notion of religions "as alternative systems of belief embodied in mutually exclusive ideological communities has become accepted." [120] The imperialistic exportation of this "distinctively western invention" resulted in viewing religions as rivals, vying for monopolistic claims and control over truth. [121] This "illicit reification, the turning of good adjectives into bad substantives to which the western mind is prone", [122], helped to produce the "inevitable perplexities in which the Christian theology of religions has become hopelessly entangled." [123] Hick argues that if Smith's proposed conceptual shift is accepted, then improper questions such as "which is the true, or truest, religion?" can be abandoned and fruitful attention paid to the diverse ways in which people have responded to the divine. [124]

An additional reason for such a paradigm shift is adduced from Smith's further investigations:

> Smith examines the development from the original religious event or idea, whether it be the life of Christ, or the teachings of Mohammed, or the insight of the Buddha, to a religion in the sense of a vast living organism with its credal backbone and institutional skin. And he shows in each case that this development

---

117. GUF p.101.
118. Hick 1978d p.ix; 1985b.
119. GUF p.101.
120. Hick 1978d p.xi.
121. GUF p.101.
122. GUF p.101.
123. Hick 1978d p.x.
124. Hick 1978d pp. x, xii.

stands in questionable relation to that original event or idea.[125]

It would seem that subjective intentionality transforms psychological absolutes, surrounding "truths and values with institutional walls which divide 'us' from 'them'."[126] It appears that even religious founders did not want institutional communities established and the subsequent divisions between "religions".

Hick argues that the value of Smith's analysis is in breaking down our conceptual grids, requiring us to view "the religious life of mankind as a dynamic continuum within which...intersections of divine grace, divine initiative, divine truth, with human faith, human response, human enlightenment" take place.[127]

Before returning to Hick's further use of Smith, it is appropriate to outline Hick's theory about the development of the religious history of humankind when viewed as a dynamic continuum of human and divine interaction. The main sources for his theory seem to be a combination of Ling's authoritative A History of Religions East and West, and more significantly Karl Jaspers' The Origin and Goal of History.[128] Hick's theory of religious history has remained constant throughout the years except that since 1980, African primal religions are promoted to the new status of one of the supernatural world faiths.[129]

The religious history of humankind is divided into three periods by Hick. The first is one of "natural religions, or religion without revelation" emerging from as far back as the third millenium BCE.[130] This phase correlates to the early tribal "group mentality that prevailed prior to the emergence of self-conscious individuality" which was to characterise the next phase.[131] Hick argues that in this primitive stage the divine "was reduced in human awareness to the dimensions of man's own

---

125. GUF pp.102-03.
126. GUF p.103.
127. GUF pp.101-02.
128. Jaspers' philosophy is, according to Macquarrie, "compatible with liberal Protestantism", and like Schleiermacher, Jaspers begins with experience - see Macquarrie 1963 p.352. Jaspers concentrates on the experience of transcendence mediated through "ciphers" or limiting situations (Grenesituationen) of finite contingency. This led Jaspers to reject any exclusivist claims for he believed that revelation was universally possible - as does Hick - see Kane 1981 on Jaspers.
129. SC p.8.
130. GMNUS p.48.
131. GMNUS p.43.

61

image" and consequently Hick concludes that in this phase "there was more human projection than divine disclosure."[132]

The first phase provided the conditions for the emergence of human individuality. Between 800 and 200 BCE there then took place a second stage of a remarkable series of revelatory experiences, in what Hick, following Jaspers, calls the "axial period": in China: Confucius and the author(s) of the Tao Te Ching; in India: Gautama, Mahāvīra, the Upanishads and later the Bhagavad Gītā; in Persia: Zoroaster; in Israel: the Hebrew prophets; in Greece: Pythagoras, Socrates, Plato and Aristotle.[133] During this period the major religious options were identified and established. Therefore, Hick views Jesus, Mohammed and Mahāyāna Buddhism, for example, as important major developments within the already existing traditions. This period, unlike the previous first phase, is one of supernatural religion "in which outstanding individuals emerged and were able to be channels of new religious awareness and understanding - in theological terms, of divine revelation."[134]

A further consideration supporting this view of multiple revelations is the relative isolation of the different cultures from one another - "for all practical purposes men inhabited different worlds."[135] Therefore, argues Hick, since such a divine revelation intended for all humankind would have taken centuries to spread to other countries, it seems more plausible to see God's revelatory activity as taking place in a number of diverse ways and at different times.[136]

Hick tentatively forsees the emergence of a third stage - if the Copernican revolution is accepted within different traditions. This phase would be analogous to the relations "between the different denominations of Christianity in Europe or the United States."[137] Hick develops Ruether's phrase, "ecclesial ethnicity", used to denote her commitment to Roman Catholicism as opposed to any other Christian denomination.[138] Hick extends this notion to religious adherence in general. Therefore, being a Christian rather than a Buddhist is finally a matter of "religious ethnicity".[139]

The term "religious ethnicity" implies that religious adherence is more often than not a result of the society into

---

132. GMNUS p.44; see also GUF pp.134-35.
133. GUF ch.10, GMN pp.52-3.
134. GMNUS p.47.
135. GUF p.136.
136. GUF p.136.
137. GUF p.147.
138. SC p.90; citing Ruether 1981 p.163.
139. SC p.90.

which one is born. This observation is the basis for a separate and further link in the argument - one which Hick has called "genetic confessionalism". [140] It is expressed thus:

> if I had been born into a devout Hindu family in India and had studied philosophy at, let us say, the University of Madras, I should have probably held a Ptolemaic Hindu theology...And if I had been born to Muslim parents say in Egypt or Pakistan, I should probably have held a Ptolemaic Muslim theology. And so on. [141]

Hick's only modification to this argument is his concession that the notion "I" used in this example is misleading. The subject "I" who is a Hindu in Madras could not be said to be the same "I" as a Muslim in Pakistan as the qualifying predicates are intrinsically substantive of the subject "I". [142] Nevertheless, the point at issue is left intact. According to Hick it is apparent that Ptolemaic theologies "tend to posit their centres on the basis of the accidents of cultural geography" and once this is recognised, one "can scarcely avoid seeing one's own Ptolemaic conviction in a new light." [143] Hick uses this argument to underscore the covert religious imperialism of the sophisticated Ptolemaic theologies which imply, in effect, that the "privilege of knowing the full truth" is dependent on one's birth place. [144]

If the arguments above are accepted, Hick offers some illuminating analogies by which the relationship between the religions may be understood. The first analogy employs a parable attributed to the Buddha:

> An elephant was brought to a group of blind men who had never encountered such an animal before. One felt a leg and reported that an elephant is a great living pillar. Another felt the trunk and reported that an elephant is a great snake...And so on. And they all quarrelled together, each claiming that his own account was the truth and all the others false. In fact of course they were

---

140.
141. Hick 1981c p.456.
142. GUF p.132.
143. Hick 1981c p.454; see also Lipner 1977 pp.254-55, who brought this point to Hick's attention.
144. GUF p.132.
     GUF p.132.

> all true, but each referring to one
> aspect of the total reality and all
> expressed in very imperfect analogies.

Hick suggests that when religions assert exclusive competing truth claims (which the old model of "religion" encouraged), the situation is analogous to the blind men quarrelling. Rather, we should consider that "many different accounts of the divine reality may be true, though all expressed in imperfect human analogies, but that none is 'the truth, the whole truth, and nothing but the truth'." [146]

Another analogy used by Hick is that of map projections. The different religions might well turn out to be "maps of different possible universes." [147] However, it may also be the case that "they were analogous to maps of the same world drawn in radically different projections, each method of projection distorting reality in a different fashion and yet enabling the traveller successfully to find his or her own way." [148]

To summarise: Hick utilises Smith's work to show that the concept of religions as competing ideological communities is a modern illicit reification contrary to the wishes of many of the founders of the great religious traditions. One is then free to see the religious life of humankind as a continuum of human and divine interaction. Added to this, the observations on genetic confessionalism cumulatively suggest that appropriate analogies for the relationship between the religions are the elephant-blind men parable, and the analogy of differing maps of the same reality. The combined strength of Hick's theological, philosophical, cultural and psychological arguments so far gains further weight when we turn to the theological and practical benefits that result from this Copernican standpoint.

(2.7). Argument 6: The argument from the theological and practical benefits of the Copernican revolution.

Hick argues that his Copernican theology results in fruitful implications for dialogue and inter-religious cooperation. These benefits may be classified as "theological" and "practical", although no sharp distinction is necessary and both allow for hitherto unforseen developments.

Theologically, the Copernican revolution removes what Hick

---

145. GUF p.140.
146. GUF p.140.
147. Hick 1981c p.462.
148. Hick 1981c p.462.

sees as the "largest difficulty in the way of religious agreement" and progressive dialogue:

> Each religion has its holy founder or scripture, or both, in which the divine reality has been revealed...And wherever the holy is revealed it claims an absolute response of faith and worship, which thus seems incompatible with a like response to any other disclosure of the holy.[149]

This stance creates what Hick calls the "confessional end of the dialogical spectrum", where each partner is convinced that his (or her) own faith "has absolute truth whilst his partner's has only relative truth."[150] Dialogue inevitably becomes monologue and a matter of proselytising for "each will be basically concerned to try and bring the others to share his own faith."[151]

However, the Copernican shift dissolves this problem. Copernicans do not regard Jesus in an exclusivist fashion because they properly understand incarnational language. This Copernican attitude may be fruitfully followed by theologians and philosophers in other traditions, although it is not Hick's task, he tells us, "as a Christian to tell Buddhists, Muslims or Hindus how to develop their symbols and belief systems".[152] However, Hick does suggest that exclusive religious claims depend on a central symbol that is best understood metaphorically or mythologically, rather than literally. This would affect the Ptolemaic Muslim, for example, who believes in the "eternal character of the Qur'an as God's final Word"; or the Ptolemaic Buddhist who believes in the "global completeness of the Buddha's insight, so that there can be no other aspects of reality than the _pratitya_ _samutpada_ of which he becomes so vividly aware in his Enlightenment." And so on.[153] If these Copernican suggestions are adopted, a major problem in the relationship between religions will be removed - as it has been, for Hick.

The Copernican perspective also broadens the scope and function of theology. If "it was hitherto reasonable to develop our theology in disregard of God's dealings with the non-Christian world, it has now ceased to be reasonable to do that."[154] In argument 5, we saw that all humankind's history

---

149. TD p.154.
150. GMN p.81.
151. GMN p.84.
152. SC p.91.
153. SC p.91.
154. GUF p.106.

65

reflects the divine activity (less so before the axial period).
Hick argues that if this is the case, theologians must reflect on
the vast data of humankind's religious history ("global"), rather
than exclusively upon their own tradition ("sectional"). [155]
Hick undertakes an exercise in global theology in Death and
Eternal Life. He is confident that this process will enrich all
religious traditions, for "whilst we can never form a totally
adequate conception of God's nature, nevertheless we may form a
less inadequate one on the basis of the full range of man's
religious experience than on the basis of a single segment of
it." [156] He affirms that those "who accept the pluralist vision
are free with good conscience to benefit from the immense
spiritual values and insights of other traditions." [157]

This shift allows the Christian to abandon confessional
dialogue and pursue what Hick calls "truth seeking dialogue." [158]
In this form of dialogue each partner

> is conscious that the transcendent Being
> is infinitely greater than his own
> limited version of it, and in which they
> accordingly seek to share their visions
> in the hope that each may be helped
> towards a fuller awareness of the Divine
> Reality before which they both stand. [159]

Finally, Hick defends himself from the possible charge that
this view invalidates mission. If the world religions are genuine
encounters with God then it makes little sense to extinguish the
richness of humankind's testimony to the divine. However, if we
recall Hick's distinction between the primitive natural religions
and the higher supernatural religions then Hick may be assumed to
qualify the scope of mission. When he asks, should "mission be
'sideways', into the cultures dominated by other world faiths, or
'downwards', into the realm of primal religion?" - we may assume

---

[155]. GUF p.103. Hick seems to suggest that in carrying out global
theology, theologians lose their own religious identity, by
saying of this new endeavour: "These will not be christian
theologies, or islamic theologies, or buddhist theologies, but
human theologies". (GUF p.103). However, Hick does not develop
this particular idea further, and elsewhwere (GUF pp.106-07, DEL
pp.26-34) he emphasises that the Copernican revolution does not
dissolve commitment to one's own religion, but only exclusive
claims arising from that commitment. In this respect, Hick's
global theology differs considerably from that of other
pluralists - see D'Costa 1986b.
[156].
[157]. GUF p.105.
[158]. SC p.90.
[159]. GMN p.81.
       GMN p.81.

66

the answer to be "downwards". [160]   One may also assume from Hick's writings [161] that Christian mission to secular society is appropriate.

What then is the role of mission regarding the great world religions? Hick thinks that because of the new political independence of old mission fields, the future role of missionaries has already been partially initiated. Missionaries, he writes, are properly engaged in "giving medical, social, educational and technical aid to developing countries. They are sharing with the needier nations, as a gift of Christian love, some of the fruits of western affluence." [162]

To summarise: the main theological implications (which have an obvious practical outcome) of the Copernican shift (commending it as well as resulting from it) are: the removal of a major obstacle to religious dialogue; providing the basis for global rather than sectional theology (allowing a richer notion of God); and the reconception of the task of mission in terms of service.

One other point is noteworthy. Hick reminds us that the English mind is supposedly "pragmatic and experimental rather than doctrinaire." [163]   Had it been more "theory-oriented" or excessively "logically minded", Ptolemaic Christians should have tried to convert, rather than help and facilitate, the adherents from other religions when they arrived in England. "They would...have sought to supersede these alien faiths by winning their adherents over to Christian baptism and church membership", rather than helping the "newly arrived Muslims, Sikhs and Hindus to establish themselves here in their own faith." [164]   Hick's point is that the practice of Ptolemaic Christians runs counter to their actual theologies - as was noted above in argument 2.

Once the Copernican shift is accepted, a situation similar to Christian ecumenism will be initiatd and "a large degree of practical co-operation" will be possible. [165]   Hick offers his own testimony. For him, Copernican Christianity involves itself in the "market place" as well as in the churches:

> I have certainly found myself...that the acceptance of all human beings (and not cnly fellow Christians) as children of God, and the acceptance of the other great world religions (and not only

---

160. GMNUS p.39.
161. SC p.88.
162. GMN p.35.
163. GMN p.36.
164. GMN p.36.
165. GUF p.147.

> Christianity) as having their own
> spiritual validity, involves activity of
> a broadly political kind, seeking through
> the work of various organizations to
> implement these attitudes in such areas
> as religious education...attention to the
> needs of the ethnic minorities in
> hospitals, prisons, etc., and to their
> treatment by the local media..[166]

Hick's list is extensive, covering many activities that he feels Christians are called to undertake in the light of their new Copernican consciousness. These many _practical_ benefits further add to the attractiveness and importance of the Copernican revolution.

(2.8). Argument 7: The argument from the infinite divine nature.

In Truth and Dialogue Hick pointed to a vexing problem arising from conflicting truth claims regarding the "differences in modes of experiencing the divine reality."[167] The main conflict revolves around "God as personal in Judaism, Christianity, Islam and...strand(s) of Hinduism", and the divine as "non-personal"[168] for example, in "Advaita Vedānta and in Buddhism." It is interesting to note that as early as 1968 Hick had indicated a possible resolution: that two apparently opposing predicates may be properly attributed to a single subject when that subject is not finite. He suggests that if we consider the Logos as "the divine self-expression in relation to creation", we can speculate that

> The divine Logos has become manifest in
> this personal way to peoples whose
> deepest presuppositions and ways of
> thinking lead them to respond to the
> personal nature of the Divine, but in
> other ways to other peoples, especially
> in the East, whose character leads them
> to a more mystical experience of the
> impersonal depths of divine being.[169]

Hick slightly develops this thesis in Truth and Dialogue. He reminds us that if, as "every profound form of theism has affirmed, God is infinite, and accordingly exceeds the scope of our finite human categories", then consequently, God "may be both

---

166. GMN p.7.
167. TD p.152.
168. TD p.152, my emphases and brackets.
169. CC p.80.

68

personal Lord and impersonal ground of being; both judge and father, source both of justice and love." [170] Hick acknowledges this answer needs further development and tantalisingly suggests Sri Aurobindo's "logic of the infinite" as a fruitful avenue for further exploration. [171]

Hick employs Hindu terms (see immediately below and 5.2) when dealing with this problem in God and the Universe of Faiths. He suggests that personal and impersonal images should be seen as contrasting emphases, rather than absolute differences, in the varying responses to God. The interaction of the two elements of "human response" and "divine initiative" account for the differences.

Although Hick does not fully develop these suggstions here, it is clear that two objectives are intended. He seems to imply that God is experienced genuinely as personal and as non-personal – and this assertion may be pursued "both as a matter of pure theology and in relation to religious experience." [172] In argument 5 above, we saw that Hick stressed the historically and culturally conditioned nature of religious experience and the resultant creeds and theologies. Accordingly he argues that it is quite likely that culture, economics, climate, psychological types, stages of individual development and a host of other factors account for, in part, the varying perceptions of God as such factors affect our ways of "becoming and being human." [173] As an example of such influences Hick refers to Ling's findings. Ling argues, using India as an example, that "among agricultural peoples, aware of the fertile earth which brings forth from itself and nourishes its progeny upon its broad bosom, it is the mother principle which seems important." The Semitic religions on the other hand, with "their origins among nomadic, pastoral, herd-keeping peoples in the Near East" find the "male principle of power and authority" most appropriate. [174] These factors apparently help to explain why the typically western conception of God is predominantly male and the eastern, predominantly female.

---

170. TD pp.152-53.
171. TD p.153. Hick cites Chubb's contribution to the Truth and Dialogue conference, where Chubb develops Aurobindo's ideas – see Chubb 1972. In GUF p.149, Hick refers to Aurobindo 1955 bk.2, ch.2.
172. GUF p.144.
173. Hick cites Berger & Luckmann's (1971 pp.66-7) study in the sociology of knowledge in DEL p.412: "the ways of becoming and being human are as numerous as man's cultures. Humanness is socio-culturally variable."
174. Both passages cited by Hick in GUF p.135; from Ling 1968 p.27.

These differences also result in varying forms of worship: from the highly formalised to the free and unstructured; from purely intellectual to richly emotional; some emphasising the remoteness and otherness of God and others, the legalistic, judgemental aspect. [175]   Hick concludes that we find these sets of "dual experience" <u>within</u> a <u>single</u> religion, not solely in inter-religious comparison.

Hick then turns his attention from "religious experience" to what he terms "pure theology". He asks whether non-theistic faiths can be "seen as encounters with the <u>same</u> <u>divine</u> <u>reality</u> that is encountered in theistic religions?" [176]   Hick attempts to argue that it is now possible to view both theistic and non-theistic religions as encounters with the "same divine reality" by means of employing the Hindu distinction between <u>nirguna</u> and <u>saguna</u> traditionally employed to designate certain aspects of <u>Brahman</u>. Hick writes:

> Detaching the distinction, then, from its Hindu context we may say that Nirguna God is the eternal self-existent divine reality, beyond the scope of all human categories, including personality; and Saguna God is God in relation to his creation and with the attributes which express this relationship, such as personality, omnipotence, goodness, love and omniscience. Thus the one ultimate reality is both Nirguna and non-personal, and Saguna and personal. [177]

Hick clarifies and develops these suggestions in 1980, eventually leading to what I shall call a Copernican "epicycle" in his theology of religions. (See chapter 5 below).

To summarise: the Copernican revolution raises some difficult questions about the nature of "God" and the coherence of viewing both theistic and non-theistic religions as equally valid apprehensions of the <u>same</u> divine reality. In so far as Hick's answers are satisfactory, they act as further arguments for a Copernican theology of religions.

(2.9). <u>Conclusion</u>.

Having outlined Hick's career and some important influences that

---

[175]. <u>GUF</u> p.144.
[176]. <u>GUF</u> p.144, my emphases.
[177]. <u>GUF</u> p.144.

helped shape his theological outlook and then situated his theology of religions within the context of the twentieth-century debate (chapter 1), I have, in this chapter, dealt with his battery of arguments for the Copernican revolution itself. We saw how Hick was dissatisfied with the Ptolemaic theology of religions which apparently consigned the majority of humankind to perdition (argument 1). However, it is evident, Hick says, that in meeting adherents from the non-Christian religions, many Christians have discovered the presence of God within these religions, suggesting that salvation is possible outside Christianity (argument 2). This fact demands a new theology of religions - which is made possible by the doctrine of a God of love who desires the salvation of all humankind (argument 3). A Copernican theology, combined with biblical and philosophical considerations, suggests and provides a new "mythological" understanding of Jesus, rather than the traditional "literal" Christology, which makes any viable theology of religions impossible (argument 4). Drawing on Smith's work, Hick also suggests that the nature of religion and religious history needs reviewing. Rather than seeing the various religions as mutually exclusive, rival ideological communities, they should be viewed as a single continuum of divine-human interaction (argument 5). This Copernican shift also commends itself by the theological and practical implications that are made possible in inter-religious dialogue and cooperation (argument 6). Finally, Hick has dealt with certain difficulties concerning the nature of "God" which arise as a result of his Copernican proposals (argument 7).

Cumulatively, the force of these arguments suggests a radical approach to the Christian theology of religions. If Hick's thesis is found to be correct and convincing, then the theology of religions faces a radical paradigm shift which Christians cannot ignore. A Copernican vanguard would herald the dawn of a new era and the overthrow of the established Ptolemaic orthodoxy. The very nature of Christian theology is called into question. A new phase of theological reflection must begin in which many old problems concerning religious pluralism and conflicting truth claims dissolve, and Copernican global theologies should thrive.

In the next two chapters I shall systematically and critically evaluate Hick's Copernican arguments. The results of this examination, I submit, will have profound implications on the question of the theology of religions, and clearly upon the very nature of Christian theology.

CHAPTER 3: AN EXAMINATION OF JOHN HICK'S ARGUMENTS - PART I

(3.1). An examination of argument 1: The argument from the untenable Ptolemaic theology of religions.

According to Hick the first and longest phase of Ptolemaic Christianity is summarised in the Catholic axiom, extra ecclesiam nulla salus. Hick thinks this teaching as "arrogant as it is cruel",[1], for it implies "that the majority of human beings are eternally lost."[2] This axiom also generates the irresolvable paradox that Ptolemaic theology fails to resolve: "can the God of love who seeks to save all mankind" ordain "that men must be saved in such a way that only a small minority can in fact receive this salvation?"[3]

There are three questions concerning Hick's criticisms: is his understanding of the extra ecclesiam teaching correct; does the doctrine imply that the majority of human beings are eternally lost, thereby generating an irresolvable paradox; and what was the reason for the retention of this doctrine despite the fact that the second and third phases of Ptolemaic Christianity acknowledged that "outside Christianity there is salvation"? In this section I try to answer these three questions. If Hick's criticisms are correct then a "Copernican revolution...is needed in the christian attitude to other faiths."[4] If his criticisms are incorrect then the Copernican revolution is not a necessity, although certain Copernican proposals may be legitimate.

(3.1.1). The first phase of Ptolemaic theology:

It is odd that Hick cites Boniface VIII (1302) and the Council of Florence (1438-45) as the major and initial exponents of the extra ecclesiam teaching, for this axiom received developed formulation ten centuries earlier by Origen (c 185-254) and Cyprian (c 206-258).[5] Augustine (c 354-430) took up Cyprian's axiom and was followed in this by his disciple Fulgentius (c 467-553), from whom the axiom entered into the theology of the middle ages. The Council of Florence text cited by Hick is in fact from Fulgentius' De fide ad Petrum.[6]

---

1. GMNUS p.29.
2. GUF p.122.
3. GUF p.132.
4. GUF p.126.
5. The roots of the axiom go even further "back to Ignatius of Antioch, Irenaeus, Clement of Alexandria, and others." - Küng 1981 p.313.
6. See Denzinger 1957 1351 n.1.

I shall trace the origin and intentions of this axiom for the following reasons. Specifically, we can then answer the three questions addressed to Hick. More generally, because most critical discussion of Hick's Copernican theology has focused entirely upon the problems consequently raised, not upon his reasons for formulating his thesis in relation to the theological tradition dealing with other religions.[7] In attending to the latter issue, I believe that the former problems will be illuminated in a manner which other critics have neglected, perhaps unintentionally.

As Cyprian is cited by Augustine and Fulgentius, and has exercised a considerable influence upon ecclesiological reflections, he is a useful starting-point for my investigation.[8] I exclude Origen because despite his "outside the Church, no one will be saved" teaching,[9], Baker argues that "the terms in which he (Origen) describes the true Church preclude identification of it with the outward visible Church."[10] Although Baker minimises Origen's grasp of the Church as an organised community with its own laws and constitutions, Kelly agrees with Baker in noticing that according to Origen's mystical sense of the Church, "Christ's body comprises the whole of creation; for according to Origen's teaching all creatures will ultimately be saved".[11] Clearly Origen does not fit Hick's category of the first phase of Ptolemaic theology although his is one of the earliest formulations of the teaching!

Cyprian's teaching at first sight seems to correspond to Hick's categorisation of the first phase of Ptolemaic theology. Soon after Cyprian's conversion (c 246) he was elected Bishop of Carthage. The Church in North Africa was a minority community fighting for its very existence, not only against heresy but also persecution. The Decian persecution (249) forced Cyprian to flee from Carthage, returning in 251 to face many lapsed Christians who had offered sacrifice to the emperor. Cyprian opposed the easy reconciliation of the lapsed and the rigorism of Novatian - who had been consecrated rival Bishop of Rome opposing Pope Cornelius. The Bishop of Carthage was faced with what Benson calls the "problem of the hour":

> Heresy had hitherto been manifold and
> fantastic. But Schism - meaning secession

---

[7]. This is true, with the exceptions of Forrester 1976; Russell 1977; Hughes 1984.
[8]. See Benson 1897 pp.200-20, 432-37; Vatican II 1964 para.9; Walker 1968 ch.5.
[9] Cited in ed. Bettenson 1978 p.243.
[10]. Baker 1903 p.363, my brackets.
[11]. Kelly 1980 p.202.

upon questions not originally doctrinal –
had been almost unknown. Now, however,
beginning from the central see, the
Church reeled with the new possibility of
being cleft in twain upon an enquiry as
to whether she possessed disciplinary
power for the reconciliation of her own
penitents. [12]

Another factor is also important in appreciating the context of
Cyprian's De Catholicae Ecclesiae Unitate. Danielou writes that
"in contrast to the apocalyptic writings of the Judaeo-Christians
and the idealism of the early Greek Fathers, the work of the
early Latin theologians is characterised by (an) extremely
concrete concept of the Church." [13] This stress on the concrete
and visible partly arose with the Church being contrasted as an
alternative society in "opposition to a hostile pagan world" [14];
and was further accentuated in this case by Cyprian's use of
"analogies borrowed from Roman law." [15]

This background illuminates Cyprian's use of the extra
ecclesiam axiom. His unquestioned premise was "that the Catholic
Church not only ought to be, but in fact is, one", [16], and this
one body represents the unity of the Godhead and of Christ. [17]
Consequently, Cyprian argued against Novatian that "unity" is
expressed in submission to one's bishop - operating within the
collegial episcopate of bishops. Irenaeus' criterion for
membership (teaching authority in doctrinal matters) failed to
deal with Novatian whose doctrinal work on the Trinity was
completely orthodox. Hence, Sage comments that Cyprian's
ecclesiology "was not the result of logical deduction or
theological examination but the sequel to various practical
considerations that arose from the continuing crisis of his term
as bishop". [18] However, Sage tends to minimise the theological
traditions and arguments utilized by Cyprian. [19]

The logical corollaries of Cyprian's theory are lucidly
summarised by Kelly:

---

12. Benson 1897 p.181.
13. Danielou 1977 p.429, my emphases and brackets.
14. Danielou 1977 p.441.
15. Kelly 1980 p.204.
16. Kelly 1980 p.204.
17. Benson 1897 p.185.
18. Sage 1975 p.335.
19. See Danielou 1977 p.436; Benson 1897 pp.186-200; Kelly 1980
pp.204-07.

> The criterion of Church membership
> is...submission to the bishop himself.
> Rebellion against him is rebellion
> against God, and the schismatic however
> correct his doctrine or virtuous his
> life, renounces Christ, bears arms
> against His Church and resists God's
> ordinances. In effect he is a heretic, so
> that Cyprian can write of Novatian
> himself: 'We are not interested in what
> he teaches, since he teaches outside the
> Church. Whatever and whatsoever kind of
> man he is, he is not a Christian who is
> not in Christ's Church'. And, since 'he
> cannot have God for his Father who has
> not the Church for his mother', there is
> no salvation outside the Church. [20]

We may note the following points. First, Cyprian's use of the axiom bore reference to <u>schismatics</u>, not adherents of the great world religions. Second, the concern behind Cyprian's teaching was a Church torn in two through what he perceived to be a lack of charity and obedience. This lack of charity, Cyprian believed, confirmed the lack of grace denied to the schismatic.

There is an important development in Cyprian's career, adding further nuance to the "traditional" understanding of the <u>extra ecclesiam</u> axiom. [21] Cyprian's thesis, if taken in an exclusively literal and negative fashion, entailed the view that grace was restricted to the Church. Consequently, outside the Church, sacraments were invalid. Benson thinks that Cyprian's lack of "distinction between a Visible and an Invisible Communion upon earth...in his next great crisis placed Cyprian himself in some danger of separatism." [22] This crisis was precipitated by the strong papal reaction against Cyprian's teaching of the invalidity of sacraments outside the Church. Pope Stephen argued for certain supernatural effects of baptism even among heretics, for the minister's role was instrumental, not substantial. The significance of Stephen's position was the acknowledgement of grace outside the visible Church - and it was Stephen's view that was finally accepted. [23]

Before pursuing my investigation, it should be noted that the Catholic Church has consistently condemned the Jansenist teaching: "Outside the Church no grace is granted". [24] De

---

[20]. Kelly 1980 p.206.
[21]. See Sage 1975 pp.295-336.
[22]. Benson 1897 p.186.
[23]. See Rahner 1963 p.42; Chadwick 1978 p.120.

Lubac shows that, with varying emphasis, the Fathers (Irenaeus, Cyprian, Hilary, Ambrose, John Chrysostom, Origen, Cyril of Alexander, the early Augustine) and Aquinas have all maintained the principle "that the grace of Christ is of universal application, and that no soul of good will lacks the concrete means of salvation". [25] It would seem that even during this "first phase", contrary to Hick's interpretation, it is "a dogma of divine faith that the Catholic Church is requisite for salvation. It is also perfectly certain that a man who dies as a non-member of the Church can attain to the beatific vision." [26] Consequently, a tentative answer to the first two questions posed to Hick would be that the extra ecclesiam doctrine is primarily concerned to express that all saving grace is God's grace, revealed in Christ the head of the Church (his mystical body) and revolves around a single issue: "is there or is there not another way of honouring the principle of the oneness of the mediator of salvation?" [27] The axiom does not imply that the "majority of human beings are eternally lost", [28] neither is it a reflection upon those who have never heard the gospel, such as Hindus or Buddhists.

Two further factors support my reading. These factors also deal with the objection that Judaism is a major world faith and thereby in principle, the extra ecclesiam teaching was applied to "other religions". The Fathers (and the medievals) viewed the world as "Gospel saturated". [29] They assumed that everyone had been confronted by the gospel. Consequently, those who were not Christians were in bad faith having, it was believed, rejected the truth of the gospel. [30] Heretics, schismatics, pagans and Jews belonged to one category: those who had properly heard of and rejected Christ. In this sense it was clear to the Fathers

---

[24]. Denzinger 1957 1379. Before Clement's condemnation, see also Pius V (Denzinger 1957 1025) and Innocent XI (Denzinger 1957 1295).
[25]. de Lubac 1950 p.108; see also Daniélou 1957 pp.22-4; Küng 1981 p.315. However, Dupuis 1966 and Cyriac 1982 ch.3 tend to have an over-optimistic interpretation of the Fathers on this question. See instead the more nuanced studies of de Lubac 1969 ch.4, and to a lesser extent, Hacker 1980 ch.2. For instance, Dupuis and Cyriac omit in their discussion of Justin Martyr's "Logos" doctrine, Justin's strong condemnation of the Hellenistic religions and that for Justin, "the truth contained in these religions is hidden and disfigured by demonic contexts." - Hacker 1980 p.37.
[26]. Fenton 1944 p.300.
[27]. Congar 1961 p.95.
[28]. GUF p.122.
[29]. Congar 1957 pp.297ff.
[30]. Congar 1957 p.298, 1961 p.119; Fransen 1967 p.84; Küng 1981 p.513; Rahner 1963 p.41.

that for those "outside the Church" there was no salvation.
Congar notes that the extra ecclesiam axiom "makes no claim to be
a judgement on the personal position of anybody", but is
developed in faithfulness to the conviction that "the Church
founded by Jesus Christ is in this world the only repository of
the principle of salvation in its authenticity and fullness."[31]

A second factor is the special position of those who lived
before Christ. This category is significant as it is applicable
to a person who has not heard the gospel objectively and properly
proclaimed. This category was understandably not extended by the
Fathers to apply post-Christ. With this qualification in mind,
let me return to the development of the axiom.

In Augustine's development of Cyprian's extra ecclesiam axiom,
the question of the salvation of those before Christ is addressed
more explicitly. Before proceeding, it must be acknowledged that
Augustine's thought developed over a long period of time and is
consequently not easily characterised.[32] Furthermore, only
some of his teachings have been accepted by the Church.[33]
However, I wish to investigate Augustine's response to the
special problem of those before Christ in the context of the
extra ecclesiam doctrine to shed further light upon the three
questions I have addressed to Hick.[34]

Some brief qualifications are in order. Baker points out (and
the same can be said of Cyprian) that the extra ecclesiam
doctrine in Augustine is applied in relation to "heretical or
schismatic societies of Christians."[35] Augustine's main works
were aimed at the Manichaeans, Donatists and Pelagians.
Furthermore, Augustine, as most Fathers, indissolubly related
the Church to Christ. For Augustine, Christ held a triple mode of
existence: as eternal Word, as God-Man Mediator, and "as the
Church, of which He is the Head and the faithful the members."[36]

---

[31]. Congar 1961 p.135.
[32]. Baker writes that "it is difficult to feel confidence in the
accuracy of any summary statement" on Augustine's work - Baker
1903 p.368.
[33]. The Council of Orange (529) affirmed Augustine's teaching on
the priority of grace to human response, but not his doctrine of
predestination.
[34]. Clement of Alexandria, Origen, Ambrosiaster, Cyril of
Alexander, John of Damascus and Oecumenius were some of the
Fathers who reflected on Christ's descent into hell as a means of
union with those who knew nothing of him - see Congar 1961
pp.136-37; ed. Vorgrimler 1969 pp.75-81; Rahner 1961b; Daniélou
1964b pp.233-48; Dalton 1965.
[35]. Baker 1903 p.368. The same can be said of Fulgentius' use of
the axiom - see Neuner 1973 p.149.
[36]. Kelly 1980 p.413.

For Augustine, the essential unity of the Church is love - just as the Holy Spirit is love personified, the mutual product of love between Father and Son. Consequently, schismatics, such as the Donatists, were excluded from the Church for they lacked, according to Augustine, love and charity in precipitating separation in the one body of Christ.[37] While Augustine stressed the visible unity of the Church in doctrinal belief, this criterion was not always applicable to schismatics whose beliefs were often "orthodox". Augustine's stress on love as entirely dependent on grace led him (in controversy with the Donatists,[38], and in the aftermath of Rome's fall,[39]) to develop his notion of the visible and invisible Church. The visible Church (communio sacramentorium) contained both sinners and the just, whereas the invisible Church (communio sanctorum) contains only the just, "the congregation and society of saints", the "holy Church".[40]

Given this context, we may turn to the question of the salvation of those before Christ. Augustine believed that the communio sanctorum exists "from the beginning of the human race until the end of the world".[41] Augustine recognised the just and righteous within the pagan and gentile "saints" of the Old Testament up to the time of Abel.[42] Consequently, in Retractationes he writes of his summary of an argument in De Vera Religione ("This is the Christian religion in our day. To know and follow it is the safest and surest salvation" - ch.10, n.9):

> This I said, bearing in mind, the name (religion) and the reality underlying the

---

[37]. Augustine 1972 pp.1007-10; Kelly 1980 p.414, n.11; Portalié 1975 pp.233, 244-5,270-76.
[38]. The Donatists claimed that the Church must be sinless and rejected the Catholic Church for accepting sacraments conferred by "traditores". Augustine held the notion of the sinless Church, but only visibly manifest in an eschatological time.
[39]. See Chadwick 1978 p.225.
[40]. Cited in Kelly 1980 pp.415-16. See also Augustine 1972 pp.45-6,593,831-32,998-99. Kelly minimises the importance of the visible Church for Augustine. He rightly says that for Augustine, even those who are "heretics or schismatics, or lead disordered lives or even are unconverted pagans, may be predestined to the fullness of grace," thereby transferring the "whole problem of the Church's nature to an altogether different plane." - Kelly 1980 p.416. However, Kelly fails to point out as does Baker (1903 p.370) that Augustine assumed "that the elect who were outside the Church were destined to come inside before their death." (my emphasis). See also Portalié 1975 ch.13. By inside is meant visible.
[41]. Daniélou 1957 p.10; see also Hacker 1980 p.55.

79

name. For the reality itself, which is
now called the Christian religion, was
already among the ancients. It had never
been wanting from the beginning of
mankind until the incarnation of Christ,
and from then on the true religion, which
had already been in existence, began to
be called Christian. For when the
Apostles began to make him (Christ) known
after his resurrection and the ascension
into heaven, and when many believed in
him, his disciples were called Christians
for the first time in Antioch, as is it
written (Acts 11:26). That is why I said:
'This is the Christian religion in our
times', not because it did not exist
formerly, but because it received this
name only later on. [43]

Clearly Augustine, a Ptolemaic theologian in Hick's eyes, is
optimistic about those before Christ, explaining theologically
they are included in God's providential plan, despite his
retention of the extra ecclesiam axiom. [44]

To return to my three questions, it would seem that Hick is
insensitive to the preoccupations of the Fathers, and the
contexts within which the extra ecclesiam doctrine was developed
and applied. After citing the Council of Florence's Decree,
without attention to the axiom's background, Hick incorrectly
applies the teaching to "the great religions of mankind". [45]   In
the Council decree itself, only eight paragraphs earlier, the
Council Fathers acknowledged "one and (the) same God as the
author of the Old and New Testament" and that the "saints of both
Testaments have spoken with the inspiration of the same Holy
Spirit"! [46]   Furthermore, Jewish "ceremonies, rites, sacrifices
and sacraments" are regarded as "suited to the divine worship"
before the coming of Christ. [47]   When Fulgentius is then cited,
obviously his presuppositions are shared: that all Jews have been
properly confronted by the Gospel and have rejected it and are

---

[42] . Hence the Ecclesia ab Abel doctrine, which is also found in
the writings of Justin, Irenaeus, Origen and later Eusebius,
Jerome and Ambrosiaster - see Neuner 1973 p.149; Congar 1952.
[43] . Augustine 1968 book 1, ch.12, para.3.
[44] . Curiously Hick uses the cited text to support his Copernican
position! - Hick 1985c p.11. See also Augustine 1972 pp.828-32,
1967 pp.135-42,113-17; Portalié 1975 p.233.
[45] . GUF p.120.
[46] . Denzinger 1957 706.
[47] . Denzinger 1957 712.

80

consequently in bad faith. The decree is also primarily intended to counter "heretical" views rather than refer to non-Christian religions. Sabellius, Ebion, the Arians, Manichaeans[48] and Macedonians are declared "foreign to the Christian body". It is in this context that the _extra_ _ecclesiam_ doctrine is proclaimed.

Regarding Boniface, Muldoon argues that Boniface's _Unam Sanctam_, from which Hick quotes, should be viewed in the broader context of his long running dispute with Philip of France and "the threat of the king's policies posed to the Church's essential unity."[49] Having dealt with the schismatic Greeks, Armenians and Georgians "Boniface and his contemporaries recognised the difficulty of ending a schism once it was established".[50] Muldoon concludes: "Thus, when the pope reminded the king that there was no salvation outside the Church, he was not only firing a salvo in the running battle over the rightful jurisdiction of the two powers; he was asserting the nature of the papal responsibility everywhere."[51] Boniface, in this teaching repeated Innocent's _Cum Simus_. Significantly this latter bull was aimed at ending the Bulgarian schism. Therefore, despite Boniface's political manoeuvrings, the teaching can be viewed in continuity with the history of the axiom's use in relation to the question of Church unity, rather than its application to other religions per se, as Hick suggests.

I have been arguing that the axiom has been developed over the ages and "applied to certain very concrete situations, to the cases of those responsible for schism, revolt or betrayal."[52] Cardinal Bea's remarks to the Fathers of the Second Vatican Council, when introducing _Nostra_ _Aetate_, supports this view of the application of the _extra_ _ecclesiam_ doctrine: "About these (world religions) it is, as far as I know, the _first_ _time_ in the history of the Church that a Council has laid down principles in such a solemn way."[53]

To summarise: it would appear that the first question (whether Hick has correctly understood the _extra_ _ecclesiam_ doctrine) must be answered negatively. Therefore the second question (whether the doctrine consigns the majority of humankind to perdition) must also be answered negatively. The Fathers, contrary to Hick's suggestions, _did_ "stop to think about...the human race who have lived and died up to the present moment...before Christ."[54]

---

48. Denzinger 1957 705.
49. Muldoon 1979 p.70.
50. Muldoon 1979 p.70.
51. Muldoon 1979 pp.70-1.
52. de Lubac 1969 p.87.
53. Cited in Cyriac 1982 p.111, my emphases.
54. GUF p.122.

Although there is some truth in Hick's comment that the Church neglected the problem of salvation "outside the borders of Christendom", [55] it must be remembered that it was commonly assumed by the Fathers (and to a large extent by the medieval Church) that the whole world was "Gospel saturated" and consequently after Christ, no one really lived outside the borders of Christendom.

Although in the middle ages it was known that there were certain countries and races outside Christendom, for the most part there was little reliable information available and regrettably even less interest. [56] Bühlmann suggests the chief motives behind the Crusades in the middle ages were "gold, slaves and territory." [57] This is somewhat polemical, although feudal and colonial interests were important forces in the medieval Church, as was the perceived military threat of Islam. [58] The missionary travels of the Jesuits and their discovery of civilised and morally good people outside the Church in the fourteenth and fifteenth centuries unfortunately became obscured in the Jansenist controversies. It should also be noted that Christianity's long and bloody engagement with Islam during the Crusades was not seen as an encounter with a major world religion, for Islam was considered a Jewish-Christian heresy, contrary to Bühlmann's opinion. [59] Incidentally, a highly developed analysis of implicit faith and invincible ignorance was in existence by the time of the middle ages. [60]

However, mainly due to the reasons outlined above, the theories of implicit desire, implicit faith, and inculpable ignorance were on the whole not applied to the question of salvation in non-Christian religions. The application of the theory of implicit faith to the question of the salvation of non-Christians characterises what Hick calls the second stage of Ptolemaic theology.

---

[55]. GUF p.122.
[56]. Congar 1957 p.96.
[57]. Bühlmann 1982 p.109.
[58]. Erdmann 1977 chs.2,3,8. Wolfram von Eschenbach's Willehalm (1220's) marks an important shift in the high middle ages attitude towards the "good pagan". The two doctrines underpinning this work are that God will not punish people for their ignorance, and that "a pagan who leads a good life not merely may receive, but merits God's grace." - Brooke 1969 p.161. See also Foster's study of Dante's treatment of the good pagan in the context of thirteenth century scholasticism - Foster 1977 chs.10-12; and Foster on Aquinas and good pagans - Foster 1977 p.154, n.25; p.172, n.3.
[59]. Cyriac 1982 p.144; see Bühlmann 1982 pp.97-9.
[60]. Council of Trent: Denzinger 1957 796; Congar 1957 pp.299ff; Rahner 1963 ch.1; Foster 1977 ch.10.

(3.1.2). The second phase of Ptolemaic theology:

Two of the three questions put to Hick have been answered negatively. The third question must now be considered: what was the reason for the retention of the extra ecclesiam doctrine which led to, according to Hick, increasingly implausible epicycles to "change its practical effects"? [61]   I have argued that the extra ecclesiam doctrine did not consign the majority of human beings to perdition, nor did it address the particular problem of salvation in the major world religions. Therefore it is questionable whether "epicycles" have been introduced to change the doctrine's "practical effects", as Hick suggests. The apparently "gigantic" paradox that necessitates a Copernican revolution in fact contains a false premise. The paradox poses the following question:

> Can we then accept the conclusion that the God of love who seeks to save all mankind has nevertheless ordained that men must be saved in such a way that only a small minority can in fact receive this salvation? [62]

The second part of the cited proposition cannot, in the light of our considerations above, be said to represent the intention and meaning of the extra ecclesiam doctrine.

Our three questions and their answers come together in Hick's attack on this second phase of Ptolemaic theology. He writes that Pius IX's Allocution is a "characteristically Catholic way of paying allegiance to the original dogma" while changing its practical effects through subsidiary epicycles. [63]   Because Hick misunderstands the central concerns and preoccupations of the Fathers and the intention of this axiom, he fails to appreciate the importance of its retention. The axiom is a development in the expression of faith that the sole mediator of grace is God, and equally affirms that this truth is indivisibly revealed in Jesus Christ who is the founder and head of the Church, his mystical body. Küng reminds us that in history when this extra ecclesiam "axiom was both formulated negatively and taken literally, it led to heresy." [64]   Consequently, the "epicycles" are in keeping with this central and necessary Christological confession within Christianity.

---

61. GUF p.123.
62. GUF p.122, Hick 1983c p.338.
63. GUF p.123.
64. Küng 1981 p.314.

83

I would contend that the "epicycles" are best viewed as the development of theology within necessary parameters defined by the extra ecclesiam doctrine. The revelation of God in Christ is the source for the two guiding premises of this discussion. The first holds that God reveals himself definitively in Christ (and his Church). And from this first premise, the second is also generated: that is, God desires the salvation of all humankind.[65]

Hick rejects the first premise, but accepts the second, betraying his misunderstanding of the extra ecclesiam doctrine. In short, the Church has tried to be faithful to the fact that the doctrine of a "God of universal love" is made known only through Jesus Christ. The notion of a God of love requires grounding. Rahner incisively remarks that this "free attitude of God, which is directed towards the salvation of every man, has only become a manifest principle, definitively and irrevocably, in Jesus Christ."[66] In other words, God's univeral love is "not a metaphysical attribute of God which can be established everywhere and always."[67] Notably, such a doctrine of God has hardly ever been propounded from philosophical argument alone. Hick, I shall later argue, has serious problems grounding his doctrine of a God of universal love, especially as he discounts philosophical proofs for such a God.[68]

However, let me return to Hick's criticism of the second phase of Ptolemaic theology to further develop my argument. The answer to my third question then, which has been implied in the first two answers, is that the retention of the extra ecclesiam axiom represents the concern for the basis of the doctrine of an all-loving God. It is the latter doctrine that Hick is keen to preserve. However, its basis is that such a God is revealed in Jesus Christ who is made visible in his mystical body the Church. If this is the case, then it is possible to view the Ptolemaic "epicycles" as part of an evolutionary development (which is also closer to the scientific intention of the term); as part of a continuous reflection upon the contents of faith within changing situations.[69] Congar calls this process a legitimate "evolution in theology".[70]

---

[65] Hence the importance of the "ab Abel" teaching. Vatican II bases its affirmation that God's "providence, evident goodness, and saving designs extend to all men (cf Wis. 8:1; Acts 14:17; Rom. 2:6-7; I Tim. 2:4)" on scriptural testimony - Vatican II 1965a para.1.
[66]. Rahner 1966b p.406.
[67]. Rahner 1966b p.406.
[68]. See 3.2 and 4.1 below.
[69]. See Ernst 1979 p.30.
[70]. Congar 1957 p.300.

In examining this phase of Ptolemaic theology a fourth question introduces itself. If we accept the necessity of the extra ecclesiam axiom as expressive of the belief in a single source of grace - explained above - then how valid are Hick's criticisms of the epicycles of the second phase? Are they, as Hick suggests, "fundamentally weak arguments" which "do not go far enough"[71] in the light of the "wider religious life of mankind?" Or do they realistically acknowledge the wider religious life of humankind and reflect upon the conditions whereby a person, who is invincibly ignorant of the gospel, may yet live and be saved by the salvific grace of God, mediated though Christ?

(3.1.3). The theology of implicit desire:

Hick's main criticisms are directed against theories of invincible ignorance and implicit desire as used and understood during the period 1854-1965. It is not clear why Hick is dissatisfied with the invincible ignorance category, other than that "only God himself knows to whom this doctrine applies."[72] Regarding this criticism, it may be noted that any doctrine that compromised the inscrutability of God's ways concerning salvation either lead to Pelagianism - in asserting that good works not merely may receive, but will merit God's grace; or, on the other hand, to a form of gnosticism whereby the holding of certain beliefs guarantees salvation.[73]

The invincible ignorance category, when applied to the non-Christian, designates those who do not know the gospel through no fault of their own.[74] This category, as suggested earlier, applies equally to certain people both before and after Christ. A more historical and existential view must account for, among other factors, "social pressure, the weight of inherited prejudices, esprit de corps, collective complexes (which) are all strong influences for altering the condition in which the presentation of a message can be considered real, effective and sufficient."[75]

---

71. GUF pp.122-23.
72. GUF p.123.
73. See Denzinger 1957 239, 1520-33 condemning these views.
74. Technically, invincible ignorance belongs to one of five sets of a division of ignorance in canon law and is contrasted with vincible or culpable ignorance. Technically, the non-Christian in invincible ignorance is known as a "negative infidel".
75. Congar 1961 pp.116-17. For the rest of this chapter I shall use the term "non-Christian" to denote those in invincible ignorance of the gospel. Whether they are saved or not is an open question.

Hick's objections to the implicit desire theory are only slightly more elaborate than his objections to the invincible ignorance category. He complains that only theists, by definition, are included in its considerations. And furthermore, by a sleight of hand, this doctrine (which is just as easily turned upon its user), renders those outside the Church as inside, even though "unconsciously" and invisibly. [76] Unfortunately, Hick does not develop these remarks. During this second phase there is a wealth of Catholic reflection on this problem, none of which is referred to by Hick. [77] This is regrettable, for the substance of Hick's objections has in fact received close attention, as I shall now demonstrate.

It is worth noting that even the requirement of explicit faith can include the possibility of salvation in Judaism, Islam and even Amida Buddhism. [78] But all three of these traditions have some form of theism or saviour figure, thereby substantiating Hick's criticism. However, a major discussion of implicit desire overcoming Hick's objections is found in Congar's The Wide World My Parish. [79] Congar argues that the doctrine of implicit desire does not require a formal theistic object of belief, consequently non-theists are properly intended within its strictures. [80] The very term "implicit" denotes that explicit belief is not the subject of consideration. However, the term "desire" may mislead by suggesting a psychological function. [81] Any psychological meaning is far from the intention of the doctrine, amusingly illustrated by Congar when arguing that the doctrine concerns a "real implication" and is not concerned with "elements of unconsciousness". [82] Congar, having just written of Martin Chauffier's comment about his communist friend's hidden love of God, writes: "Do not the communists themselves tell us that, by refusing to commit ourselves to certain opinions (theirs) on the grounds of not taking sides in matters which divide men from one another, the Church in reality gives her

---

76. GUF p.123.
77. Eminyan 1960 offers a wide-ranging survey of Catholic opinion during this period. See also Rahner 1963 pp.1-88; Journet 1955 pp.31-40.
78. Lombardi 1956 p.208.
79. Congar's advisory position in the drafting of Vatican II 1965a is significant. The strong influence of de Lubac, Rahner and Congar on the Conciliar documents has been acknowledged - see ed. Vorgrimler 1969 pp.86, 93.
80. How otherwise could Vatican II (1964 para.16, 1965a para.2) acknowledge the presence of the divine in non-theistic religions and also the possibility of salvation for the non-culpable atheist? See also Lombardi 1956 p.24.
81. This seems to be Hick's understanding - GUF p.123.
82. Congar 1961 pp.121, 120, respectively.

86

support to the 'forces of reaction'".[83]   Congar argues that
whether or not one knows God, every event in history calls forth
a fundamental decision, expressed in various ways and in
different forms of commitment, for or against God implicitly or
explicitly. In the same way that the Church must either belong to
the "forces of reaction" or side with the communists, Congar
analogously points out that there is no "neutrality in the great
conflict between Jesus Christ and Satan." But, and very
importantly, he adds, "only God can read hearts."[84]

Although I cannot now examine the presuppositions of Congar's
argument concerning implicit faith, it is illuminating to note
his careful qualifications of this doctrine which are closer than
Hick realises to his own Copernican sympathies. There is, for
instance, a clear shift away from knowledge to the life lived
without minimising the importance of explicit faith. Congar
argues that every historical event is capable of mediating God,
however imperfectly, unclearly and implicitly, by calling forth a
response of absolute self-forgetful love.[85]   This may be found,
for example, in some people's commitment to "Duty, Peace,
Justice, Brotherhood", often at the cost of "their own personal
interests and comfort, at the cost of themselves, and even
sometimes of life."[86]   This opportunity of genuine
self-forgetful love is most fully presented in relation to that
which people are able to manifest their deepest commitment -
their neighbour, who can call forth an "absolute that strikes a
spark of love."[87]

Congar is conscious of the dangers that beset such a thesis.
Until now it may appear that he is in agreement with Hick's
suggestion that the epicycles need to be developed "to the point
at which salvation is understood in terms of right relationship
to the divine reality".[88]   However, the rest of Hick's sentence
highlights the wide gulf in method and presuppositions between
Copernicans and Ptolemaics (or Hick and Congar more
specifically), when Hick adds that "right relationship to the
divine reality" should be understood "as variously known in the
different religious traditions".[89]   Hick's suggestion seems to

---

[83]. Congar 1961 p.121. See also Rahner 1972 p.154
[84]. Congar 1961 p.121.
[85]. For the biblical basis of Congar's argument - see Congar 1961
pp.104-21.
[86]. Congar 1961 p.124.
[87]. Congar 1961 p.121. Congar offers four arguments supporting
this point of view - see pp.124-26. Rahner's similar assertion is
based on an elaboration of Congar's third point: "man" as mystery
orientated towards the Absolute mystery, God - Rahner 1979 ch.16,
1961a chs.9,10.
[88]. GUF p.124, my emphases.
[89]. GUF p.124.

imply that the notion of "right relationship" and "divine reality" should be determined by a phenomenological analysis of the world religions, thereby giving normative revelatory status to none. Congar, on the other hand, is clear that such an inspection of other religions requires, for the Christian, Christocentric presuppositions concerning the nature of "divine reality" and "right relationship". The consequences of Hick's method and presuppositions will be further analysed below.

Let me return to Congar's defence of implicit faith to quell Hick's objections. Congar carefully qualifies his argument. First, a "properly transcendent" absolute is required such that people give themselves in true love and charity.[90] There can be false absolutes to which people commit themselves, such as hatred and pride which produce self-seeking and egotism. True absolutes are also in real danger of "the human absorbing the divine."[91] This is where the "real implication" of an action contradicts faith and charity, when for instance a "man can have a passion for justice which in fact betrays justice, because it excludes certain people; or a love which betrays charity, because in practice it denies charity's universality or disinterestedness or some other essential value."[92] The human element may also absorb the divine through idolatry, whereby properly transcendent absolutes "lose their malleability as signs and become idols falsely worshipped instead of God."[93]

I have tried to show that Hick's objections fail to address the deeper issues implied in theories that characterise the second phase. Invincible ignorance is not invalidated by the fact that only God knows to whom this doctrine applies. Furthermore, implicit desire cannot be dismissed on the grounds of its supposed exclusion of non-theists. During the second phase there was much reflection on this teaching bringing forth an emphasis on practice and a life of charity as entailing the possible conditions for salvation.[94]

My contention that Hick misunderstands Catholic teaching is clearly demonstrated in his own use of this type of theory! He writes of the good humanist and atheist:[95]

---

[90]. Congar 1961 p.121.
[91]. Congar 1961 p.126.
[92]. Congar 1961 p.127.
[93]. Congar 1961 p.127. These comments and warnings apply to Christians.
[94]. We may recall in the discussion of Cyprian and Augustine that charity is of prime importance. Aquinas places the virtue of charity higher than the virtue of religion - see Foster 1977 pp.227-30, 253.
[95]. In this passage "Reality" replaces the term "God" - see 5.2 below.

> From the religious point of view such
> secular servants of humanity are
> involved, <u>without</u> <u>knowing</u> <u>it</u>, in the
> transition from self-centredness to
> Reality-centredness; and the religious
> communities have a mission to show them
> the <u>further</u> <u>dimension</u> <u>of</u> <u>reality</u> of which
> they are at present <u>unaware</u>.[96]

Eight pages before this quote, Hick reiterates his criticism of implicit faith!

Hick's criticism that the implicit faith theory can just as easily be adopted by other religions may rightly seem somewhat irrelevant. If Hick's "secular servants of humanity" complained at Hick's "arrogance" and suggested that Hick and his co-religionists actually participated in a transition towards secularity-centredness, Hick would not, I suspect, deny his claim. Rather, as he has done concerning the positivist attacks, and in relation to humanism, he would try to argue for the reasonableness, intelligibility and comprehensiveness of his position.

In conclusion, the implicit desire teaching is not a sleight of hand creating "unconscious" Christians, but an attempt to remain faithful to two central tenets. The first is shared by both Catholic and Protestant theologians. The second, according to Hick, constitutes the divide between these two groups. The first is that the sole source of salvific grace is God, revealed in and through Jesus Christ. The second, which is intrinsically linked to the first for the majority of Catholics, is that since all grace is the grace of Christ and since all grace is by its nature ecclesial (because grace is necessarily manifest in history and community), then salvation must always come through, and be related to, the Church.[97] Hick, I have argued, has failed to show that the epicycles are "fundamentally weak arguments." His original misunderstanding of the <u>extra</u> <u>ecclesiam</u> axiom results in his misconstruing most of Christian history. This is exemplified in his characterisation of the third phase's

---

96
. <u>SC</u> p.88, my emphases.
97
. On this, see Rahner 1963 ch.1. He argues against an understanding of the "votum ecclesiae" in purely interior terms, suggesting, by means of an analogy of the Church as sacrament (thereby denoting two aspects of one reality: sign and reality signified) that if the reality of grace is present to the non-Catholic (or non-Christian), then the votum ecclesiae "has a <u>quasi-sacramental</u> <u>visible</u> <u>aspect</u> in the concrete" which then "can and must be included in the visible nature of the Church." (p.77).

implausibility when he writes, "theological ingenuity goes to its limits to hold together the two propositions that outside Christianity there is no salvation, and that outside Christianity there is salvation."[98]

Hick's characterisation just quoted above is polemical. As a way of summarising this section I shall try to express the real intention of what only appears to be, and is sometimes falsely set up as, a contradictory statement. In the light of my defence of what I would prefer to term inclusivist rather than Ptolemaic theology,[99], a sympathetic reading of the tradition may run thus: theological reflection has tried to explain that although the single source of all salvific grace is God, revealed through Jesus Christ and his mystical body the Church, this salvific grace has always been present and has sometimes been responded to affirmatively in various ways from the beginning of humankind's history. Even after the incarnation, the Catholic tradition has always held that those who have not properly confronted the gospel may, under certain circumstances, be saved. It has never been specified who or how many of these people there are. This would compromise the inscrutability of God's ways. The teachings of the Catholic tradition brought to fruition in Vatican II, in no way deny that there is much that is "true and holy" in non-Christian religions and that salvation is found by the adherents of these religions under certain conditions.[100]

(3.1.4). Conclusion:

I do not intend to examine Hick's criticisms of the third phase as my initial three questions to Hick have been answered in the foregoing discussion. The major point of disagreement with the Catholic tradition in its many phases, is that for Hick, salvation in the other religions must be viewed theocentrically (at least before his later epicycles), not Christocentrically or ecclesiocentrically. This section has tried to demonstrate that for most of Christian history, God, Christ and the Church have been indivisibly related for complex, diverse and valid theological reasons. Hick is aware of this relation for this is precisely the focus of his atttack. What he seems to be less aware of, as my analysis I hope has demonstrated, is why and how theologians have been concerned to maintain the unity of God, Christ and the Church. Regrettably, Hick does not engage seriously enough with the early or later Christian tradition

---

[98]. GMNUS p.33-4.
[99]. See my characterisation of the inclusivist paradigm in 1.3 above, and D'Costa 1986a ch.4.
[100]. See Vatican II 1964 para.16, 1965a para.2, 1965b para.7: and also D'Costa 1984a; ed. Vorgrimler 1969 pp.1-154; Kunnumpuram 1971; Cyriac 1982 ch.9; SNC 1984, 1985.

while trying to establish the necessity of his Copernican theology, thereby failing to demonstrate adequately its necessity. A major reason for Hick's misunderstanding of much of the Christian tradition, I have argued, is his literal and unhistorical interpretation of the extra ecclesiam doctrine. This literalism is the cause of further problems in his Christological understanding.[101]

A number of further points are in order. Hick's hermeneutical insensitivity to the Christian tradition concerning the salvation of non-Christians extends to his assessment of the Bible. Hick argues that the New Testament writers knew nothing of the major world faiths, except Judaism, so that their insights are illegitimately applied[102] to the world faiths for the problem is an entirely new one. It is inappropriate here to enter into discussion of the biblical texts concerning our problem.[103]

In redressing the balance Hick's positive and valuable insights should not be ignored. Because of Hick's special attention to Catholic theology, I have one-sidedly focused upon this tradition which of course is not unanimous concerning the assessment of non-Christian religions - both now and in past history. Hick is right when he says that some Christians, such as "fundamentalist evangelical groups", literally and strictly hold that "outside Christianity, there is no salvation."[104] Many of Hick's questions and criticisms may rightly bear upon such literalist positions. Hick is also right in saying that for centuries this issue has not been in the forefront of the theological agenda. However, he is, as I have shown, sometimes too sweeping and historically inaccurate, and often hermeneutically insensitive. A major strand of inclusivist theology, which I have briefly outlined above, cannot be said, as Hick claims, to contradict[105] the very doctrine of "God which it presupposes." And the apparent paradox (whereby an all-loving God consigns the majority of humankind to perdition) which generates the "necessity" of the Copernican revolution is also seen to be questionable.

---

101. See 4.1 below.
102. Contrary to this see Ernst 1979 p.31; Hughes 1984 pp.15-6. This lack of attention to the traditional determinants of Christian theology such as scripture, tradition (and the authority of the Church) often mar Hick's reflections on certain theological questions (see 4.1 below). Louth 1983 offers a perceptive analysis of this tendency and its problems in contemporary British theology.
103. On this issue see Daniélou 1957 pp.11-19; Legrand 1973; Ariarajah 1985; Cracknell 1986.
104. GUF p.121. However, even evangelical attitudes are not unanimous - see Stott 1975, 1981; Scott 1981; Hughes 1984.
105. GMNUS p.31.

If this section has shown Hick's deficient understanding of the origin, intention and context of the extra ecclesiam teaching, I will have succeeded in alerting the reader to some of the difficulties encountered in Hick's Copernican revolution. I have tried to show why much of Christian history has sought to closely relate Christ, his Church and God. By incorrectly understanding the theological importance and concern behind this identification Hick, it will be seen below, runs into some serious problems. Furthermore, by misinterpreting the tradition, Hick fails seriously to undermine what I shall be defending as an inclusivist theology of religions (or in Hick's categories - the second and third Ptolemaic phases).

Despite my criticisms, Hick's Copernican revolution may still presents itself as a challenging and viable theology of religions. It fails, however, to present itself as a pressing necessity. In other words, if the Copernican revolution fails we are not necessarily left with an imperialistic and untenable "Ptolemaic" theology.

Rather than turning to Hick's argument 2, I now turn to argument 3: "The argument from an all-loving God". The necessity for grounding the doctrine of God in Christology has been constantly alluded to. Therefore, its crucial importance demands prior consideration to argument 2. [106]

(3.2). An examination of argument 3: The argument from an all-loving God.

Before examining the basis and grounding for Hick's premise of an all-loving God, there are a number of issues that require clarification. There are two strands in Hick's use of this argument. The first can be denoted as an argument from universalism. Hick argues that the doctrine of hell would "be incompatible with God's sovereignty or with his perfect goodness." [107] Employing such a supposition, Hick realises that a form of universalism is inevitable as it seems

> impossible that the infinite resourcefulness of infinite love working in unlimited time should be eternally frustrated, and the creature reject its own good, presented to it in an endless range of ways. [108]

---

[106]. Argument 2 is dealt with in 4.4 below.
[107]. EGL p.378; see 2.4 above.
[108]. EGL p.380.

Consequently, the first strand of the argument supposes that if God is all-loving and gracious, then not a single person will be lost.

The second strand is closely related for it goes on to affirm that if God is all-loving, then surely such a God would provide non-Christians the means to salvation: "If God is the God of the whole world, we must presume that the whole religious life of mankind is part of a continuous and universal human relationship with him."[109] This is also because the majority of humankind have never heard of Christianity. The two strands of the argument can be joined together in the following way: since God saves all people - and since God must be working in all religions to do this - then the Copernican revolution is necessary to take cognisance of these insights.

In this section I wish to pursue three questions. The first two are related to both parts of Hick's arguments outlined above. The third is addressed to the basis of Hick's presupposition. The questions may be summarised as follows. First, does the notion of an all-loving God necessarily entail such a universalism? Second, and relatedly, is the notion of an all-loving God incompatible with the idea that such a God only acts salvifically within one religious tradition? Third, what is the basis for Hick's belief in an all-loving God and is such a basis compatible with his other Copernican presuppositions? Although both parts (outlined above) of Hick's arguments are inter-related they are not, I will argue, inseparable. Hence, if we find fault with one part, the other, may on its own, entail a Copernican rethinking. Furthermore, even if both parts of the argument stand up to scrutiny, it is possible that in answering the third question, the Copernican alternative may turn out to be indefensible.

(3.2.1). Universalism and the Copernican revolution:

It should be said at the outset that a belief in universalism does not in itself require a Copernican revolution. Hick was, after all, a "Ptolemaic" theologian while also a universalist, as were the later Barth (possibly) and Origen (certainly).[110] Consequently, if it is possible for inclusivist theologians to argue coherently for the salvation of non-Christians as was shown above, then it is quite coherent and possible to be a "Ptolemaic" universalist. In itself, universalism is compatible with the second and third phases of "Ptolemaic" theology (as Hick defines it), and does not logically entail a Copernican shift. In Hick's "Ptolemaic" days, his own choice of "epicycle" related to a

---

[109]. GUF p.101.
[110]. In the light of EGL pp.371-81, it is not quite clear why Hick writes that he had always thought, up until 1972, that all non-Christians were "damned or lost" - GUF p.121.

post-mortem confrontation with Jesus. [111]   In 3.1 above, I tried to show that Hick's arguments against the Ptolemaic epicycles are not convincing. Hence on the basis that Hick was himself at one time a "Ptolemaic" universalist and that Hick's arguments against the Ptolemaic epicycles are inconclusive, we may proceed with the assumption that Hick has not shown that universalism is incompatible with the later stages of "Ptolemaic"-type theologies, i.e. with inclusivist theologies.

Another point requires clarification before proceeding. God's desire to save all people does not in itself require a concomitant belief in universalism. Many Christians have thought that to affirm universalism in such an unqualified manner entails the denial of human freedom freely to choose or reject God. Thus, the Catholic Church both proclaims the universal salvific will of God, while formally condemning universalism as an error. [112]

Hick in fact seems to hold a qualified form of universalism, for he recognises that "despite the logical possibility of failure" (i.e. of God not saving all people), "the probability of His success amounts, as it seems to me, to a practical certainty." [113]   He goes on to define this practical certainty: "In the traditional language of theology this practical certainty is an aspect of the Christian hope." [114]   While Hick does not press for a strong form of universalism, thereby proportionately undermining the force of the first part of his argument as outlined above, there is one serious objection to Hick's form of universalism arising within his own epistemological presuppositions.

In Faith and Knowledge Hick expounds the notion of "epistemic distance" which is central to his whole theological outlook. [115] Hick argues that God creates people at an "epistemic distance", so that they find themselves in an ambiguous universe. Hence all experience, including religious experience, is a matter of interpretation. [116]   This is because Hick wishes to safeguard two issues which he sees as central to theism. The first is that theism is non-coercive; and relatedly, that revelation involves a free act of interpretation which does not encroach upon human freedom. For real faith there must be real freedom. His thrust is aptly summarised thus:

> If human analogies entitle us to speak

---

[111]. See CC p.106.
[112]. Vatican II 1965a para.1; Denzinger 1957 209, 211; Rahner 1966a pp.405-09.
[113]. EGL p.380.
[114]. EGL p.381, my emphases.
[115]. FK2 chs.5-6.
[116]. FK2 p.97.

about God at all, we must insist that such a universe (i.e.: in which a loving response to God is guaranteed) could be only a poor second best to one in which created beings, whose response to Himself God has thus not 'fixed' in advance, come freely to love, trust and worship Him. And if we attribute the latter and higher aim to God, we must declare to be self-contradictory the idea of God so creating men that they will inevitably respond positively to him.[117]

There are two possibly insurmountable problems that are raised in the light of Hick's theory of epistemic distance and his belief in a near practically certain universalism. Hick posits "resurrection worlds" as being the place where future human development takes place, and in which, over many lives, people will eventually be saved.[118] For the moment I will accept the possibility of such resurrection worlds.[119] We may then ask: are there good reasons for Hick's optimism concerning universalism? The reason for a more qualified optimism than Hick's is that in the resurrection world the epistemic distance must be the same as it is now, because Hick maintains that our present epistemic distance is the right distance from God and in fact, is the only final justification for the degree and extent of evil experienced in this world. Otherwise, there would be unnecessary suffering for the critic could rightly argue that God could have created this world in a less ambiguous fashion, lessening the extent and "justifiable" intensity of evil. The point of the epistemic distance which now exists, is such that people can come "freely to love, trust and worship" God.[120] If this is the case, there is no reason why there should be a greater number of people saved in the next world(s) than in this. Because, if the epistemic distance is narrowed or modified,

> then the Hickian theodicist is left in a dilemma. For as a logical consequence we must admit that either as a result of the changes men are no longer free in the degree required for them to fulfil God's purpose or that not every evil can be

---

117. EGL pp.310-11, my brackets.
118. DEL chs.15,20; and embyronically suggested in CC p.106; EGL p.283.
119. However, see the criticisms of Nielsen 1963; Bean 1964; Duff-Forbes 1969; Davis 1975; Kavka 1976; Tooley 1976; Lipner 1979; Loughlin 1985b. See Badham 1976 for a critical development of Hick's thesis.
120. EGL p.310.

121   justified by the soul-making theodicy.

Hick sits uneasily on the prongs of this dilemma.

However, in order to avoid the dilemma, Hick introduces a "divine therapist" and therefore the possiblity of more

> direct operations of divine grace, corresponding in their effect to that of the chemical and electric shock treatments used in our psychiatric hospitals...In an analogous way the divine therapist may perhaps dissolve inhibiting blockages and distortions in order that the inherent needs of our nature may eventually lead us freely to respond to him. [122]

It is curious that Hick employs such an argument for he criticises a very similar suggestion made by Flew, who argues that God could be conceived as a "divine hypnotist". [123] Hick argues that such "miraculous manipulations" should be dismissed for it "would not be logically possible for God so to make men that they could be guaranteed freely to respond to Himself in genuine love and trust." [124] Consequently, Hick's suggestion of an interventionary "divine therapist" runs foul of his own strictures, not least because the notion of interventionist "direct operations" contradicts Hick's epistemic principle and the essentially non-coercive nature of revelation.

With such internal logical difficulties, it is difficult to maintain that universalism is a near "practical certainty". Certainly, an all-loving God gives grounds for such a hope (as Hick himself acknowledges), but does not provide, on Hick's own suppositions, such an optimistic outcome which he describes as a "practical certainty". My point is this: although universalism, in whatever form, is not incompatible with an inclusivist outlook, Hick's use of the Christian's practical certainty of universalism as a reason for the Copernican revolution is found wanting. This is because there seems to be insurmountable internal logical difficulties within Hick's own form of universalism. However, I do not believe that this undermines Hick's argument from an all-loving God altogether, as there is

---

121. Kane 1975a p.30; and also, Kane 1975b; and Ward 1969 pp.250-53.
122. DEL p.253.
123. Flew 1955 pp.161f.
124. EGL p.310, my emphasis; see also the criticisms of Griffin 1976 p.195.

96

the second part of his argument which is not ultimately dependent on the first. [125]

(3.2.2). **The God of love and those who have never encountered Christianity:**

The second part of Hick's argument has a "stronger" and "weaker" form. Both aim at showing that if "God is the God of the whole world, we must presume that the whole religious life of mankind is part of a continuous and universal relationship with him." [126] Hick himself does not distinguish between such a weak and strong form, but these distinctions will be fruitful in exploring the issues in further detail.

The strong form of the argument may be said to apply to all non-culpable non-Christians. In effect,

> the large majority of the human race who have lived and died up to the present moment have lived either before Christ or outside the borders of Christendom. Can we then accept the conclusion that the God of love...has nevertheless ordained that men must be saved in such a way that only a small minority can in fact receive this salvation? [127]

The trouble with Hick's use of this perfectly profound and legitimate insight is his assumption that the "weight of this moral contradiction...has driven christian thinkers in modern times to explore other ways of understanding the human religious situation." [128] While Hick is correct in thinking that modern thinkers have attended to this apparent "moral contradiction", is he correct in assuming that this "moral contradiction" constitutes a "paradox of gigantic proportions" which has existed for virtually fifteen centuries in Christian history; a paradox ignored and seriously entertained by generations of Christians? [129]
I have argued against such an assumption.

---

[125]. The following qualifications to my critcisms are in order: a) the possibility of constantly rejecting God is not limited to non-Christians; b) therefore, my criticisms do not imply a decision positively or negatively about the question of non-Christians being saved; c) even given this less than practically certain hope, such a hope is only given further specificity in terms of the second part of Hick's argument.
[126]
[127]. GUF p.101, my emphases.
[128]. GUF p.122, my emphases.
[129]. GUF p.123, my emphases.
. GUF p.122.

97

We have seen that the status of the non-culpable non-Christian is in fact given some consideration within the Christian tradition. We also noted the prevalent assumption that all people had heard the gospel, so admittedly, little attention was paid to the problem in the form in which it is posed today. However, and this is important, it is a generally accepted part of the Christian tradition that before the coming of Christ, the Old Covenant was "valid" and "legitimate" in as much as Israel's history was a history of God's salvific dealings with his people. Hence, Marcion was deemed a heretic as early as the second century for his exclusion of the Old Testament. And Augustine, a staunch defender of the extra ecclesiam teaching, believed that the Church extended in reality "ab Abel" - to the beginnings of humankind, including all those who had acted out of goodness and charity. Augustine was not alone among the Fathers in thinking this. It is also the case that the New Testament writers were not embarrassed to acknowledge the saving faith of Israel and even those outside of Israel before the time of Christm.[130]

It may therefore be concluded (with Hick) that a legitimate "moral contradiction" would occur if it was held that non-culpable non-Christians were lost through no fault of their own. It may also be said, against Hick, that such a moral contradiction was resolved or at the least, seriously attended to, in much of Christian history if we take into consideration the common assumption of a "Gospel saturated" world; and that before the time of Christ, as many Christians have argued, the non-culpable non-Christian was not lost.

However, using the resources of the inclusivist tradition, I now wish to further argue that the principle of non-culpability applied to those before Christ may be legitimately extended to those after the time of Christ. It is time to explore the category of those after the time of Christ more carefully than before and justify the assumptions made earlier in my argument. In considering certain people after the time of Christ who should be classified in the same category of those before the time of Christ we can usefully distinguish two sub-categories.

First, there are those who have not encountered the gospel in their historical situation because, for whatever reasons, the Christian message has not, even today, been preached to all people. An undiscovered Amazonian tribe would constitute such a group. If salvific revelation was possible in Israel before the time of Christ, we cannot deny a priori that this may also be the case with Hinduism or Buddhism - while still acknowledging the historical and theological differences within these religions.

The case of the Portuguese Roman Catholic explorer Martin de

---

[130]. See for example Acts 10; Heb. 1:1,11.

Encisco illuminates the necessity for a second sub-category. De Encisco travelled widely in South America. He also composed what is called the Regnerimiento, which consists of a solemn reading to the native Indians of a manifesto, written in Spanish or Latin, which sets forth a brief history of the world since its creation, the coming of Christ, followed by an account of the institution of the papacy. The preaching of the "gospel" concluded with the grant, by Pope Alexander VI, to the King of Spain of certain islands and territories. The Indians were required to recognise the Church and pope as sovereign authorities over the world, and representing the pope's name and place, the King of Spain and his Queen, Joanna. [131] This example sharply poses the question of what conditions constitute the real entry of the gospel into the historical and existential situation of an individual. When precisely does the absolute nature of the gospel supposedly invalidate non-Christian religions? For de Encisco, the answer consisted in the point when they heard his Regnerimiento, regardless of whether they understood Latin or Spanish. The result of supposedly rejecting the gospel led to the enslavement of the Indians as they could now be considered wilful idolators. Was de Encisco right in regarding the Indians as wilful idolators because of their rejection of the gospel?

A polemical example perhaps, but it does indicate the multiplicity of factors to be considered even when the gospel is preached to non-Christians. On one level there is the issue of the language of proclamation. By this, I do not mean de Encisco's insensitivity to whether the Indians understood Latin or not. The problem goes much deeper. Ludwig Wittgenstein's notion of "language games" can, I think, throw some light on the situation. Wittgenstein argued that "language games" are linguistic aspects of different "forms of life" and that the "speaking of language is part of an activity, or a form of life." [132] In effect, linguistic meaning can only be discerned when close attention is paid to the intimacy between language, context and action; the "form of life" in which "language games" operate. Certainly, a resultant implication is that one can only determine the meaning of terms such as "God", "love", "prayer" and "salvation" by looking at and living within the community that use these words and explaining their criteria and methods for determining their use of language. A number of important points result from Wittgenstein's reflections which are pertinent to this category of people who have, one might say, "heard", but not heard, the gospel, through no fault of their own.

There is the question of whether a missionary can actually be understood within the non-Christian's thought world, which is

---

131. Cited in Congar 1961 p.116.
132. Wittgenstein 1968 para.23.

formed by their culture, practice and religion. There is a danger of assuming that language from one "form of life" has the same meaning and even relevance within another. An example from science may help. Thomas Kuhn points out that those who called Copernicus mad for saying that the "earth" moved were not straightforwardly wrong. For them part of what "earth" meant was a fixed position. Their "earth" could not be moved. [133] The confusion that results when two different religions (paradigms) meet is similar to that when two different "language games" operate. [134] To take another example, the apparently single and simple word "mass" has quite different meanings within the constellation of an Einsteinian or Newtonian physics - or within a Catholic church! Regarding religious language, too often in the past, some missionaries have been content to demand repentance for sin, when both concepts have had little currency, or even quite different meanings, to the people they addressed.

If the gospel is to be communicated effectively, the thought world, religions and culture of the non-Christian have to be carefully and sensitively appreciated. Furthermore, this will inevitably result in the indigenisation of the gospel to the extent that it is made intelligible, without detracting from its "scandal". Although indigenisation is not entirely new and has in fact been going on from the beginning of Christian history, [135] there are good grounds to consider whether simply hearing the gospel actually entails its proper and real entrance into the historical and existential situation of the non-Christian hearer.

This leads to a further point. If "language games" have their meaning in "forms of life", then the historical, political and psychological "forms of life" accompanying evangelisation need also be considered in an inquiry into the conditions for the gospel's "real entry" into a person's situation. The colonial context of de Encisco's preaching is painfully obvious. In the post-colonial environment, Stanley Samartha tells of the fear of political and colonial manipulation in a Hindu's reply to an invitation to a dialogue meeting:

> Do not think that I am against dialogue...On the contrary, I am fully convinced that dialogue is an essential part of human life, and therefore of religious life itself...yet, to be frank with you, there is something which makes me uneasy in the way in which you Christians are now trying so eagerly to

---

[133]. Kuhn 1970 chs.9,10.
[134]. See further D'Costa 1985d; Smith's (1986) response and subsequently D'Costa 1986c.
[135]. See Newman 1906 esp. pt.II, chs.5-8.

> enter into official and formal dialogue
> with us...Until a few years ago, and
> often still today, your relations with us
> were confined, either to merely the
> social plane, or to preaching in order to
> convert us to your dharma...For all
> matters concerning dharma you were deadly
> against us, violently or stealthily
> according to cases. It was plain to see
> from your preaching...or from your, at
> best, condescending attitude towards us
> in your pamphlets and magazines. And the
> pity was that your attacks and derogatory
> remarks were founded on sheer ignorance
> of what we really are, or what we believe
> and worship.[136]

It would be inaccurate and dishonest to think that Christian
missionaries have always been a cause for such scandal and
painful insensitivity, but such factors do play a considerable
part in providing the conditions, (the appropriate "forms of
life") for the real entrance of the gospel into a person's life.
To disassociate the preaching of the gospel from political
colonialism, racial superiority and western culture is surely
necessary for its meaning to shine clearly through the "forms of
life" within which it is confronted.

To summarise: I am suggesting that when we inspect the
category of those who have not encountered the gospel through no
fault of their own, this category applies to those before and
after the time of Christ, within the purview of the
qualifications made above. I have not touched upon those who have
heard the gospel and properly understood it and yet rejected it.
This category of people takes us to Hick's weaker form of the
argument.

If the above argument is accepted, then I have arrived at and
defended a position which Hick must logically describe as a
"Ptolemaic epicycle" and dismiss accordingly. Nevertheless, it is
clear that on inclusivist grounds it is quite legitimate to
acknowledge salvation outside Christianity when a person has not
properly encountered the gospel. In this respect, Hick's point
that the majority of humankind living outside the boundaries of
Christendom cannot be lost by virtue of such a geographical
accident is correct, and a strong argument from an all-loving God
is legitimate - although ineffectual against its target of
inclusivism. One might say that Hick proposes a valid argument
for the Copernican theology, but not a valid criticism of
inclusivist theology. This point does not necessarily imply that

---

[136]. Cited in Samartha 1981 p.9.

an inclusivist Ptolemaic theology is not without its own internal problems. Admittedly, the extension of the principle regarding Judaism before the time of Christ, to after the time of Christ in the way that I have done, is something of a recent development;[137] but, be it noted, partly because of the assumption of a "gospel saturated" world, not because such a "moral contradiction" was entertained seriously by generations of Christians.

A weaker form of Hick's argument from an all-loving God entails the assumption that because God is "the God of the whole world, we must presume that the whole religious life of mankind is part of a continuous and universal relationship with him."[138] I will concentrate on one particular difficulty arising from this thesis. Such an argument assumes that even when someone is confronted with the gospel and truly understands it, they may still reject it and adhere to their own religion without blame or fault. Hick does not employ my distinctions, so it is not absolutely clear that he intends such an implication - although his writing would seem to support such a reading. The reason why such a supposition is contentious is that even if it is assumed that God acts salvifically within other religions (a position which is defensible on both inclusivist and Copernican lines), to affirm that a person can reject the gospel without guilt or sin implies that they have rejected the definitive and normative self-disclosure of a God of love, mercy and judgement - without sin! Such an assumption implies that the revelation of God in Jesus should not be considered any more authoritative or definitive than the revelations of God within other religious traditions.

This latter implication raises a major difficulty for Hick. If all the different revelations are taken with equal authority and none is more normative than another, what of the normative premise of the Copernican revolution regarding a God of universal love? It is part of Hick's thesis that the God of love disclosed in Christianity actually entails and necessitates the Copernican revolution! I believe that Hick severs the ground from under his Copernican feet. This is so because in arguing for the Copernican revolution on the premise of a God of universal love, such a position entails precisely that one form of revelation of God is definitive and normative compared to others.

Within the context of Christian theology the problem can be posed in the following way: can Hick's God of love be divorced from the events which disclose such a God - that is Christ? If not, then Hick's move away from Christocentricism is untenable. If theocentricism can be severed from Christocentricism then the

---

137. For example, see Congar 1961 ch.10; Küng 1976 pp.89-116.
138. GUF p.101.

Copernican revolution is still a valid option. In considering this question we are led to my third and final question: what is the basis and grounding for Hick's belief in an all-loving God, and is the basis for such a belief compatible with his Copernican presuppositions?

(3.2.3). The basis for Hick's supposition of a God of love:

As seen in 2.4 above the Ptolemaic position (most explicitly in its earliest form) is presented as posing a "paradox of gigantic proportions" when we emphasise the "Christian understanding of God. For does not the divine love of all mankind...exclude the idea that salvation occurs in one strand of human history"?[139] Hick argued that a gigantic paradigm shift is required to solve an equally gigantic paradox. Christianity must shift from an ecclesiocentric and/or Christocentric paradigm to a theocentric paradigm initiated by the Copernican revolution. In 3.1 above I argued that one part of the paradox was untrue: i.e. that the traditional Christian conception of God entails that salvation is witheld from non-Christians. Now I wish to inspect and question the basis for Hick's affirmation of the second part of the paradox: God's universal salvific will. This discussion will lead into, and partially include, Christological issues relating to 2.5 above and are further discussed in 4.1 below.

My question to Hick concerns the basis for asserting an all-loving God in Christianity, if Christianity must renounce Christocentricism (and ecclesiocentricism).[140] In other words, how credibly can Hick expound a doctrine of God's universal salvific will if he does not ground this crucial truth in the revelation of God in Christ, thereby bringing Christology back into centre-stage?

To answer this question let us briefly glance at Hick's pre-Copernican thought on the matter. In his earliest Christological reflections Hick unequivocally realises the indivisibility of Christology and the doctrine of God. He argues that the most important attributes of God are revealed in the life, death and resurrection of Christ. The "condemnation of greed, pride and uncharitableness", the "limitless ideals of the Sermon on the Mount", the "world ruled by divine love", in fact "God ruling, God loving, and God forgiving were words made flesh in Jesus Christ."[141] For Hick, the Christian doctrine of God

---

139. GUF pp.122, 100-01, my emphasis.
140. I will deal later with the defence that Christianity is not alone in affirming a God of love. For the moment I will confine myself to the internal Christian issue of the basis of such a doctrine of God.
141. FK1 pp.203-05.

is exclusively based on Christ's life, death and resurrection. To speak of God apart from Christology would be unimaginable:

> it was the experience of the disciples
> that God's fatherly love was revealed in
> the life of Christ. Jesus told men that
> God loves and cares for each of them with
> an infinitely gracious, tender, and wise
> love; and the assertions were credible on
> his lips because this supernatural agapē
> was apparent in his own dealings with
> them.[142]

Some pages later, Hick makes his underlying supposition abundantly clear when he argues that "the event from which the Christian conception of providence is derived, is the death of Jesus Christ."[143] Nine years later Hick tried to give the notion of "supernatural agapē" in Christ some philosophical precision, still maintaining that any viable doctrine of God is necessarily grounded in Christology.[144]

Two further complementary points are important. First, Hick has consistently argued that the traditional proofs for the existence of God are unsatisfactory. After outlining and briefly criticising each of the traditional proofs, Hick concludes in 1983, as he did in 1963: "None of the arguments which we have examined seem qualified to compel belief in God in the mind of one who lacks that belief."[145] Hick rejects all proofs for the existence of God related to a priori arguments, a posteriori arguments and arguments based on probability.[146] It is not necessary for the purpose of my thesis to ask whether Hick's rejection of such arguments is valid, but simply to note this fact. Hick's rejection of such arguments is part and parcel of his epistemological suppositions. Curiously, Hick's answer to the problem of grounding his concept of an all-loving God undermines his Copernican thesis in a number of ways.

(3.2.4). The equality of religious experience as a basis for belief in God:

---

142. FK2 p.206.
143. FK1 p.211.
144. Hick 1966e p.164.
145. PR1 p.30, PR3 p.30.
146. TEG pp.18-19. It should be noted that philosophers like Swinburne (1979) would argue that it is possible to arrive at Hick's notion of God from philosophical argument. If such an argument was used for the basis of the Copernican revolution we would have to employ other counter-arguments utilised elsewhere in our criticisms.

First, I will examine an implication of his belief that all cognitive religious belief is based on _experience_ and not argument. Then I will focus my question more decisively regarding which particular religious experience is necessary for a legitimate basis to the Copernican revolution.

First, Hick argues that the basis of belief in God is certainly not from philosophical and theological argument, but, it would seem, from _religious experience_.[147] This is in keeping with his epistemological theory and his Schleiermacherian roots. Hick argues that if one grants cognitive validity to one's own Christian experience, then by implication cognitive validity must be granted equally to the experience of non-Christians. However, it is difficult to see how this principle can be coherently and intelligibly applied - both generally and more specifically in relation to the Copernican revolution.

Generally, it would entail that obvious logical contradictories, which may operate at a variety of levels, could be entertained at the same time. For instance, if the religious experience of one community led to the testimony that Jesus _died on the cross_ and was raised on the third day, such an account is either true or false. Such an account is therefore incompatible with the assertion that Jesus did _not die_ on the cross, but was in fact taken down before death and proceeded to visit India; or alternatively, Jesus was not the person nailed to the cross in the first place.[148] Similar examples abound. William Christian has charted the multiple levels on which such _genuine_ and _irresolvable_ conflicts may occur between religions, such as those related to courses of action, proposals of valuation and proposals of belief.[149] Admittedly, there are many situations where there may be only _apparent_ conflict, which can be mutually resolved when the real import of each partner's beliefs or proposals is properly understood. Such an instance may occur when an atheist denies the existence of "God", and in further conversation, it is discovered that what the atheist intends and means by the word "God" has nothing to do with what a Christian may understand and intend by the word "God".[150] Of course, there are also situations where religious beliefs from different traditions may be held by two people without any conflict. For instance, there is not even an apparent conflict when the claim is made for the historical existence of Gautama and Jesus.

---

147. _GUF_ chs.3,6. This emphasis on religious _experience_ rather than the _object_ of experience has led Hick to his latest position.
148. The former is the belief of the Ahmadīyah Muslims; the latter of most Muslims based on the Qur'an (sura 4).
149. Christian 1972 chs.3-6.
150. See Solomon's interesting story in Solomon 1986 pp.23-4, and n.46; Rahner 1969 p.38.

Hick distinguishes three levels of conflict in matters of religious belief, but does not see them as damaging his case. They are matters of history; matters which he classifies as quasi-historical and matters concerning the different responses to and experiences of the divine reality.[151] For the moment I will concentrate on the first two levels and will return to the third in greater detail in 5.3.

Hick acknowledges difficulties and conflicts over historical matters and cites the example of Jesus <u>dying</u> or <u>not</u> <u>dying</u> on the cross.[152] He suggests three considerations which apparently neutralise the force of this difficulty. First, he argues that the evidence over such matters is "fragmentary and inconclusive." Second, despite the disagreement, one must admit that, for example, the Ahmadīyah Muslim may be "closer to the Divine Reality than I". Finally, he argues that such matters of historical judgement can only be "penultimately important".[153]
Cne may question whether Hick actually deals with the real issues at stake. Although historical criticism has brought into question the nature of the resurrection appearances, there is little doubt among New Testament scholars that Jesus <u>did</u> die on the cross. Furthermore, it is difficult to understand why Hick is so sceptical about the historical evidence on this matter, especially in the light of his other works, where he always supposes that Jesus <u>did</u> die on the cross and never questions the New Testament on this point, when he has on other points such as the resurrection.[154]

Even despite this internal discrepancy in Hick's work and his over-hasty dismissal of the evidence concerning Jesus' death as "fragmentary and inconclusive", thereby apparently conceding to the Ahmadīyah position, it seems that Hick vastly overstates the case when he argues that such differences are only "penultimately important".[155] For the Semitic religions the events of history tend to be all important and decisive. For example, if Jesus did not die on the cross, then by implication the resurrection appearances and the events that followed would be cast in a

---

151.
152. Hick 1983d pp.485-87.
. He rightly adds that such conflicts are intra-religious as well as inter-religious - Hick 1983d p.485.
153.
154. Hick 1983d p.486.
. See <u>SC</u> pp.20ff, where Jesus' death is taken for granted. Concerning the nature of the resurrection, Hick writes: "It appears to me that we shall never know with any certainty whether the resurrection of Jesus was a bodily event; or consisted of visions". (<u>SC</u> p.25).
155. . See Anderson's criticisms of the Ahmadīyah case and his argument for the historical accuracy and reliability of the evidence concerning Jesus' death on the cross - Anderson 1970 esp. ch.4, 1984 pp.67-8, 74-7.

vastly different light. [156]   Without exaggeration, it could be said that the whole significance and meaning of Jesus' life would need to be reconsidered. One may say that if Jesus did not die on the cross and in fact travelled to Kashmir, then much of the Christian faith is based on a falsehood. This neglect of the important implications of possibly irreconcilable historical differences of interpretation is far-reaching.

A most surprising feature of Hick's assessment of the gravity of such historical questions is his own evaluation of the significance of Jesus' death on the cross. The point he concedes, regarding the so-called "quasi or trans-historical" differences is equally relevant to the first level. That is, he would not "deny" their [157] "genuine significance and...extensive ramifications." The extensive ramifications of the significance of the cross cause Hick to write elsewhere, in the same year as the article under discussion, that "Jesus' life, and the stark revelation in his death of the meaning of his life, [158] have changed our religious situation." Furthermore, he writes that "Jesus' death on the cross has always been so significant for Christians", because "the result of that death has been that God's claim upon us has only been intensified...So through the centuries the cross of Christ has become the turning point towards faith in the experience of millions." [159]   His Copernican atonement theory affirms that the significance of the cross illustrates that "the divine love, the divine attitude to mankind, was incarnated in the life of Jesus." [160]

I do not wish to examine the coherence and adequacy of Hick's doctrine of the atonement but simply to point out that Hick himself acknowledges that by implication, the question of whether or not Jesus died on the cross is central for the Christian tradition. Hence, to return to my argument, it would appear that if all experiences be given equal cognitive validity, even in principle, then it would not be logically possible to apply this to the claims of Ahmadīyah Muslims and Christians (including Hick). Clearly, it would be pragmatically possible, and indeed even desirable, to allow for the co-existence of religious

---

[156]. Admittedly there is a plurality of views among Christians, but Christians who deny the death of Jesus on the cross are exceptionally rare - see for example, Schonfield 1965.
[157]. Hick 1983d p.487.
[158]. SC p.24.
[159]. SC pp. 21, 23. Hick affirms the importance of the cross while rejecting the "satisfaction" theory of atonement - SC p.21; IM pp.77-84; and see Moule's criticism of Hick's atonement theory - IM pp.85-6.
[160]. IM p.84; see also SC pp.20-4. In FK1 p.211 Hick writes that "Jesus' death is an act of divine grace, the climax of God's work for man's salvation."

believers holding opposing views. Furthermore, this is not to say that Ahmadīyah Muslims may not eventually produce more conclusive and decisive evidence, but until that point, it is self-contradictory for Hick, in the light of his own work, to allow either the equal cognitive status of differing religious claims or that the conflicts over straightforward historical claims are unimportant.

The significance of certain key historical events in many religious traditions of the world cannot be divorced from the actual factuality of the events. This point of course applies differently to the various religions. What I have been arguing is this: when we turn to consider the way in which Hick grounds and justifies his doctrine of God, his attempt to give equal cognitive status to all religious experiences runs into considerable difficulties. This is partly because Hick's equality principle pays undue attention to the knowing subject rather than the "object" of knowledge. [161]

The problem is now sharply focused upon when we ask which type of religious experience, for Hick, discloses the all-loving God so central to the Copernican revolution.

(3.2.5). Upon which religious experience is the Copernican revolution based?:

Before 1985, Hick grounded the belief in an all-loving God in the specific fact that Christians experience their life "in greater or lesser degree, as being lived in the presence of God, as made known to us by Jesus". He writes, a few sentences later, of the impact of Jesus' life and teachings: "to be thus decisively influenced by him is, I suppose, the basic definition of a Christian." [162] If Hick is to rely on experience rather than arguments for the existence of God, it is clear that not all experiences equally disclose the type of God which Hick wishes to defend and requires for his Copernican revolution. Some experiences can be more "decisive" or "normative" than others and I believe that when pressed, Hick would have to justify his Copernican premise with the implicit claim of a "decisive" status and role for Jesus' disclosure of God. [163] This would be

---

[161]. This is the same problem inherited in Jasper's theology of religions who, like Hick, strongly relies on Kant - see Kane 1981 pp. 130-31; and 1.2.1, 1.2.2 above.
[162]. Hick 1981b p.47, my emphases.
[163]. See 4.1 below for a further exploration of the coherence of Hick's Copernican claims concerning the nature of the incarnation. For the moment, I shall accept Hick's statement concerning "our concept of God, which we have received from
(Footnote continued)

necessary in order to sustain the status of the claim of an all-loving God against competing "images" of "God". Examples are cited by Hick such as a "blood-thirsty tribal deity"[164]; or that "God is identical with nature or with the world"; or "an 'absentee' god who long ago set the universe in motion and has thereafter left it alone."[165]

However, to claim such a decisive status for the revelation of God disclosed in Christ raises the question whether Hick is forced into a covert "Ptolemaic" position, implicitly holding a special place for Christianity, or at least Christ's revelation. This criticism can be developed in two ways. First, if Hick's God of love is disclosed in the person of Jesus, is it coherent to suggest a distinction between theocentricism and Christocentricism, for is not the doctrine of God indissoluble from the events which disclose such a God - as Hick himself held in his pre-Copernican days? Second, if the above is true then Hick's Copernican revolution contains an implicit Christologically normative criterion that runs counter to his own Copernican suggestions as well as his criticisms of "Ptolemaic" epicycles. Can Hick viably sustain his distinction between Christocentricism and theocentricism? Haddon Willmer criticises the following tendency in Hick's work, whereby one puts

> the emphasis on the God revealed in Jesus, as though we can know him (God) apart from Jesus Christ. Then we can make statements like 'God is love' and use them apart from and even against much of this history of Jesus and the history from Jesus.[166]

This kind of manoeuvre and its problematic implications found in the "history of Christian liberalism and enlightenment" is open to a number of criticisms.[167] Many such criticisms will be further developed (in 4.1 below) when I turn to Hick's "incarnational" suggestions. For the moment it should be asked whether Hick can successfully relativise the events which disclose such a God and not thereby consequently relativise the disclosure of God derived from these events. The fact that Hick's concept of God relies on religious experience alone and not on any sort of logical argument implies that the answer to the

---

[163](continued)
Jesus" (1981b p.48), without relating it to his criticisms of the incarnation.
[164]. GMNUS p.115.
[165]. PR2 pp.5,4 respectively.
[166]. Willmer 1977 p.166. Willmer also goes on to criticise the dissolution of Christology from ecclesiology - pp.168ff.
[167]. Willmer 1977 p.166.

question is "no". Hick seems to be driven back to the events of Jesus' life, death and resurrection to justify and sustain his interpretation and understanding of God.

In 1983 he is content to say that:

> God has not revealed religious truths or theological propositions to us but has indeed revealed his own nature by expressing it in his actions in relation to mankind. He has revealed his presence and his character in basically the same way that a human being does - by acting so that others feel the impact of his presence and become conscious of the attitudes, values and purposes embodied in his actions. [168]

For Hick, the "human being" through whom God's "nature" and "purposes" are revealed is Jesus, although admittedly not exclusively. But my point is that the revelation of God through Jesus is a necessarily decisive revelation and this is all important. Consequently, it is incoherent and contrary to Hick's wider and implicit theological assumptions to argue that a "God of love" and not thereby "Christ" be placed at the centre of the universe of faiths.

If my arguments are accepted we can now see a number of serious flaws in Hick's whole Copernican enterprise. His Copernican revolution does not overcome the possible charge of "triumphalism". If, as he argues, putting Christ at the centre is triumphalist, surely it is equally so to put his notion of God at the centre (with its attendant difficulties), which is after all a specific and particular notion of God which is incompatible with a number of theistic views, and even more so with non-theistic views. [169] Furthermore, his criticisms of inclusivism are evidence of his failure to recognise the central conviction upheld by inclusivists that "God" is normatively and decisively revealed in Christ. Hence, the "Ptolemaic" epicycles are employed to theologically explain the same phenomena as Hick's Copernican revolution: that God is salvifically active outside Christianity. But where an inclusivist's theology, such as I have defended, takes leave of Hick, is in maintaining that God's revelatory activity can only be recognised through Christological spectacles. How else can the Christian recognise the activity and work of God? It is because Hick neglects this question that he misunderstands the later stages of inclusivist theology. I have argued elsewhere, in an analogous manner, that

---

168. SC p.56.
169. See GMNUS p.15, PR2 pp.4-5.

Christology cannot be totally divorced from ecclesiology for if
the affirmation of God's action in Christ is not to become an
abstract principle or purely a concept, then the life of the
Christian community, the Church, is central to Christology. [170]
However, my argument as it stands is appropriate for my present
circumspect purposes.

(3.2.6). A non-Christological basis for Hick's doctrine of God:

At this point Hick could argue that the doctrine of an all-loving [171]
God is not exclusive to Christianity. He could argue that
within Judaism and Islam, two other major theistic religions,
there are similar doctrines of God's love for all humankind and
therefore the claim that such a doctrine requires a
Christocentric grounding is invalid. Hick has not developed this
type of counter-argument in any detail, but from certain of his
writings it is clearly a line of defence implicit and possible [172]
within his Copernican position.

To this type of counter-argument I would wish to pursue two
questions. Although neither of these questions is decisive on its
own, cumulatively they suggest that such a counter-argument fails
to resolve satisfactorily the difficulties pin-pointed in the
Copernican position. First, although Christianity, Judaism and
Islam are all undoubtedly monotheistic, can one simply assume
that the doctrines of "God" in these three religions are
compatible and similar? Can one properly abstract doctrines of
"God" without reference to the historical contexts and
particulars that disclose and reveal that "God"? Relatedly, one
may further ask whether such a manoeuvre ends up with
sophisticated "Ptolemaic" or inclusivist Islamic theologies,
Jewish theologies and Christian theologies rather than a
neutrally based Copernican theology? The second question may be
asked regardless of the answer to the first: does a theocentric
Copernican revolution properly accommodate non-theistic religions
on their own terms?

Let me explore the first question, with a comment from Robert
Caspar, an Islamicist and Christian theologian, regarding
monotheism in Christianity and Islam:

---

[170]. D'Costa 1986a chs. 4-5; see also Newbigin 1969 pp.76-7;
Rahner 1969 ch.17, 1978 pt.8.
[171]. Hick, May 2 1985 (private letter), criticises ch.2 of
D'Costa 1986a on the grounds that "your assumption that Jesus is
the only source of belief in a universally loving God is, surely,
parochial to say the least". See also Manzoor 1984 who argues
that universalism is central to the three monotheistic
traditions.
[172]. See for example Hick 1985c pp.5-6, Hick 1984d,e; GMNUS p.40.

From as early as the Koran, Christianity
is presented as unfaithful to the
monotheism preached by Jesus (3,51;
4,172; 5,116-117). In particular, the
Christians adore three gods (4,171;5,73),
namely God, Jesus - and Mary (5,116).
They say that Jesus is God...or the Son
of God (9,30). The Koran also denies the
crucifixion of Jesus (4,157-158·). There
are a few Moslem theologians who
recognise, like Ghazali, that
Christianity is indeed a monotheism,
although different from Moslem
monotheism.[173]

Caspar's work is not cast in a polemical or antagonistic mode.[174] Nor does he deny the salvific activity of God within Islam.[175] The main point of his article, from which the quotation above is cited, is to clarify substantial and significant points of difference in Christianity's <u>Trinitarian</u> monotheism (often viewed as <u>tritheism</u> by Muslims) and Islam's <u>unitary</u> monotheism. Furthermore, it may also be argued that Christianity's <u>Trinitarian</u> monotheism is different from Jewish <u>monotheism</u>. Hence, although Judaism, Christianity and Islam may all be theistic, one cannot simply equate the various doctrines of "God" owing to these substantial underlying differences.

In recent dialogue there is much evidence of a move away from contrasting differences alone - often in a polemical manner - to elaborating, exploring and developing the substantial areas of agreement.[176] Also, old areas of disagreement are being approached afresh. However, it would be rash and facile to conclude that many substantial differences regarding the doctrine of "God" between the three "monotheistic religions" have been overcome.[177] It should also be noted that a Christian unitarian may have much in common with a Muslim's understanding of God. Cross-religious and intra-religious permutations such as this could be multiplied. What really is at stake regarding Hick's theocentric grounding is what notion of "God" determines and occupies the Copernican centre? If unitarian, then clearly

---

[173]. Caspar 1985 p.72.
[174]. Caspar 1985 p.76.
[175]. Caspar 1985 p.75. He also cites Duquoc (1985) in this regard, whose arguments confirm Caspar's remarks.
[176]. See for example with Islam: Caspar 1985 p.72; Kerr 1984 who charts the changing Christian attitudes towards Muhammed; Cragg 1984, a pioneer in this field; and Farias 1984.
[177]. See Arinze 1985 pp.118-24 and the material referred to therein, esp. SNC 1971; eds. Samartha & Taylor 1973; Maybaum 1973; ed. Wood 1971; eds. Sherbok & Kerr 1985; Lash 1986 p.186.

Trinitarian Christians would have cause to disagree. If Trinitarian, then unitarian Muslims may seriously disagree. If neither, then both groups may find grounds for disagreement.

Furthermore, the related question as to whether one may abstract doctrines of "God" without reference to the historical contexts and particulars that disclose and reveal that God takes on a special significance. For instance, can the doctrine of the incarnation - so central and determinative of Christian Trinitarian monotheism - be acceptable or permissible to the Muslim or Jew? Or, to take another example, can the claim that Muhammad is the final prophet, which has substantial implications for the Muslim view of both Judaism and Christianity, be acceptable or permissible for Jews and Christians?[178] Examples could be multiplied.

The point of these comments is to indicate that in practice and also in theology, doctrines of God within the three religions are intrinsically related to historical contexts and particulars, which if taken seriously should cause certain apprehension in adopting Hick's possible non-particularist theocentricism. Unless the Copernican was to abstract a synthetic and syncretistic common-denominator "God", it would be difficult to ground the Copernican revolution with equal weighting and support from the three theistic religions. For the Christian, Jesus' significance is central to the understanding of God which entails that the Muslim claim that Muhammad is the final prophet of God cannot be accepted at face value. Hence, the Muslim concept of God is thereby affected. Furthermore, such a synthetic and syncretistic notion of "God" would of course constitute yet one more particular alongside other particulars - in effect, creating a Copernican theism alongside Trinitarian and unitarian theism. The necessity of grounding such a theocentric revolution in some sort of particular revelatory history is necessary and inevitable.

My argument is supported by some important evidence of thinkers from different religions who argue in common that the various religions can be viewed as alternative and complementary paths to "God" (or the divine reality, etc.). Just such a set of essays is found in a collection co-edited by Hick! In The Experience of Religious Diversity, Hick and Hasan Askari (the co-editor) note in the preface that the various contributors, from Buddhism, Christianity, Hinduism, Judaism and Islam "offer...convergent approaches" regarding the relation between religions. Hick also notes that the contributors reject "'exclusivism'" and "accept the fact of religious pluralism."[179]

---

[178]. See Cragg 1984 for a perceptive and illuminating discussion of some issues related to this, and also Parrinder 1976; Kerr 1984.
[179]. eds. Askari & Hick 1985 p.5.

While this is true, I would argue that the particular contributors to this volume do so on <u>inclusivist</u> (ie. "Ptolemaic") lines. [180]

This Ptolemaic inclusivism is especially highlighted in the contribution of the Zen Buddhist Masao Abe and the Process Christian theologian John Cobb. [181] It is also interesting that in Hick's introductory chapter he seems to be aware of this inclusivism and develops Abe's position in a way which Abe may not accept, and criticises Cobb in a similar fashion. [182] For instance, he notes that Abe potentially suggests a "form of Buddhist imperialism" - a point that Abe is aware of, and which correlates to the alleged imperialism of Christian inclusivist theology. This "Buddhist imperialism" is present, for Abe "adopts the Mahāyāna conception of the Ultimate as <u>sunyata</u>, 'Emptiness'." [183] Hick's alternative suggestion, however, seems to run counter to the integrity of the basic beliefs of Abe, for Hick writes (perhaps equally imperialistically): "Now this Zen experience is, I would suggest, on the same level as theistic awareness of the Ultimate as a Personal Being". [184] Such a suggestion would clearly be unacceptable to Abe. [185] Let me develop the relevance of these remarks.

The acceptance of religious plurality on <u>inclusivist</u> lines seems to be recognised in Hick's introductory essay to the volume when he writes: "There are also, however, significant contrary trends <u>within</u> all of the traditions. <u>Each</u> has inner resources of its own, by developing which it can come to accept the fact of religious pluralism." [186] In a private letter, Hick explicitly acknowledges that "most of the contributions to the <u>The Experience of Religious Diversity</u> are inclusivist from their different points of view." [187] These two quotes and the arguments above support my thesis that an allegedly common theistic God within Islam, Christianity and Judaism, does not allow Hick to escape from the difficulties of the Copernican revolution. Of course, there are thinkers who argue that religions other than their own have validity (in varying degrees), but nevertheless their position is based on specific doctrines of God or the Ultimate found <u>within</u> their own tradition. While there may be similar doctrines, such as universalism, one can only stand within a particular tradition or set of revelatory events to substantiate the doctrine of God that

---

180. See D'Costa 1986e.
181. eds. Askari & Hick 1985 chs.11,10, respectively.
182. eds. Askari & Hick 1985 pp.19; 21-2, respectively.
183. eds. Askari & Hick 1985 p.18.
184. eds. Askari & Hick 1985 pp.18-9.
185. Abe 1985 pp.182-7.
186. eds. Askari & Hick 1985 p.5.
187. Hick 9 December 1985 (private letter).

114

entails the acceptance of pluralism. Hence, we can have Christian, Muslim or Jewish inclusivist - and one might add,[188] given the logic of Hick's position, Copernican inclusivists!

Hick's disagreement with Abe leads to my next criticism. We may ask whether a theocentric Copernican revolution properly accommodates non-theistic religions on their own terms? We have had reason to question whether Hick's non-particularist theocentricism is viable. Now we turn to the question of whether a theocentric Copernican universe can accommodate the non-theistic religions.

(3.2.7). The theocentric Copernican revolution and non-theistic religions:

First, whether or not non-theistic religions have a valid apprehension of an aspect of God, it is important to note that Hick only accepts their "validity" on his own Copernican terms[189] and not on their own terms. Take for instance, a considered Buddhist critique against any notion of a personal God,[190] and the espousal of a non-personal Absolute for which "love" and other such theistic terms would be totally inappropriate. Now, if such a Buddhist and his or her religion were viewed as part of the Copernican universe of faiths this could only be done by: a) reducing the ontological import of the Buddhist's claim, for if taken absolutely seriously he or she would deny and question the very basis of the Copernican view; b) insisting that this Buddhist did not properly understand his or her own beliefs, and that the Copernican theologian did! Why this is not as objectionable or offensive as calling the other person an "anonymous Christian" is unclear. It involves and evokes the same criticism adduced by Hick against proponents of the anonymous Christian theory.[191] Consequently, even if certain insights of Buddhism are thought to be "valid", they cannot be seen as valid in their own right or within their own context, for such a view may entail the holding of two mutually exclusive beliefs: that the God of love at the centre of, and the basis of, the Copernican revolution, both does and does not exist. Such contradictions, I would suggest, can only be held within a wider

---

[188]. See also Moses 1950 pt.2 for a criticism of Radhakrishnan's alleged pluralism (see Radhakrishnan 1927), and Kraemer 1938 p.109, 1956 p.66 for his incisive criticisms of Troeltsch's alleged pluralism.
[189]. See above regarding Hick's response and criticisms to Abe.
[190]. Dharmasiri 1974.
[191]. 1. Stalemate in dialogue. 2. Designating the non-Christian in terms which they would not wish to use. 3. An imperialistic strategy whereby the other is characterised in a way which they would not chose - see SC p.88.

context in which the personal is acknowledged as one side of a creative tension in the description of God, but also the decisive dominant and normative side.

A second and related problem facing Hick is his admission that certain beliefs cannot be given equal weighting. For instance, he criticises Smith's thesis that whatever is sincerely believed and practised is true. Could Hick's reply be turned against his own Copernican thesis? He argues that Smith's thesis entails that:

> Nazism was also a true faith, as is warlock worship, and faith in witchcraft and in astrology. To say that whatever is sincerely believed and practised is by definition true, would be the end of all critical discrimination, both intellectual and moral...Surely we must insist that religion involves knowledge of God as well as a way of life. To be sure, the knowledge is no good without the life...But equally the life is no good if the 'knowledge' on which it is based is not knowledge at all but delusion. [192]

This latter quotation comes from Hick's earlier work, in the first year of his Copernican revolution. Although he may now wish to change the expression of his objection, one may still conjecture that the substance of his objection would be the same. [193]
This is so because of his persistent view that religious language must be cognitively meaningful if it is to be true. Hence, logically speaking (and given that there is a proper understanding of mutually used terms of reference) it cannot both be true that "God" does and does not exist, although it could be true that certain non-personalist insights from Buddhism and Hinduism, for example, can help to throw light on or correct over-anthropomorphic ways of speaking of God. [194] Hick is correct in pointing to the latter situation as being a positive encouragement to dialogue. However, he is wrong when he utilises this insight to circumvent the very real [195] and possibly irresolvable clash of beliefs within religions.

---

192. TD p.148.
193. However, in his Copernican epicycles there is admittedly a shift of emphasis away from correct knowledge - see 5.5.2 below.
194. See for example: Smart 1968, 1981; the first exploring Hinduism, the second Buddhism. In both books Smart argues that Christians have much to learn from the non-personal strands within Eastern religions.
195. The question of whether salvation is possible despite formally incorrect beliefs is left open for the moment.

To summarise: in 3.2 I have addressed the question as to the basis of Hick's notion of an "all-loving God", and whether Hick can coherently move away from Christocentricism to theocentricism. In the analysis above, I argued that Hick's notion of God, in terms of his own presuppositions, is grounded in the person of Jesus Christ, both in his pre-Copernican and Copernican days. To sever and abstract this view of God from the particulars that disclose such a view is untenable. It is untenable because Hick is forced back to Jesus to defend such a view against possible rival images of God. I then argued that even if Hick were able to sever the relation between theocentricism and Christocentricism, his Copernican revolution fails to succeed in finding a non-particularist grounding and also fails because of its exclusion of non-theistic religions on their own terms. To include non-theistic religions within his Copernican universe of faiths involves the holding of principles subject to Hick's own criticisms against the alleged triumphalism and arrogance of inclusivist theology. However, as I have argued that the logic of inclusivism is not triumphalist or arrogant, Hick would nevertheless need to explain why this Copernican triumphalism was any better than the latter stages of "Ptolemaic triumphalism". Finally and most importantly, the fact that the Copernican revolution requires, at the very least, a <u>theistic God of love</u> presents a long-term problem in as much as <u>non-theistic religions</u> would be loath to say that union with such a God was their real goal and purpose.[196]

Having examined two major arguments presented by Hick, I will turn to the rest of Hick's arguments in the next chapter.

---

[196]. In Hick's Copernican "epicycle" he has tried to respond to these criticisms and I shall return to this development in ch.5. Even though Hick's position has recently developed (post 1980), the above section is important in an examination of Hick's theological development specifically, but also in relation to <u>theocentricism</u> as opposed to <u>Christocentricism</u> or <u>ecclesiocentricism</u>, a position held by a number of theologians in formulating a theology of religions. See D'Costa 1986b; and also Coward 1985 ch.2.

CHAPTER 4: AN EXAMINATION OF JOHN HICK'S ARGUMENTS - PART II.

(4.1). An examination of argument 4: The argument from the proper understanding of Jesus.

In this section I will critically examine Hick's distinction between "myth" and "literal" as applied to Christological language. I will argue that, despite his mythological Christology, Hick fails to escape from my criticisms above (chapter 3) regarding his attempt to replace an ecclesiocentric or Christocentric centre with a theocentric and Copernican centre to the universe of faiths.

In employing this mythic/literal distinction, Hick is clearly trying to avoid an understanding of the incarnation as the absolutely unique and only disclosure of God to human beings. According to Hick, such an understanding inevitably requires adherence to this single disclosure for salvation. [1] Although he does not discount the possibility of a unique revelation, he suggests that there are "many positive reasons...for thinking that this is not true." [2] We have seen his reasons in chapter 3 above - primarily the universal salvific will of God. Although Hick is trying to sever an exclusive ontological linking of Jesus and God, I believe that his mythological understanding still maintains (implicitly, if not explicitly) a normative ontological linking of Jesus and God, which is in fact necessary to support his central axiom of a God of universal love. Without this latter premise, the Copernican enterprise would collapse. However, with this premise, and its inevitable Christological implications, the Copernican revolution [3] looks rather like yet another ingenious Ptolemaic epicycle! I will proceed to examine Hick's arguments for a mythological understanding of the incarnation to develop this criticism further.

(4.1.1).Other religions:

Hick noted a cross-cultural natural religious tendency to exalt a human founder to an elevated divine status, thereby transposing psychological absolutes into ontological (and often exclusive) absolutes. While the notion of "divinity" in the examples cited by Hick differs considerably, [4] it is also necessary to guard

---

1. [blank]
2. See his supposed logical chain of inference: GMNUS p.58.
3. Hick 1983c p.338.
4. For a summary of these criticisms see D'Costa 1984b.
   See Anderson 1978 ch.3; Newbigin 1969 pp.50ff. For two
   (Footnote continued)

against a particular danger arising from Hick's observation. He seems to recognise that there is a Feuerbachian note underpinning his argument: "Feuerbach's account of the idea of God as a projection of human ideals has a certain application here", whereby the Christian projects his or her own "spiritual needs" on to Jesus. [5] The danger is that this argument, taken to its logical conclusion, implies that religious language may be reduced to a subjectivist expressionism without any real reference - the emphasis purely upon the projecting and not that on which it is projected. Although this view is held by a number of theologians such as Dewi Phillips, Don Cupitt and Richard Braithwaite, Hick has constantly rejected a non-cognitive, non-referential view of religious language, and has criticised Phillips, Cupitt and Braithwaite on this very point. [6] Hick makes it clear that the believer's language concerning Jesus does express the cognitive and ontological claim that through Jesus, Christians encounter the God of love: "of what kind is the love of God? The Christian answer points to the love for men and women that Jesus both taught and lived out in his own life." [7] After all, Hick acknowledges that "'love' is a many coloured word" and requires precise specification. [8] Hick's specification derives from Jesus. So even if the language of incarnation is mythological, it clearly has ontological import. This therefore has the inclusivist or "Ptolemaic" implication that the God of universal love requires grounding in a normative Christology. For Christians the God of universal love at the centre cannot be spoken of or recognised without Jesus, an implication which Hick unjustifiably rejects in his attempt to shift away from Christocentricism to theocentricism.

Furthermore, simply because there may be a natural religious tendency to exalt a human founder to an exalted divine status, one cannot deny such claims a priori - unless Feuerbach's thesis is accepted a priori. Hence, John Rodwell is correct when he points out that "it matters not one jot for the legitimacy of a hypothesis how it came to be formed." [9] This surely applies to Hick's argument about a natural religious tendency invalidating the "literal" status of the incarnation. We may conclude that the

---

[4] (continued)
especially good studies distinguishing some critical differences between avatar and incarnation, see Parrinder 1970; Robinson 1979 ch.3.
[5]. MGI p.168.
[6]. Braithwaite 1955; Phillips 1965; Cupitt 1980, 1982. For Hick's criticism of Braithwaite: PR1 pp.90-3; on Cupitt: WBG pp.102-11; on Phillips: 1964b p.237, PR3 pp.90-3.
[7]. SC p.39.
[8]. SC p.39.
[9]. IM p.68.

argument based on a natural religious tendency to deify founders or leaders does not in itself invalidate: a) the cognitive claims that God is disclosed in Christ - for Hick seems to allow this; b) the possiblity that God could have so chosen to reveal himself through Christ; c) the possibility that God may have also disclosed himself in other revelations although according to the inclusivist Christians, most <u>definitively</u> and <u>normatively</u> (rather than exclusively) in Christ.

The argument that incarnational language tells us more about the culture and times, rather than the real status of Jesus is interesting but tangential to the issue at stake. It is pure hypothesis that if Christianity had expanded eastwards, Jesus would have been identified as a Bodhisattva or Avatar. In fact, it is interesting to note that when Christianity did spread eastwards at a very early date, if the tradition of St Thomas' arrival in India is true, no such process occured. [10] The history of Christianity's meeting with various and diverse cultures testifies to a process of incorporation and indigenization. For instance, Greek philosophy was utilized to <u>express</u> the significance of Christ rather than <u>determine</u> the significance of Christ. [11] John Henry Newman's masterly study, <u>An Essay on the Development of Christian Doctrine</u> testifies to this process taking place doctrinally as well as liturgically and cultically. Certainly, incarnational language does tell us much about the culture of the times - in as much as a proper understanding of Christological language requires a close knowledge of the meaning and use of incarnational terminology before, and then after, its use by Christians. However, it cannot be said that incarnational language does not relate to the perceived status of Jesus. Consequently, it is not pertinent to the discussion whether or not Jesus would have been called a "Bodhisattva" or "Avatar", but what those who would have called him such would have meant. Rodwell's comment about the "genetic" fallacy underlying the methodology of the contributions to the <u>Myth of God Incarnate</u> is worth quoting again: "it matters not one jot for the legitimacy of a hypothesis how it came to be framed."

The final part of the argument concerning the transposition of psychological absolutes into ontological absolutes will be dealt with below. However, if Hick's argument from a general tendency in all religions to deify founders is found wanting, he still relies on other arguments. Hick has also asked whether the claim for a literal incarnation can be philosophically intelligible.

---

[10]. See Neill 1964 pp.142-44, 1984b ch.2, pts.1,2; Brown 1956. The Syriac culture of the Thomas Christians withstood penetration by the Hindu culture.
[11]. Stead 1977 esp. chs.8,9; Lonergan 1974 ch.2, and pp.251-53. Admittedly, the relationship between culture and the shaping of theology is far more complex - see Schreiter 1985.

(4.1.2). Philosophical difficulties:

The use, meaning and status of Christological language is indeed a complex and difficult issue. Here, I wish to pursue only the criticism that Hick's myth/literal distinction does not circumvent the necessity of grounding our understanding of God in Christology. If this is shown then Hick's move from Christocentricism to theocentricism is problematic.

Let us recall Hick's example of the distinction between mythic and literal language:

> I may say of a certain happening that it is the work of the devil. If this is not literally true, the statement is mythic in character, and it is a true statement in so far as the attitude which it tends to evoke is <u>appropriate</u> to the <u>actual character</u> of the event in question. [12]

The difficulty inherent in Hick's distinction becomes evident when we ask what constitutes an "appropriate" response? Let me say that Hick's "certain happening" is a car crash. If this accident was the work of the devil in a mythical sense, would such language make any sense if the accident did not bear some relation to an entity or force called "the devil"? For such a statement about the accident to make any sense, the language must be "appropriate" to the "actual character" of the event. Or why, for instance, is it inappropriate to think of the same accident as resulting from the stupidity of the human driver or even the work of God? Does the notion of "appropriate" or "inappropriate" indicate the purely subjective attitude of a person to a situation without real concern for, or reference to, the "literal" truth of the situation, its "actual character" ? If such language about the accident is not purely subjective, then mythic truth has more to do with the real character of events than simply denoting attitudes, otherwise the notions of "appropriate" and "inappropriate" become vacuous.

We approach the heart of the issue when Hick answers the above questions, precisely in relation to Christology. "If, then, the <u>appropriate</u> attitude to Jesus the Christ is the attitude of saved to saviour, how can this be justified if he is not <u>literally</u> God incarnate?". [13]   Hick answers:

> Through their responses to the person of

---

12. <u>GUF</u> p.167, my emphasis.
13. <u>GUF</u> p.176.

> Jesus countless people have been opened
> to the divine presence; changed in the
> direction of their lives; reconciled to
> themselves, to their neighbours and to
> God; have become conscious of the reality
> of their loving heavenly Father who has
> forgiven and accepted them...It was not
> he (Jesus) but his heavenly Father who
> saved. But Jesus was so fully God's
> agent, so completely conscious of living
> in God's presence and serving God's love,
> that the divine reality was mediated
> through him to others.[14]

The "appropriate" or "practical truth" seems not to lie
exclusively in the believer's subjective response, but in the
"reality" of "God's presence...mediated through" Jesus. Hence, an
appropriate response refers to the "real character of that which
is being identified."[15] If Hick is saying this much, and we
have already seen his disavowal of a purely subjectivist
non-cognitive view of religious language, then surely he is
saying too much! If Christian discourse about God takes on its
coherence and appropriateness in terms of Jesus, and this
discourse concerns truth, then Hick has clearly failed to sever
the normative and ontological import of Christological language.

Hick's concern with ontological significance is clear
elsewhere when he criticises the subjectivist tones of his fellow
pluralist, Smith. In counter-balancing Smith's emphasis upon
personal response, Hick writes:

> Just as revelation is only real when it
> is responded to, but on the other hand
> can only be responded to because it is
> already 'there' to be responded to, so a
> religion...can only become
> personalistically true in a man's life
> because those beliefs were already true
> beliefs, pointing towards and not away
> from the divine reality, and because
> those practices were already appropriate
> rather than inappropriate as ways in
> which to worship and serve the divine
> reality.[16]

Hick's distinction between mythic and literal runs into

14
15. GUF pp.176-77, my emphases and brackets.
. GUF p.176. Consequently, Lash's charge (IM p.21) against
Hick's "subjectivism" is incorrect.
16
. TD p.146.

further difficulties when we examine his notion of literal truth.[17]
He defines literal truth as theoretical truth, and writes
the following: "A theory is true or false (or partly true and
partly false); and any theory that can be of interest to human
beings must be capable, in principle at least, of confirmation or
disconfirmation within human experience."[18] Hick has
consistently maintained that religious language about God can be
verified, at least in principle, in the after-life. He has held
this view against all forms of non-cognitive religious discourse
as was noted above. Hence, language about God has the status of
theoretical and literal truth. But if talk of God derives from
Jesus, then by implication Christological language must also have
some literal or theoretical truth. Hick's criticism that the
incarnation is as intelligible as a square-circle has been
appropriately criticised. Herbert Macabe argues that the
square-circle analogy is confusing precisely because it is not
clear that God is incompatible, in his domain of activity, with
man.[19] One may legitimately ask Hick to explain the meaning
of his own assertion that God's love is "mediated through" Jesus
in the light of his square-circle analogy. It is this
insensitivity to incarnational language which leads Lash to
notice that "according to Hick, the fathers of Nicaea unwittingly
taught meaningless nonsense."[20]

    In the light of the above discussion we may now return to one
further aspect of Hick's argument - it concerns the transposing
of psychological language into the language of absolutes.
Regarding the lover's language, this transposing process is
exemplified in the claim that his "Helen is the sweetest girl in
the world".[21] According to Hick, such language should not be
taken as affirming an absolute and exclusive claim, but as a
psychological expression of importance. The same applies to
incarnational language. Hick's point has a certain but limited
application in relation to the issue at stake. Although some
Christians claim that Christ need not be regarded as exclusively
absolute (i.e. the latter stages of "Ptolemaic" theology), if
incarnational language is to have any cognitive meaning at all
then a certain absoluteness is necessary. This is all-important.
If Jesus is regarded as disclosing God, then ultimate questions
concerning the nature and purpose of reality are at stake. The
analogy of the lover's language and religious language breaks
down because, even on Hick's own premises, talk of God concerns

---

[17]. GUF pp.165-66, MGI pp.176-77, SC p.32.

[18]. GUF p.166.
[19]. Macabe 1977 p.353. See also IM 2.B, 3.B.iv; Hebblethwaite
1977.
[20]. IM p.22.
[21]. GMNUS p.57; SC p.32; see also Knitter 1985 p.185; Ariarajah
1985 pp.25-6.

talk about the nature of reality, not simply an expression of subjective feelings, attitudes, or preferences. Therefore, Hick is correct in arguing that the tendency to absolutise psychologically significant claims may lead to an unnecessary exclusivism. But he is incorrect in implying that this absolutising tendency invalidates the normativeness of Christological language. Consequently, Hick is only partially correct when he writes that:

> We do not suppose that because our own love or insight or loyalty has the unqualified character that it has, other people's love, insight or loyalty must be less authentic...and (consequently) we can be sure of the authenticity of our own (religious) experience without supposing that we thereby impugn that of others.[22]

In terms of subjective attitudes regarding the person we love, clearly this experience does not impugn the love or loyalty of another. However, when the "object" of our "love" is God, the cognitive significance of Christian language may often impugn and contradict the love and loyalty of another. For instance, the Nazi, warlock worshipper or astrologer may have very different and incompatible notions and experiences of the nature of reality, [23]; and equally so the Advaitin Hindu or Theravādin Buddhist in as much as their views about ultimate reality are not, taken in their totality, compatible with that disclosed by Christ.[24]

(4.1.3). Biblical criticism:

In the light of the above comments, I shall not pursue the biblical side of Hick's thesis in great detail as I have already shown that on Hick's own premises, credible Christian discourse about God requires grounding in Christology. I have been arguing that if this is acknowledged, Hick's move away from Christocentricism to theocentricism is undermined. However, a number of observations concerning Hick's analysis of the biblical evidence may further strengthen my argument.

Norman Anderson has noted that "Hick greatly exaggerates the

---

22. GUF p.173, my brackets.
23. See TD p.148.
24. This cannot be stated absolutely, as there are of course variants within developing traditions. But see Kraemer 1938 ch.4, esp. p.134 for an illuminating discussion of the necessity of viewing religions as "totalitarian"; and my qualified criticisms of Kraemer's thesis - D'Costa 1986a pp.62-3.

paucity of positive evidence we have about the one to whom he refers as the 'largely unknown man of Nazareth.'" [25]   Anderson goes on to show how, despite this, Hick still makes strong claims concerning Jesus' disclosure of God's presence and love which run contrary to his biblical scepticism about our knowledge of the historical Jesus. Anderson's criticisms highlight some significant issues. First, Hick's Copernican writings seem to [26] contain a strong element of internal contradiction.   For instance, when writing that Jesus is the "largerly unknown man of Nazareth" lying "behind this gallery of ideal portraits" (the New Testament books), later in the same essay, Hick writes that "we do nevertheless receive, mainly from the synoptic gospels, an impression of a real person with a real message, lying behind the often conflicting indications preserved in the tradition." [27] Hick goes on to state his own conclusions about what may be legitimately said of Jesus. I quote at length, for what Hick says of Jesus in this passage indicates that Hick minimises the strength of the New Testament evidence while making some fairly substantial claims about Jesus that cannot be based on the scanty evidence that Hick supposes to exist:

> I see the Narazene, then, as intensely
> and overwhelmingly conscious of ·the
> reality of God. He was a man of God,
> living in the unseen presence of God, and
> addressing God as abba, father. His
> spirit was open to God and his life a
> continuous response to the divine love as
> both utterly gracious and utterly
> demanding. He was so powerfully God
> conscious that his life vibrated, as it
> were, to the divine life; and as a result
> his hands could heal the sick, and the
> 'poor in spirit' were kindled to new life
> in his presence. If you or I had met him
> in first century Palestine we would - we
> may hope - have felt deeply disturbed and
> challenged by his presence. We would have
> felt the absolute claim of God

---

[25]. Anderson 1978 p.64; citing MGI p.168; see also Lewis 1981 p.107.
[26]. This does not refer to the internal contradiction found in comparing his pre-Copernican with his Copernican work. A gradual development and shift of position is perfectly legitimate. However, it does refer to the contradiction, or at least difficulty, that one notices that in the various re-editings of CC where Hick leaves much of his Christological reflection unchanged: compare, for example, CC pp.46-9, TCC pp.20-6, SC pp.20-6.
[27]. MGI pp.168, 172, respectively.

confronting us, summoning us to give
ourselves wholly to him and to be born
again as his children and as agents of
his purposes on earth. To respond with
our whole being might have involved
danger, poverty, ridicule. And such is
the interaction of body and mind that in
deciding to give ourselves to God, in
response to his claim mediated through
Jesus, we might have found ourselves
trembling or in tears or uttering the
strange sounds that is called speaking
with tongues...Thus in Jesus' presence,
we should have felt that we are in the
presence of God, but not in the sense
that the man Jesus literally is God, but
in the sense that he was so totally
conscious of God that we could catch
something of that consciousness by
spiritual contagion. At least this was
what might happen. But there was also the
possiblity of turning away from this
challenging presence, being unable or
unwilling to recognize God's call as
commanding us through a wholly
unpretentious working-class young man,
and so closing ourselves to him and at
the same time to God.[28]

A number of observations arise which pose serious problems to
Hick's overall Copernican strategy. First, recalling points made
immediately above and in chapter 3, it is difficult to see what
import the myth/literal distinction has if Hick is able to say
that in Jesus we have "the absolute claim of God confronting us"
and that we would be called to "give ourselves to God, in
response to his claim mediated through Jesus"; or that in
rejecting Jesus we are "closing ourselves to him and at the same
time to God." It would appear that unless the use of the term
"God" has no literal or cognitive significance, the claim that
God is "mediated through Jesus" cannot be regarded as other than
having some "literal" and cognitive import - to employ Hick's
terminology. Otherwise, Hick's language here would run counter to
his concern for the cognitive validity of religious language.

Furthermore, it is difficult to see what Hick means when he
writes that his account in no way implies that "the man Jesus is
literally God", especially in the light of the implications of
his own language and description of Jesus. One may presume that
the meaning of "is" implies what Hick argues leads to the

---

[28]. MGI p.172, my emphases, except might.

square-circle dilemma. This is where the doctrine of the incarnation is said to be analogous to a square being called a circle because "how one person can be both eternal and yet born in time; omnipotent and yet with the limited capacity of a human being", and so on, is impossible to defend. [29] However, it is difficult to see why Hick thinks that this quite crude use of is should be the only use available, especially in the light of the implications of his own language and description of Jesus quoted immediately above. Taking our cue from Lash's comment that "according to Hick, the fathers of Nicaea unwittingly taught meaningless nonsense", [30], we may explore other possible meanings of "is" - by in fact turning to Hick's earlier work where he discusses the status of the term "is" with far greater sensitivity! [31] Clearly in Hick's later criticisms, the underlying assumption is that there is a "common logical world inhabited in a mutual exclusion by God and man." [32] However, in the light of Hick's own quotation (above) regarding Jesus and God, it is difficult to see how Hick can justify his own assertions. Given this difficulty, it is odd that Hick defended and defined a way in which the use of "is" may be applied to incarnational language and has never subsequently explicitly [33] criticised his own earlier suggestions.

In 1966 Hick tried to interpret the Chalcedonian formula of "homoousios" in terms of "agapé", a more dynamic rather than static notion of conveying God's action, or the "inhistorisation" of God in Jesus. [34] Hick argued that there were four usages of the word "is": a) predication, b) class membership, c) [35] definitional or equivalence-of-symbols, d) identification. He then goes on to define two forms of identification - qualitative and quantitative. He argues that the "is" in speaking of Jesus as both God and man, in relation to manhood, indicates class membership. But in referring to God, it indicates identification. This latter case, understood qualitatively, is analogous to saying: "that the love of Mrs A for her children is identical in quality with the love of Mrs B for her children". [36] In an analogous sense, Hick argues that this is one way in

---

29. SC p.31.
30. IM p.22.
31. Hick 1967a, and GUF ch.11. Cupitt also discusses three forms of "is": identity, predication and acclamation - IM p.36, to which Lash makes a pertinent and interesting response - IM p.41.
32. Macabe 1977 p.353.
33. He includes the 1966 essay in its entirety in GUF ch.11!
34. GUF pp.152-54. He initially developed these ideas in 1959 - see Hick 1959a. The term "inhistorisation" is borrowed from Farmer 1952 p.12; see Farmer's discussion (1952 pp.5-7) for the context of his usage.
35. GUF p.154.
36. GUF p.156.

which the term "God" may be used in relation to Jesus. However, by itself, it leads to what Hick calls a degree Christology; that is, that "incarnation is something that is capable of degrees and approximations." [37] However, Hick wants to go a step further, for he thinks that Nicaea and Chalcedon did not stop at affirming Jesus' difference from others as a difference in degree, but as a difference in kind; that is [38] "that Christ is uniquely the incarnation of God the Son". [38] Consequently, on an analogy with numerical and qualitative identity, keeping in mind the uniqueness of the divine nature, [39] Hick employs the notion of identity by continuity or inclusion. For example, when an amoeba puts forth a temporary extension of itself we can describe such a pseudopodium as being one, or continuous, with the amoeba as a whole. He then uses this meaning of qualitative and numerical identity to signify the type of "is" in the affirmation that Jesus "is" God. [40] Hence, employing analogies used by Tertullian and Athanasius concerning the continuity between a source of illumination and the light which radiates from it, Hick argues that we may claim a similar numerical identity between Jesus and God's agapé thereby affirming "a direct causal connection between Jesus' attitudes to his fellow human beings and God's attitudes to them." [41]

Hick's earlier sensitivity to the richness and complexity of the term "is" creates a vivid contrast to his rather crude and unimaginative use of the term in his later work. In his early essay he seems to acknowledge that "is" understood "actually and literally" involves analogy and metaphor. [42] This earlier sensitivity seems to be totally excluded from his later understanding. [43] None of the above comments are intended to

---

37. GUF p.157.
38. GUF p.157.
39. It is clearly nonsense to say that A's love is numerically identical with B's love, when speaking of two finite beings. However, Hick points out that when we speak of finite agapé (the specificity of Jesus) being numerically identitical with the infinite agapé (of God's), it has meaning because "the infinite is not excluded by the finite." (GUF p.158). He employs a distinction used by others such as Robinson 1979 p.104, that Jesus was "totus deus" (wholly God) not "totum dei" (the whole of God) - GUF p.159.
40. Rather than, a) self-identity, when we say something is identical with itself; or b) identity through time: i.e. O at t1 = O at t2 - GUF p.159-60. It is not clear how a) is in fact different from the option that Hick develops.
41. GUF p.162. Even at this stage it is possible to claim, as Mascall does, that Hick's arguments indicate the weakness of his particular defense of "kind" Christology - Mascall 1978 p.124. Although Mascall's criticisms are pertinent, they do not
(Footnote continued)

129

indicate easy alternatives to giving expression and insight into kind or degree Christologies, but simply to indicate that Hick's criticism of the incarnation is unfocused and indecisive. More significantly, he fails to justify a severing of the intimate relation between Christology and understanding of God. Consequently, his argument for a theocentric, rather than a Christocentric universe of faiths is weakened.

One further difficulty arises from the <u>Myth</u> <u>of</u> <u>God</u> <u>Incarnate</u>[44] passage quoted above. Again, this point concerns method. Hick's criticisms of the <u>development</u> of incarnational language is that John's gospel and later patristic formulations of Christology which were also based on it, were formulated on a "pre-critical acceptance of the Fourth Gospel reports of Jesus' teaching as historical"[45], and represent a "process whereby the church sought to interpret to itself the <u>meaning</u> of the Christ event, and...(such interpretations were)...<u>not part</u> of that event itself."[46] What is at stake is the question of the continuity of intention in Christological language. Did the understanding of Jesus take on "a new meaning as it took root in Graeco-Roman culture"?[47]

This is a complicated and controversial issue and Hick's analysis is in keeping with much of the liberal Protestant tradition. I would stray from the purpose of my argument in exploring this question in any great depth, but a few critical remarks are appropriate.[48] First, it is by no means unanimous in post-critical circles that John's Gospel should be regarded as relying on traditions that are far removed from the historical Jesus. It is also not unanimous in post-critical circles that

---

[41](continued)
seriously undermine the type of model employed by Hick, but rather his use of it.
[42]. GUF pp.154,161-63. See also Barbour 1974 who carries out a sensitive analysis of the different types of language employed in religious discourse and also Mondin 1963; Donovan 1976.
[43]. See MGI p.175. See Lonergan's argument that the Nicene creed uses metaphorical language for its most important doctrines, without thereby impugning its cognitive import - Lonergan 1974 pp.22-7. Stead 1977 offers a masterly account of the complexities of patristic language.
[44]. See further, Williams 1977; Coventry 1978.
[45]. MGI p.175.
[46]. GUF p.114, my emphases and brackets.
[47]. GUF p.116.
[48]. On the Christology of the Councils, see the following useful works: Daniélou 1964b ch.7; Davies 1965 pp.191-99; Pollard 1970; Lonergan 1974 chs.2,17; 1985 ch.6; Grillmeier 1975 esp. ch.2; Turner 1976 chs. 2-5,7; Kelly 1980 chs. 6,11,12; Gunton 1983 esp. ch.1.

John's Gospel represents reflections rooted in an altogether alien culture from that of Jesus. [49]   Furthermore, it is not clear that Hick's distinction between the Church's seeking to interpret the "meaning of the Christ event" is different or separable from "that event itself". In effect, is it true that a particular interpretation is less valid in proportion to its chronological distance from the events being interpreted?

Two critical objections may be developed concerning the latter point. The first is whether it is possible to so divide the "event itself" from the "meaning" and "interpretation" of that event. In fact, Hick's own epistemological theory insists that "all experiencing is experiencing-as", so that "all conscious perceiving goes beyond what the senses report to a significance which has not as such been given to the senses." [50] Consequently, it is difficult to assume an uninterpreted neutral Jesus who can be discovered or recovered from "behind" the Church's attempt to "interpret to itself the meaning of the Christ event". Furthermore, it is difficult to make sense of Hick's distinction between the Church's interpretation of the Christ event, and the event itself, for the only substantial records upon which we - and Hick - rely, are in fact a product of the Church. The New Testament is nothing but the Church's testimony to the import and significance of Christ. [51]

Second, the a priori assumption that later interpretations are less valid than earlier ones is questionable. Regarding the humanities, one need only look at the writings on Hitler, to take one example [52] to argue that this principle is not generally applicable.   Reflecting on the evidence and bringing to bear new evidence and insights regarding a particular event can provide the conditions whereby later interpretations of that event may be more truthful and valid than earlier interpretations. Historians especially are often aware of this problem.   In the sciences, for example, successive scientific paradigms may explain and interpret evidence in a way that contradicts earlier interpretations of the significance of a given event or experiment, even when such events are not repeatable such as the eruption of a particular volcano, the destruction of a particular star, or the creation of the world. [53]   In relation to the New Testament and Church history, there

---

[49]. See Dodd 1963; Brown 1966/1970; Lindars 1972 pp.23-74; Robinson 1985.
[50]. GUF pp.41-2.
[51]. This point is concisely made and developed by Willmer 1977 pp.166-77.
[52]. See for example the way in which Taylor 1964 overturned the established "authority" of Bullock 1952, on Hitler.
[53]. See Kuhn 1970; and Bernstein 1983 pt.2 for an interesting discussion of Kuhn; and also Mason 1962 esp. pts.5,6.

is no reason why one should assume that earlier interpretations are necessarily more valid than later ones. Hick in fact contravenes his own principle in his criticism of what he takes to be the biblical theory of the atonement supported by some of the Fathers and Paul. [54] He argues that later interpretations of the atonement, such as that propounded by Irenaeus, are more valid and meaningful than earlier ones. [55]

Third, there is an assumption in Hick's work that in the synoptics there is a "low" Christology compared to the later, developed and new "high" Christology of John and Paul, which was further elaborated upon by the Fathers. However, Charles Moule for one has offered substantial counter-evidence in The Origins of Christology. Elsewhere, he summarises one theme of his book in the following way:

> It is not even necessary to appeal to the so-called 'titles' of Jesus, though these do appear, as a matter of fact, to be rooted firmly in the earliest understandings of him - in some cases, even in his own sayings. But, apart from any titles, the experience of Jesus reflected in the earliest epistles as an inclusive divine presence, as personal indeed but more than individual, and as closely associated with God himself in the bestowal of spiritual blessings, gives the lie absolutely to any theory that relies on the lapse of time and on evolutionary mutations to produce a 'high' christology from the original impact of Jesus. [56]

I do not wish to imply that because there is another way of reading the evidence contrary to Hick, we can dismiss his questions. Rather, I wish to argue that there are substantial internal difficulties within Hick's Christological arguments. Furthermore, in the light of his own comments on Jesus (quoted extensively above), there are difficult problems within Hick's own Jesuology that he neglects.

There are a number of issues which I have left untouched, such as Hick's actual analysis of New Testament Christology, and his understanding of the patristic Christological formulae. I have chosen to omit discussion on these points as my main purpose in this section is to show that: a) even on Hick's apparently

---

54. IM pp.77-84.
55. EGL pt.3.
56. Moule in IM p.137.

mythical understanding of incarnational language, he believes (not without considerable difficulties, as I have shown above) that God is encountered in Jesus; b) that such a belief entails that talk of God is normatively grounded in the person of Christ; c) that if this is so, the whole issue concerning mythical and literal language fails to justify a shift from Christocentricism to theocentricism in the Copernican revolution; d) that Hick's assumption that literal Christological language implies that God has not acted outside of the incarnation is historically false and theologically unnecessary. The main thrust of Christological language[57] is that God has acted decisively and normatively in Jesus. Consequently, it is only in the light of this single normative revelation that other claims that God has revealed himself or herself must be judged. As is seen from the latter stages of Ptolemaic theology, the normativeness of Christ does not exclude the action of God outside the incarnation, but must necessarily relate these other events to Christ's revelation.

To summarise: I have dealt in some detail with Hick's Christological arguments to establish two points. First, I have maintained that Hick's pluralist axiom concerning the universal salvific will of God requires grounding in Christology. Second, if this is true, Hick's pluralist move from Christocentricism to theocentricism is difficult to justify. Furthermore, we can see that Hick has failed to appreciate the inclusivist and exclusivist preoccupation with the axiom that he discards: that is, salvation is found only through the grace of God in Christ. In so much as Hick accepts the former part of this sentence, I have been trying to show that he must then also accept the latter part: "in Christ". For if salvation, whether in Christianity or in other religions, comes from God, then the Christian can only assert, identify and maintain this claim by the use of Christological criteria.

(4.2). An examination of argument 5: The argument from the nature of religion and religious history.

Having criticised the theological foundations of the Copernican revolution, I wish to pursue some of the subsidiary arguments that Hick puts forward as part of his overall Copernican strategy. In much of what follows, I am taking the tentative conclusions which I have arrived at above for granted. It is necessary to consider the force of the Copernican suggestions both individually and cumulatively.

Hick's argument from the nature of religion and religious history initially centres around the contribution of Smith

---

[57]. I will return to the one outstanding point concerning Hick's notion of "images" and "pictures" of God in ch.5 below.

regarding the reification of "religion", leading to the view of rival religious communities. Smith's thesis, which is utilised and developed by Hick, suggests a shift in perspective whereby a question such as "which is the true, or truest, religion?", and the notion that God does not act throughout history in all religions - is declared invalid. [58]

(4.2.1). "Faith" and "cumulative traditions":

First, let me turn to Hick's adoption of Smith's distinction between faith and cumulative tradition. There is much to be said in favour of Smith's thesis. Certainly, the notion of competitive and rival ideological religious communities has led to the most barbaric persecution and hatred. And certainly, within each religion there are many internal differences that sometimes render meaningless an umbrella term like "Hinduism", as it accommodates major theistic, non-theistic and materialist schools. Furthermore, religious life must be viewed in terms of the persons who believe, and not only in terms of propositional statements of belief. The latter in fact take their meaning from the life and context of the community in which they operate. But does all this really invalidate the use of terms such as "Christian", "Muslim", and so on, let alone circumvent the possibility of conflicting religious truth claims? This latter point is the main issue at stake.

We can learn from an application of Ludwig Wittgenstein's classical analysis of "games"; that we may still use a term (e.g. Christian), although the different expressions of the term may have only "family resemblances" rather than a fixed and static content. [59] Allowing for exceptions, surely central paradigm cases of what it is to be a Christian, involve belief in a God with reference to Jesus; of what it is to be a Muslim, involve belief in the final authority of the Qur'an and Muhammad's words. Although we might have to say "a Theravādin Buddhist" rather than "a Buddhist", or an "Advaitin" or "Viśiṣṭādvaitin" rather than a "Hindu", the principle of a determinative paradigm with its founder, scriptures, sacred traditions, teachings and practices uniting a community of believers is surely necessary if language and religious and cultural identity are to retain any meaning at all. [60]

Given this, and Hick's support of religious language as cognitively referential, Hugo Meynell's criticism of Smith's

---

[58]. MER p.x.
[59]. See Wittgenstein 1968 paras.66-7; and D'Costa 1985d where I develop this point further; and 3.2.2 above.
[60]. Hick seems to accept this, both in his use of language and in an essay in GUF ch. 8; see the interesting contributions in support of my position: Sykes 1984 pt.3; Lindbeck 1985 chs.2,4,6.

pluralist thesis is especially pertinent:

> Once the chips are down, all differences
> in expression due to culture and
> intellectual development taken into
> account, and all ambiguities removed,
> there cannot both be and not be a God;
> and the Qur'an bestowed through Muhammad
> both be and not be the final and
> culminating expression by him of his
> nature and will to humankind...so long as
> the religious believer actually believes
> anything, as opposed to merely having a
> set of aesthetic or practical attitudes,
> he is inevitably <u>liable</u> to this kind of
> disagreement with other religious
> believers and unbelievers. Vague talk of
> a 'transcendent' to which all religious
> believers are committed conceals rather
> than disposes of this awkward fact. [61]

Although Meynell's final comment about vague talk of a "transcendent" was aimed at Smith, could the same be said of Hick's "God" at the centre of the universe of faiths? I shall develop this point further in chapter 5. Nevertheless, Hick and Smith are right in saying that thinking of religions as "distinct and bounded historical phenomena" is primarily a western invention. However, even if such a habit of thought is a western innovation, its usefulness and appropriateness is not thereby called into question. In fact, most religions and their development, for better or worse, can be mapped out in terms of certain historical and geographical boundaries, however much these shift and change. [62] Furthermore, many religions organise themselves around a particular founder, scripture, set of beliefs and practices, and so on - although the ways in which they do this will differ. Consequently, the adherents of religious movements might actually wish to be identified with their common origin and source, as is seen in Hick's own confessional Copernican statements. [63] Therefore it follows that these "isms" are not necessarily illicit reifications, for as Ninian Smart points out in his criticism of Smith:

> The fact that new terms are used (e.g.
> "Sikhism") in the modern context does not
> show that they are inapplicable. The

---

[61]. Meynell 1985 p.154, my emphasis and brackets.
[62]. This is clearly evident from even a survey of the contents page of Ling 1968. Hick's theory of religious history also contains such a view - see <u>GUF</u> ch.11; <u>GMNUS</u> ch.3.
[63]. <u>GUF</u> ch.8, p.121; Hick 1981b; most recently 1986a pp.1-2.

non-traditional nature of western terms
does not <u>by itself</u> mean that there is a
distorting reification. 'Gamesmanship' is
of fairly recent coinage, but
gamesmanship preceded the coinage (hence
the success of the coinage).[64]

Smart also makes another pertinent point that challenges
Smith's Protestant emphasis on the "faith" or "commitment" of
<u>individuals</u>, rather than of communities:

It is possible that attacks on the notion
of 'a religion' arise from a kind of
individualism, since superficially the
concepts of 'being faithful', 'having
faith', 'being committed', etc., apply
primarily to individuals. But first this
is doubtful (the attention to the first
person singular in western philosophy
being possibly a legacy of Protestantism)
and second these concepts do not, in any
case, have universal application.[65]

The notion of a "person" as relational is gaining much ground in
philosophy and the social sciences, and more significantly, is
advocated by Hick.[66] Consequently, to speak of a person's
"faith" as distinct from his or her beliefs and practices
(cumulative tradition) by which and <u>through</u> which they are formed
and form is itself an illict reification. To divorce a person's
"faith" from that person's community of believers and their
practices involves an ahistorical and asocial reification. Can
one meaningfully say that the "faith" of <u>X</u> (a materialist
humanist), <u>Y</u> (a Roman Catholic) and <u>Z</u> (a Theravādin Buddhist) is
the same thing, let alone identify any characteristics by which
to make such an assertion without reference to the community and
its practices to which <u>X</u>, <u>Y</u>, and <u>Z</u> belong?

(4.2.2). <u>The relation of founders and the subsequent traditions</u>:

In the light of the above comments, we may also question the
coherence of Hick's argument that the "religious reality"
(whether it be Buddha, Muhammad, Christ or the Vedas) stands in
questionable relation to the tradition which develops and
continues around it.[67] To claim that a disclosure of religious

---

64. TD p.46.
65. TD p.46; see also the differing ways in which the
contributors to ed. Whaling 1984 have qualified Smith's
individualism.
66. See <u>DEL</u> chs.2,15,22; Hick 1984d.

reality does not demand theological doctrines or codes of behaviour to form some boundary conditions for the group of people responding to that disclosure is highly contentious. If, as Hick claims, the religious reality demands and challenges us to a new way of life and a new vision of reality, then in as much as these new aspects receive articulation and practice, communities will form, and necessarily so, due to the social nature of personhood. Even in his Copernican days Hick writes that "the function of a religion is to bring us to a right relationship with the ultimate divine reality, to awareness of our true nature and our place in the whole, into the presence of God."[68] To imply that such a function can generally be facilitated without the development of institutions or codes of behaviour or a "cumulative tradition" is both ahistorical and unfaithful to the teachings of many of the great teachers and religious leaders. Furthermore, these developments will no doubt lead to differences and distinctiveness between different religions that cannot be lightly passed over.

However, distinctiveness and differences should not in themselves be good reason for persecution, superiority or isolationism. Hick's version of Copernican Christianity is not the only form of Christianity which condemns these traits.[69]

There is a further reason to question Hick's contention that religions stand in questionable relation to their founding events. From the point of view of certain doctrines, Hick often argues from "tradition" to support his contentions, thereby suggesting the legitimacy of the continuity of tradition. For instance, concerning the cognitive claims in religious language, Hick writes against the non-cognitive understanding of Christianity:

> Thus from the point of view of one whose faith forms part of history going back through generations of the church's life to the faith of the New Testament, and behind that to the insights of the great Hebrew prophets, the non-cognitivist is not offering an objective analysis of the language of faith as living speech but is recommending a quite new use of it.[70]

In another context, Hick argues that the historical durability of a religious tradition helps to establish that it represents a

67. GUF p.103.
68. GUF p.147.
69. See for example Vatican II 1965c ch.2, para.9; 1965b ch.1, para.6; and SNC 1984 pp.132,139.
70. GUF p.8, my emphases; and also PRP p.16.

"genuine encounter with the divine reality." [71]   This would imply the authenticity of the tradition and the legitimacy of an institutional development, in some cases, centring upon a founder or revealing event(s). No doubt there is a variety of beliefs within any religious community, many of which will overlap. However, this fact does not preclude the legitimate evaluation of the status or truthfulness of elements within one's own or within another's religious tradition. Hick shows such discrimination in regard to non-cognitive and predestinarian forms of Christianity: he argues that they are inappropriate with respect to their founder and to the historical tradition. [72]   Other examples are his Irenaean theodicy, which is to be found in second-century Christianity, and Chalcedon, safeguarding the truth of the myth of the incarnation! [73]   This element of my argument reduces itself to the viable claim that some strands of historical Christianity are more appropriate than others - hence, the history of heresy. [74]

Historically it is also difficult to substantiate the claim that in all cases the institutional nature of religious communities was unintended and undesired by their founders. This may be true in some cases, but as the claim stands, it is not applicable. For instance, the sangha would appear to be indispensable in relation to the teachings and practice of Gautama; and it is arguable that Jesus did intend a community of believers which would continue to preach the "kingdom of God", and be a "sign of the times". [75]

This whole area is formidably complex, but the dismissal of organised religious communities as being either contrary to the founders' intentions, or deliberately divisive of people by creating an "us"-"them" mentality, [76], cannot be justified without much more analysis.

(4.2.3). "Truth" and "falsity" in religion:

If Hick (and Smith's) analysis of religion and the consequent implications of their analysis are problematic, what of Hick's arguments that we cannot speak of true or false in religions, just as we cannot speak of true or false in cultures and

---

[71]. GUF p.141.
[72]. GUF p.8; PRP p.16; EGL pp.127-32.
[73]. See EGL pts.3-4; GUF pp.170-1.
[74]. See Rahner 1964.
[75]. Schnackenberg 1974 pt.1, pt.4 ch.1; Küng 1981 pt.B; Flew 1943 ch.3; Rahner 1978 pt.7; and the much neglected book of MacKinnon (1940). There is admittedly much debate about whether Jesus founded the Church.
[76]. GUF p.103.

civilisations. This is true at a high level of generality - e.g. "the Hindu religion and culture is false". Such a statement is as absurd as it is unfocused. However, a certain amount of discriminative evaluation cannot be bypassed, for if culture includes laws and institutions, one may perhaps speak of the falsehood of the South African apartheid system, or certain aspects of the caste system that permeated Hindu society, or the treatment and place of women in certain strands of Islamic society or within the Christian Church. Moral "falsehood" in the above instances would imply a discriminative judgement about the morality of certain structural elements existing within religions or/and societies. Clearly, in making such judgements it should be acknowledged that one may be operating with a different set of moral criteria from the person or cultures in question. But unless all morality is deemed to be relative, such judgement may be intellectually permissible and sometimes practically necessary. In fact, Hick has made the judgements cited above in recent years.[77] Consequently, it is possible, contrary to Hick's injunction, that judgements can be made about cultures, societies and religions.

(4.2.4). Hick's phenomenological considerations regarding genetic confessionalism:

If Hick's theological considerations have serious internal difficulties, can he rest his case on the phenomenological considerations he has put forward?[78] What of Hick's argument that if in the majority of cases one's place of birth determines one's religion, to claim that one religion is more valid than another amounts to a form of genetic confessionalism?[79] Religious adherence, like racial identity, should therefore be viewed in terms of "religious ethnicity".[80]

Hick is surely right in pointing out that one's religion is often determined by one's birthplace. However, to imply then that all religions should be viewed as equal paths to the truth tends to make truth a function of birth. This underlying assumption, which is required if the argument is to have any decisive weight, runs into considerable difficulties. Elsewhere, Hick acknowledges this difficulty when he writes of Nazism, warlock worship and witchcraft (which could be chosen because of the family and culture into which one is born): "To say that whatever is sincerely believed and practised is, by definition, true, would be the end of all critical discrimination, both intellectual and

---

[77]. Hick 1981c pp.465ff; GMN p.94.
[78]. Loughlin 1985a has argued that Hick's case rests on phenomenological considerations alone and not theological arguments.
[79]. Hick 1981c p.456.
[80]. SC p.96.

moral."[81]   Hick eschews this total relativisation of religious truth, although admittedly some Christian pluralists do not.[82] However, it is difficult to see how Christian relativists could combat the claims that Nazism and witchcraft represent true responses to the divine reality. Furthermore, if Hick's argument was pushed to its logical limit it would result in a theory of determinism - a notion which Hick firmly rejects.[83]

Given the above qualifications and criticisms of a strong form of Hick's claim, it can be further argued that his genetic confessionalism only takes on its importance in the light of two suppositions - both of which I have shown are questionable. The first is that all those outside Christianity are consigned to eternal perdition. The second is that a monopoly of religious truth and religious insight is claimed for one religion alone. Given these suppositions one can clearly see the force of Hick's argument. However, remove them and include the criticisms above and the genetic confessionalism argument does not amount to much, especially if a further consideration (following) is introduced.

If it is acknowledged freely that God has acted throughout human history in various and particular ways, there is no a priori reason why one act within the complex series of acts should not be viewed as the climax and high-point of all the rest. Moule writes:

> it is impossible not to believe that God's creative work of reconciliation permeates the whole of his creation and all history...But such a belief is not in the least incompatible with the belief that this continuous process comes to complete and perfect expression at a particular point. On the contrary, it is arguable that God's immanence, involvement, and participation in his whole creation should reach its climax at some time and some place: the 'scandal of particularity' is by no means a denial but rather a confirmation of the ubiquity and continuity of God's activity.[84]

Interestingly, this scandal of particularity (not exclusivity) is partially accepted by Hick in a restricted context. In 1980 he wrote that as an historian he would be unable to answer the

---

81. TD p.148. Interestingly, this criticism is aimed at Smith.
82. See my criticisms of Smith and Race in D'Costa 1986b; and of Troeltsch in D'Costa 1986d.
83. DEL p.116.
84. IM p.86; see also Newbigin's comments in IM pp.197-210.

question of whether Jesus is the fullest incarnation of God's love. However, he adds that as "a Christian I can say that so far as my knowledge extends this is so."[85] If this comment is to have any cognitive import it clearly undermines the force of his genetic confessionalism argument. Ultimately the claim for the normativeness of Christ is not a human claim of superiority or special favour, but the recognition of the possibility that certain moments in history are more decisive and normative than others. Again, Hick contradicts his genetic confessionalism argument in his theory of religious history, whereby generations of people in the pre-axial period existed with "natural religions, or religions without revelation."[86] It could be argued, using Hick's form of reasoning, that his theory of religious history entails a form of "chronological confessionalism" whereby only those born after a certain date can have access to God!

If Hick's contention that Smith's thesis requires the Christian to adopt a Copernican standpoint has been shown to be problematic, I do not wish to imply that some of the "conclusions" of Hick's reflections are invalid. However, these conclusions can be generated from an inclusivist standpoint. For instance, on an inclusivist view it is openly acknowledged that history can also be viewed as a divine-human continuum. This view is implicit in the Old Testament doctrine of a cosmic covenant established through Adam and Noah, a teaching not absent in the New Testament.[87] It is my contention that we do not require a Copernican revolution to affirm that God has always been at work in history in various ways and in sundry times. Furthermore, the Ptolemaic view does not entail that religions should view each other as rival communities or that mutual hospitality, cooperation and openness are inappropriate.[88]

(4.2.5). Hick's Copernican analogies:

Finally, the two analogies that Hick employs to illuminate his Copernican thesis succinctly highlight some of the central contentious issues that I have been discussing. Hick seems to assume that the Copernican revolution implies a form of religious equality whereby no one religion can claim a special vantage point or particularly decisive revelation. I have argued that such a position eventually entails an apparent lack of explicit truth criteria, with attendant difficulties, or at the least, a set of implicit truth criteria not openly acknowledged. The point I am making becomes clear when we turn to the analogies that Hick offers.

---

85. Hick 1981d p.9.
86. GMNUS p.48.
87. Ariarajah 1985 ch.1; Cracknell 1986 ch.2-3.
88. See 4.3 below.

Allowing that these analogies are employed in limited ways and should not be pressed inappropriately, I think that my point still holds. For instance, the elephant and blind man analogy only works if it is assumed that at least one person is not blind and can see that the blind men are touching different parts of the same elephant. The original parable tells of a prince who conducted this experiment and if it was not for the prince's special vantage point, the blind men may have quarrelled endlessly - or alternatively, there would be no guarantee that they were not indeed touching and describing different objects.[89]

The special vantage point for Hick is his belief in a Christian God of universal love and his consequent problem is in trying to disassociate this notion of God from any religion (ecclesiocentricity/Christianity) or any particular revelation (Jesus Christ). Even if Hick were successful in this, a theistic vantage point is implicitly assumed. This is done at the cost of finally rendering the non-theistic religions as blind men in as much as they claim that their own revelations are decisive and definitive, and in as much as Hick claims that their revelations are incomplete and partial.

The importance of particularity in assessing any self-disclosure of God is further highlighted in Don Cupitt's criticism of Hick's astronomical analogy:

> The religions are very different from each other. Each is a highly complex symbol-system. It is by no means clear that they all point towards and converge upon a common focus, and we have no independent knowledge of or way of speaking about that which is supposed to be their common focus. We have many myths and symbols and we have ways of describing and explaining their use in particular traditions, but we have no independent access to the thing symbolised.[90]

The important point that Cupitt is making is that it is only through the particularities of the religious communities' beliefs and practices that their particular revelations may be spoken of.[91] To assume a non-partisan vantage point in asserting any

---

[89]. This criticism is made by Almond 1983 p.37, who in turn cites Smart's criticsm of the use of this parable in a Hindu context: see Smart 1968 p.132.
[90]. Cupitt 1982 p.23, my emphases.
[91]. Howard 1981 p.337 also notes the difficulties with this analogy regarding different practices.

particular "common focus" is difficult, if not impossible.

It should be noted that in response to the above types of criticism, Hick has defended his use of the elephant and blind men analogy as not implying any privileged vantage point, but rather that the analogy is "arrived at inductively". He writes:

> We start from the phenomenological data of the form of religious experience and thought presented by the history of religions. We then seek to interpret these data from the standpoint of the basic conviction that religious experience is not, as such and in toto, a realm of illusory projection but is also, at least in part, an effect within consciousness of the presence and pressure $_{92}$of a transcendent divine Reality.

Hick argues that from this basis, and not a privileged vantage point, one arrives at the elephant-blind men parable. But this answer, I would argue, has one major difficulty which drives Hick back implicitly into a Ptolemaic situation. How is Hick to discriminate between the "illusory projection" possible within religions and a valid interpretation and response to the divine, without some view of the nature and purpose of God? We have already seen that there are many manifestations of religions occuring in different cultures that Hick has criticised as distorted or false. This is because they contradict his central and implicit presupposition of a God of love, creating all "human animals into children of God", such that "the fulfilment of the human potential in an ultimate perfect human community in the divine presence" becomes a necessary criterion for truthful belief. ^{93} I am arguing that it would be impossible to come "neutrally" to the data, as Hick seems to claim, and inductively arrive at the elephant-blind men parable. For the only way in which one could even postulate that the blind men were not in fact in contact with totally different realities is the assumption of some privileged vantage point, or in effect, some view of God or divine reality that justified such an interpretation against an opposite assumption. Otherwise, why should one not assume that the blind men did confront different "objects", rather than a single elephant, or, as would a Barthian, that most maps are really distorted?

To summarise: from much of the above it will be clear by now

---

^{92}. Hick 1983c p.336.
^{93}. Hick 1981d p.5; see also Hick 1982a; DEL chs.8,19,22.

that many of my criticisms of Hick concern his theological and phenomenological assumptions and their implications. I have also tried to show that my criticisms do not entail my adopting what Hick calls (the first phase of) "Ptolemaic" theology. This will become even more evident as I now turn to Hick's argument from the theological and practical benefits of the Copernican revolution.

(4.3). An examination of argument 6: The argument from the theological and practical benefits of the Copernican revolution.

Throughout this chapter I have suggested that Hick's Copernican revolution involves deeply problematic assumptions and in this section I shall argue - sometimes directly in the light of my earlier criticisms, and sometimes for new reasons outlined below - that its supposed implications are equally problematic.

Hick argues that when religions meet on non-Copernican premises, a form of confessional dialogue inevitably results. One partner will always think that he or she possesses the absolute truth, and his or her dialogue partner possesses only a relative truth. Inevitably, according to Hick, the main aim of dialogue will be conversion. The Copernican shift apparently overcomes these objectionable implications and a form of truth-seeking rather than confessional dialogue arises. In truth-seeking dialogue each partner realises that the "transcendent Being is infinitely greater than his own limited vision of it" and partners can "accordingly seek to share their visions" to facilitate a mutual growth in "awareness of the Divine Reality before which they both stand."[94]

I have touched on a number of issues related to dialogue and confession above. For the moment, however, I wish to argue that: a) on Hick's own Copernican premises there is an implicit confessional form of dialogue operating; b) that Hick caricatures confessional dialogue in a way that obscures the main issues at stake and the openness and mutual enrichment possible on inclusivist premises.

(4.3.1). Is Copernican inter-religious dialogue confessional?:

Let me begin with point (a). I would argue that the Copernican approach to dialogue implicitly involves a "confessional" form of dialogue which entails the same principles that Hick criticises in the so-called Ptolemaic confessional form of dialogue. First, the idea that the partner possesses a relative truth as compared

---

[94]. GMN p.81. For a criticism of these assumptions in the works of other pluralists such as Knitter, Race, and Smith - see D'Costa 1986b.

to one's own absolute truth is supposed to create a block in "Ptolemaic" dialogue. However, this same logic is necessarily operative in Hick's position if the partner is not also a Copernican theologian or philosopher. For instance, Hick's position requires that Buddhists who hold "that there can be no other aspects of reality than the pratitya samputpada" cannot be taken with absolute seriousness. They are to be viewed as making only a partial claim, presumably despite themselves. He argues that such a Buddhist should be encouraged to understand that their central symbol of reality is "best understood metaphorically, or mythologically, rather than literally", and that they "will sooner or later find that it (their religious tradition) will develop" in this way. [95] Unless Copernicans limit their dialogue exclusively to other like-minded Copernicans within other religious traditions, they will implicitly entertain a view which holds that the partner has a relative truth compared to their own absolute Copernican perspective, in which the partner's insights are "accepted" - but not always on the partner's terms! This strategy involves the same logic criticised by Hick as "confessional".

Second, Hick writes that when inter-religious dialogue takes place on a confessional level, with:

> people bearing mutual witness to their
> own faiths, each in the firm conviction
> that his is the final truth and in the
> hope of converting the other, (dialogue)
> can only result either in conversion or
> in a hardening of differences... [96]

It is difficult to see, if my argument above is valid, why the Copernican partner would be in a different position if he or she was in dialogue with a non-Copernican from another religion. The Copernican partner would be convinced that their Copernican view represented the best position and they would accordingly be indifferent to the non-Copernican position of their partner. In the process of dialogue, may our Copernican not question the legitimacy and authority of any non-Copernican view of the relation between religions? Hick does precisely this with his partners in dialogue (when they are inclusivist Christians reflecting on the theology of religions).

If the Copernican responded that there may still be a "lot of mileage" in dialogue and that exploring rather than "hardening" of differences would take place - then mutatis mutandis, this can be applied to the inclusivist position. Karl Rahner writes of the open-ended and inspiring nature of dialogue in the following way

---

95
. SC p.91.
96
. GMN p.85, my brackets.

after pointing out the immensely complex hermeneutical problems involved in attempting to understand "the other". He notes that this very difficulty "also gives it (dialogue) a meaning before any agreement is reached, viz.: that one can learn an infinite amount from each other."[97]

Furthermore, is there an inherent tension in Hick's apparent "liberalism" when he writes "it is not my task as a Christian to tell Buddhists, Muslims or Hindus how to develop their symbols and belief systems"?[98]   Only a few lines earlier he suggests that the way forward for inter-religious unity is that each tradition re-evaluates its traditional symbols and views. Consequently, he suggests the following claims should be reinterpreted as mythological and metaphorical rather than as literal:

> In Hinduism this central symbol is the eternal and absolute character of the Vedas as containing all truth without exception; in Buddhism, the global completeness of the Buddha's insight, so that there can be no other aspects of reality than the pratitya samutpada of which he became so vividly aware in his Enlightenment; in Judaism, the absolute character of the Torah, given to God's chosen people...[99]

Hick's list contains suggestions for Hinduism, Buddhism, Judaism, Islam - and Christianity! Elsewhere, he writes that Christianity's "gift to the other great religious traditions can now be its own experience of modernization" in the light of its coming of age in a scientific culture.[100]   He then goes on to pose questions to all the world religions from this new Copernican consciousness.[101]   In the light of Hick's various comments, it is not clear why he says that it is not his "task...to tell Buddhists" and others how to develop their own religious systems. If it means that unjust coercion is ruled out, then is his position on this point very different from the later phases of "Ptolemaic" theology? I shall show below that unjust coercion is totally rejected by some inclusivist theologies - without contradiction or compromise on the priority given to preaching the gospel. It is this form of inclusivism that I am defending.

---

97. Rahner 1969 p.40, my brackets.
98. SC p.91.
99. SC p.91.
100. GMN p.88. This is precisely the "gift" that many Muslims least desire.
101. GMN pp.93-7.

(4.3.2). Has Hick mischaracterised "Ptolemaic" dialogue?:

I now wish to develop the second of my two points. If Hick's
Copernican premises actually entail an implicit form of
confessional dialogue, which he criticises in others - how
appropriate is his characterisation of "Ptolemaic dialogue"? Hick
seems to foster a crude assumption that "Ptolemaic" Christians
cannot, without contradicting their own principles, tolerate, or
contribute to, the existence of other religions. This is most
clear when he writes that when "Ptolemaic" Christians had helped
non-Christians in Birmingham to actually establish their own
places of worship, or helped and co-operated with non-Christians
they had unwittingly solved the problem of religious plurality.
The problem was "solved, not in theory but in practice, by
allowing human needs to take precedence over the implications of
the accepted theological language." [102] The suggestion, in its
strongest form, is that clearly the implications of a
non-Copernican theology would require that no help and care could
be given to non-Christians without demanding their conversion! [103]
However, this type of position has been rejected by even
some first phase Ptolemaic theologians. [104]

A weaker form of Hick's comments would suggest that on
Ptolemaic principles, the absoluteness of Christianity implies
that it cannot tolerate any other equal and therefore Christians
should try to convert their neighbours whenever possible. To do
otherwise entails internal contradiction. [105] However, it is
possible to view the non-Christian religions as possibly false or
as partial revelations of God; and at the same time to argue that
all people of whatever religious persuasion should, under
reasonable circumstances, be allowed religious liberties. The
"Ptolemaic" Second Vatican Council held just such a position.
Citing the conciliar document Dignitatis Humanae (DH), issued
thirteen years before Hick's cited article, a recent official
Roman Catholic document affirmed that:

> Mission must always revolve around man in
> full respect of his freedom. For this
> reason, the Second Vatican Council,
> having affirmed for the whole church the
> necessity and urgency of Christ, "the
> light of life", with all its apostolic
> faithfulness and fortitude...confirms the

102.
103. GMN p.41, my emphasis.
. This is the implication to which Hick seems to subscribe in
GMN p.36, lines 13-18.
104. . See Stott 1975; Hesslegrave 1981; Stott 1981; School of
World Mission 1981 pp.192-5; Scott 1981.
105. . See GMN p.36, lines 8-10.

need to promote and respect the true
freedom of other persons, rejecting any
form of coercion whatsoever most
especially in the religious sphere.

"Truth, however, is to be sought in a
manner proper to the dignity of the human
person and his social nature. The inquiry
is to be free, carried on with the aid of
teaching or instruction, communication
and dialogue. In the course of these, men
explain to one another the truth they
have discovered...in order to help one
another in their search for truth..." (DH
3.)

"In spreading religious faith and
introducing religious practices, everyone
ought at all times to refrain from any
manner of action which could seem to
carry a hint of coercion or of a kind of
persuasion which would be dishonourable
or unworthy, especially when dealing with
poor or uneducated people. Such a manner
of action would have to be considered an
abuse of one's rights and a violation of
the rights of others." (DH 4). [106]

I have quoted at such length to make a number of points in
contrast to Hick's potrayal of Ptolemaic dialogue. First, in
relation to my immediate point, it is clear that the Catholic
Church without compromising its "apostolic faithfulness" not only
"respects", but "promotes" the freedom and rights of all persons
of whatever religion. Rather than running counter to the
"implications" of its "Ptolemaic" theology as Hick suggests, such
a respect is in fact founded in the revelation of God in Christ,
and by means of natural law: "The Council further declares that
the right to religious freedom is based on the very dignity of
the human person as known through the revealed word of God and by
reason itself." [107] Second, Hick's assumption that mutual
seeking after truth is incompatible with a "Ptolemaic" theology,
[108], is also thrown into question when the document explicitly
states that dialogue should facilitate each partner in his or her
own search for truth. [109] The view that non-Christian religions
have nothing to teach, illuminate and share in relation to
Christianity is not concomitant with the principles of

---

106. SNC 1984 p.132, my emphases.
107. Vatican II 1965c ch.1, para.2 (including footnote).
108. GMN p.81.
109. SNC 1984 p.138 para. 35; 1985 p.113 para. 5, p.130, para.
entitled "Contribution of non-Christian religions to
Christianity".

inclusivist "Ptolemaic" theology. Hence, it is curious and possibly polemical when Hick writes that pluralists "are free with good conscience to benefit from the immense spiritual values and insights of other traditions" thereby suggesting that others are not.[110] There are volumes of "Ptolemaic" testimony that such a process can take place "with good conscience".[111]

Third, when the Vatican documents speak of promoting and respecting the rights of all people, this comment should be viewed in the light of other conciliar documents which insist that all forms of social service are implied in the Christian injunction to love one's brother and sister. An official Vatican document summarises the various forms of mission as constituted by: a) "the single presence and living witness of the Christian life"; b) "concrete commitment to the service of mankind and all forms of activity for social development and for the struggle against poverty and the structures which produce it"; c) the "liturgical life and that of prayer and contemplation"; d) "dialogue" in order to "walk together towards truth and to work together in projects of common concern" ; e) the "announcement and catechesis in which the good news of the Gospel is proclaimed and its consequences for life and culture are analysed."[112]

Hick seems to affirm the first four but he is keen to eliminate the fifth from dialogue. This seems to be because of his theological assumption that mission towards other major religions implies an unjustified superiority and also implies that God has not acted within these religions. It is because of these unjustified assumptions (regarding the nature of inclusivist "Ptolemaic" theology) that Hick allows for mission only in regard to "secular servants of humanity" (humanists, atheists and naturalists) and the "primal religions" where there has been "no revelation of God."[113] Politically, the notion of Christian mission also seems to echo colonial rule, a memory which Hick is keen to overcome and eliminate.[114] Hick has not given enough detailed attention to this issue. It is therefore inappropriate to take up his thought in any great detail, except to note the minimisation of the proclamation of Christ in Hick's notion of mission. It is also worth noting that an inclusivist Christian may share the commitment to the type of goals that missions ought to have according to Hick, but the commitments are

---

110. SC p.90.
111. Many of these testimonies are brought together by Camps 1983 pt.3 and Schreiter 1985. See also D'Costa 1986a ch.5, 1987, introductory essay section to each chapter.
112. SNC 1984 pp.129-30.
113. GMNUS p.44.
114. GMN p.35, 1986a.

a result of his or her "Ptolemaic" discipleship to Christ. These attitudes are not exclusively Copernican!

Hick is also incorrect when he writes that once the Copernican shift has been accepted "a large degree of practical co-operation" will be possible, for as noted above, a large degree of practical co-operation is already possible and indeed encouraged on inclusivist principles.

(4.3.3). Global theology:

One further issue requires comment at this stage. Hick's proposals for a global theology reflect the Copernican attitude that God has revealed himself throughout history. Consequently, the data from all aspects of human religious life must be taken into account when considering any religious topic. We have already noted that this attitude towards history is not exclusive to Copernicans, but for the moment there is only one point I wish to make which will be developed in chapter 5. Hick has not gone as far as some other pluralists in their claims about the purpose and nature of a global theology. I have dealt with these other pluralist suggestions elsewhere.[115] Hick has given details of the methodology and aims of his global theology most fully in Death and Eternal Life,[116] where he has attempted to write a "global theology of death." Methodologically, such a theology requires attention to "any potential source of light" on the subject, which thereby takes "seriously the variety of human views concerning man's destiny".[117] Hick's aim in so doing is to examine whether the "central witness" of the "great faiths of east and west...point towards, a common conception of human destiny."[118] His tentative answer is in the affirmative.

Hick acknowledges at the outset of Death and Eternal Life that the "present enquiry is undertaken from a christian standpoint", and that this is all he may and can do.[119] He writes that to "renounce all concrete human patterns would be to exist in a vacuum."[120] Hence, although a Copernican theologian, Hick acknowledges that a certain standpoint is inevitable and necessary when coming to evaluate the global data. What he wishes to avoid is a (supposedly) "Ptolemaic" attitude which would dismiss such an enterprise, claiming that the resources for answering all questions are to be found within the Christian tradition alone.[121] From the point of view of the later stages

---

115. D'Costa 1986b.
116. DEL p.29.
117. DEL pp.26,27.
118. DEL p.34.
119. DEL pp.27, 28-9.
120. DEL p.29.
121. DEL p.30.

of Ptolemaic theology - a position which I have been developing and defending - Hick's global theology is a welcome and interesting enterprise. I would only add that, of necessity, the Christian carrying out such global reflections would employ Christocentric truth criteria in discering the activity of God. This process would allow for the clarifying and enlargement of the Christian understanding of God, humankind and the world. Some criteria are necessary and the centrality of Christ (and all this implies about the Church) is central to the Christian global theologian. Otherwise, in the words of Küng, one would lose "all criteria for the discernment of spirits".[122]

(4.4). <u>An</u> <u>examination</u> <u>of</u> <u>argument</u> 2: <u>The</u> <u>argument</u> <u>from</u> <u>encountering</u> <u>saintly</u> <u>and</u> <u>holy</u> <u>people</u> <u>from</u> <u>the</u> <u>non-Christian</u> <u>religions</u>.

My response to this particular argument has been implicitly addressed in a number of previous sections. It will suffice to reiterate my comments briefly. It can be acknowledged that God's salvific will revealed and made historically present, definitive and irreversible in Christ is operative outside Christianity. Therefore, the Ptolemaic theologian should gladly and without reserve or contradiction admit that God is present in the life of <u>individuals</u> and consequently, due to the social nature of persons, mediated in varying degrees through the <u>religions</u> of these said individuals. The holy pagans and saints of the Old Testament and the validity of Israel's covenant before the time of Christ (and by extension, in principle, to other religions), have all been acknowledged without embarrassment or contradiction in inclusivist "Ptolemaic" theology. In fact, such a recognition is also the basis whereby inclusivist Christians realise that they have much to learn from the world religions. In the light of the above considerations brought to bear against Hick, it may be concluded that the existence of saintly and holy people from other religions does not in itself call for a Copernican revolution. If anything, such findings are actually implied in the inclusivist position.

(4.5). <u>An</u> <u>examination</u> <u>of</u> <u>argument</u> 7: <u>The</u> <u>argument</u> <u>from</u> <u>the</u> <u>divine</u> <u>nature</u> <u>-</u> <u>personal</u> <u>and</u> <u>non-personal</u>.

My criticism of this argument has been expressed throughout this and the previous chapter. I will therefore briefly reiterate my objections and direct the reader to the pertinent sections where they are discussed in greater detail. However, in chapter 5 I will point out how in trying to deal with some of these difficulties, Hick has developed an epicycle to his Copernican theory which requires an entirely fresh assessment of the

---

[122]. Küng 1986 p.122.

Copernican revolution.

To summarise the criticisms levelled at this argument of Hick's: I argued that as a God of universal love was decisive and in fact the very presupposition of the Copernican revolution, the universe of faiths was implicitly theistic and therefore did not properly accommodate non-theistic religions.[123] Furthermore, in attempting to ground such a normative theism it was seen how Hick is inevitably pushed back to Christology, from which he tries to escape by means of the Copernican revolution.[124] Consequently, a normative theism in this instance was forced back to a normative Christocentricism and therefore, the conclusion that Hick was a covert Ptolemaic theologian! I argued that even if non-theistic religions could be seen to have partial insights into the nature of ultimate reality, in the final analysis they could not all be accommodated on their own terms for this may entail the explicit rejection of the Copernican God at the centre.[125] These and my other criticisms should cause Hick to re-think the Copernican position. There is evidence that he has, in his attempt to revitalise the Copernican revolution by means of a further epicycle. It is to these epicyclic developments that I shall now turn. The credibility of the Copernican enterprise relies on these developments within Hick's position.

---

123. See 3.2 above.
124. See 4.1 above.
125. See 3.2 above.

CHAPTER 5: AN EXAMINATION OF JOHN HICK'S COPERNICAN EPICYCLE

(5.1). Introduction.
In the previous two chapters I criticised various aspects of Hick's Copernican revolution. One major argument was aimed at Hick's severing of theocentricism from Christocentricism. However, since the 1980's Hick has developed an "epicycle" which requires critical attention. His epicycle attempts to overcome many of the objections above, but a number of critics have failed to notice this development in Hick's thought. [1] This epicyclic development means that Hick now occupies a unique position regarding the gamut of Christian responses to religious pluralism - as outlined in chapter 1.

(5.2). Hick's Copernican "epicycle".

I argued that even if Hick's theocentricism could float free from some normative grounding event(s), such as Jesus' life, death and resurrection, his Copernican revolution was still deficient (on his own premises) in assuming a theistic God at the centre of all religions. I further argued that the Theravādin Buddhist or Advaitin Hindu could not be properly accommodated on their own terms within Hick's proposals. Hick's epicycle attempting to circumvent these difficulties can be found as early as 1970. [2] Hick addressed these two problems by employing the Hindu distinction regarding Nirguna and Saguna Brahman:

> Detaching the distinction, then, from its Hindu context we may say that Nirguna God is the eternal self-existent divine reality, beyond the scope of all human categories, including personality; and Saguna God is God in relation to his creation and with the attributes which express this relationship, such as personality, omnipotence, goodness, love and omniscience. Thus the one ultimate reality is both Nirguna and non-personal, and Saguna and personal... [3]

Two ambiguities arise from his admittedly brief remarks. The Nirguna aspect seems somewhat redundant in explaining the divine

_____

[1]. Race 1983 pp.82ff; Hughes 1984 p.18; Knitter 1985 p.147.
[2]. GUF ch.10 was delivered as a lecture in 1972, and although published a year before TD, Hick's suggestions in TD pp.152-3 were made in 1970, three years before the actual publication of GUF.
[3]. GUF p.144.

153

as experienced as non-personal, for if Hick's Nirguṇa "God" is by implication not in relation to creation it cannot be experienced by those who belong to that creation. If it is in relation to creation and therefore accessible to experience, then by Hick's own definition it is Saguṇa, not Nirguṇa "God" that is being spoken of.

Hick was forced to clarify his concept of "God" due to the incisive criticisms made by Julius Lipner and Duncan Forrester that I have developed in the two chapters above.[4] It was pointed out that in the Advaita Vedānta tradition, Nirguṇa Brahman is of greater ontological validity, thereby elevating the impersonal as ultimately normative. In the Viśiṣṭādvāita tradition, the personal Īśvara is given ontological prominence, thereby denying (as Rāmānuja did) the featureless non-dual Nirguṇa of Śankara's Advaita.[5]

On the one hand Lipner asks: "Is the 'God' at the centre of the universe of faiths a Christian God...?".[6] This impression is reinforced as the

> whole problem is discussed within a Christian framework;...he (Hick) appeals to a Christian notion of God as an all-loving creator and Father of mankind (a description that neither Theravāda Buddhists nor Muslims, for example, for different reasons, will accept)...[7]

This reading of Hick's position is similar to the Viśiṣṭādvāitin use of Saguṇa Brahman. Lipner highlights Hick's implicit theism.

On the other hand, Forrester argues that the centre of Hick's universe of faiths is inhabited by "either the Unknown God whom people ignorantly worship and whose nature cannot be declared because it has not been revealed, or a God without attributes, the nirguṇa Brahman of Hindu thought". Forrester suggests that Hick's ideas would only be acceptable to a "Vedāntic Hindu" (presumably an Advaitin Hindu).[8] This ambiguity in Hick's position, resulting in two opposing interpretations, pushed Hick into an either/or dilemma. Either the ultimate nature of the divine is to be thought of as impersonal (Advaita); or like Viśiṣṭādvāita, the ultimate nature of the divine is to be thought

---

[4]. Lipner 1975,1976, 1977; Forrester 1976.
[5]. See Dasgupta 1975a ch.10, 1975b ch.11, 1975c chs. 18,20, esp. pp.304-451; Lott 1980 chs.4,5; Lipner 1986 ch.5; for a detailed account of the issues and debates between Rāmānuja and Śankara.
[6]. Lipner 1977 p.253.
[7]. Lipner 1977 p.253, first set of brackets mine.
[8]. Forrester 1976 p.69.

of as personal and theistic.

The critical articles were published between 1977 and 1978 and it was not until 1980 that Hick addressed this dilemma - which, since then, has constantly preoccupied him. [9]   After 1980, Hick believes that the answer to this problem has been resolved (as shown above) and his writings since then represent only further refinements, rather than significant changes, to his new position.

Hick's response may be classified as an "epicycle" - i.e. it is an attempt to modify and develop the Copernican theory in the light of objections. Hick's epicycle is highlighted with reference to his pre-epicyclic Copernican position when he says that both Nirguna and Saguna "God" are viewed as equally valid representations of the Real that is above and behind both impersonal and personal manifestations and disclosures. [10]   If Hick was criticised as giving priority to either the personal Saguna or the impersonal and unknown Nirguna, he responds by implicitly denying both criticisms and develops a further option in 1980. He writes that we must distinguish:

> between God, and God as conceived by human beings. God is neither a person nor a thing, but is the transcendent reality which is conceived and experienced by different human mentalities in both personal and non-personal ways. [11]

He justifies the use of this distinction on philosophical grounds as well as on the grounds that this type of distinction is found in many religions. The following table indicates the distinctions within various traditions referred to by Hick in defending his thesis: [12]

---

[9]. Hick 1980b. Hick's silence may have been due to the following factors. GUF was closely followed by MGI which took up much of Hick's energies in the ensuing debate. Hick also delivered the Stanton Lectures in Cambridge (1974-1975; 1975-1976) and the Wescott (Teape) lectures in India (1975-1976). In Hick October 1985 (private letter), Hick expresses "surprise" that his one response to Lipner's article was not accepted by the Scottish Journal of Theology.

[10]. Hick 1980b pp.133-35, GMNUS pp.83-7, PRP pp.39-44.

[11]. Hick 1980b p.133.

[12]. Hick 1980b pp.133-34.

"God" experienced under both personal and impersonal modes within
various religious traditions

Impersonal mode   Personal mode

Eckhart: Deitas(Godhead)   Deus(God)

Sankara: Nirguna Brahman   Saguna Brahman

Tao Te Ching: The Tao

Jewish Kabbal: En Soph   God of the Bible

P.Tillich: "God above the God of theism"

A.Whitehead:Primordial nature of God   Consequent
                                          nature of God

G.Kaufmann: "Utterly unknowable x",   "available God",
                                          "real God";
                                                 "mental   or
                                                 imaginative
                                                 constructions"

Traditional Christian:
            Infinite self-existent   in relation to
                                          mankind
Mahayana Buddhism:
            Dharmakaya/Sunyata   nirmankaya

However, these distinctions do not seem to differ greatly from Hick's earlier position, for the Nirguṇa/Saguṇa distinctions seem to operate as before. But the significant difference (an epicycle!) is to be found when Hick gives this Nirguṇa/Saguṇa distinction philosophical precision using a __modified__ Kantian model. [13]   Hick loosely borrows Kant's distinction between the

> noumenal world, which exists independently of and outside man's perception of it, and the phenomenal world, which is that world as it appears to our human consciousness. All that we are entitled to say about the noumenal world is that it is the unknown reality whose informational input produces, in collaboration with the human mind, the phenomenal world of our experience. [14]

When Hick develops this Kantian model, the shift and epicyclic development in his position becomes clear. If it initially seemed that Nirguṇa=noumenal and Saguṇa=phenomenal, the epicycle becomes evident for he now seems to argue that both nirguṇa and saguṇa are phenomenal images of the one noumenal "Eternal One" or "Real". [15]   In effect: Nirguṇa=Saguṇa=phenomena and the unknown Real=noumenon. Hick notes that for Kant, reality is only known through the categories of understanding:

> In Kant's system the pure categories, or pure concepts of Understanding (for example, substance), are schematised in terms of temporality to produce the more concrete categories which are exhibited in our actual experience of the world. (For example, the pure concept of substances is schematised as the concept of an object enduring through time). Something analogous to this, I am suggesting, takes place in our awareness of God. [16]

Hick argues that historical and cultural conditioning is

---

[13]. Hick 1980b pp.141ff; GMNUS pp.53,67,83; PR3 pp.119ff. Hick is aware of differences between Kant and himself: 1980b pp.141-43; and the difficulties in interpreting Kant. Below I shall show that Hick's Kantian epistemology gets him into similar difficulties as did Kant with his epistemology.
[14]. Hick 1980b p.142.
[15]. GMNUS p.42; see also below.
[16]. Hick 1980b p.142.

analogous to the schematisation imposed by the categories. He suggests "that God is to be thought of as the divine noumenon, experienced by mankind as a range of divine phenomena which takes both theistic and non-theistic forms."[17] And within theistic and non-theistic forms there are further concretisations through the amalgam of the "continuum of historical factors which have produced our different religious cultures."[18] In theistic forms these concretisations are seen in the various "personae" such as, Jahweh, Krishna, Śiva, Allah and the Father of Jesus Christ. Initially Hick does not clearly define the term "persona" but in 1984 he writes that a "divine persona is concrete, implicitly finite, sometimes visualizable and even capable of being pictured."[19] In non-theistic religions the divine "impersonae" are experienced as "Brahman, Nirvana, Sunyata, the Dharma, the Dharmakaya, the Tao."[20] Hick writes that impersonae are not as concrete as personae, but nevertheless an impersona is "not a 'thing' in contrast to a person...It is thus not so much an entity as a field of spiritual force, or the ultimate reality of everything, that which gives final meaning and joy."[21]

To summarise: the eternal noumenal expresses itself through both theistic and non-theistic traditions in an equally valid fashion, and more specifically within each tradition in different personae and impersonae. In 1980 Hick used the word "God" to denote the noumenal reality despite its theistic connotations. Hick argues that there is "no fully tradition-neutral term or tradition-transcending term", therefore "as a Christian I shall accordingly use the word 'God', but not use it in a straightforwardly theistic sense."[22] However, later that year and since 1981 Hick circumvents theistic echoes in the term "God" by using the terms "Eternal One", "Ultimate Reality" or "the Real"[23] to denote the noumenal which previously he had called "God". (From now on I shall use the term "Real" rather then repeat Hick's variations). These terms strive towards the neutrality which Hick had previously thought impossible to achieve.

---

[17]. Hick 1980b p.146.
[18]. Hick 1980b pp.142-43.
[19]. 1984j p.162. Earlier, in GMNUS p.52 he briefly refers to its traditional Latin meaning as a "face or image or icon" (representing God).
[20]. PR3 p.120, 1980b pp.142-3, 1984j pp.159-64.
[21]. Hick 1984j p.163.
[22]. Hick 1980b p.133, my emphasis.
[23]. These terms can be dated from 16 October 1980 onwards. On this date Hick delivered the lecture published in GMNUS ch.3. In GMNUS ch.5, Hick also employs these terms and this chapter was first published in 1981 - see 1981a. See GMNUS p.42 for the rationale of these terms.

Hick argues that the noumenal Real is experienced phenomenally as a personal God in Christianity and also experienced phenomenally as the impersonal "sunyata of Mahayana Buddhism" in an equally "genuine, authentic, valid" fashion. [24] Nirguna Brahman can no longer be equated with the divine noumenon, but is now one of many divine phenomena (impersona) alongside the differing personae such as Saguna Brahman.

It will be useful to summarise diagrammatically Hick's epicycle before further developing my exposition of Hick's position. [25]

24. GMNUS p.53.
25. References: Hick 1980b pp.135ff.

Hick's Epicycle: The Nature of the Divine Reality and its
Manifestations.

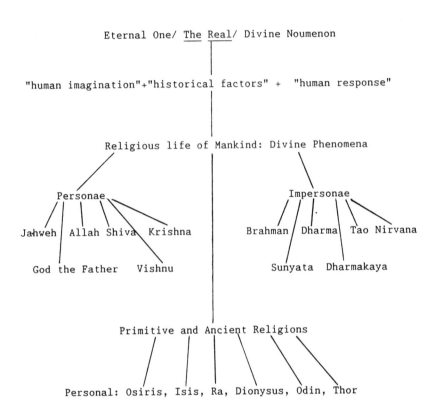

The creation of an epicycle is confirmed by three qualifications that Hick appends to his theory. First, Hick explicitly disavows either an Advaitin or Viśiṣṭādvāitin type of position. He distinguishes his position from the Advaitin's where "God" is ultimately non-personal, the personal aspect being relegated to a "lower and preliminary stage". [26] Hick also distinguishes his position from that of Viśiṣṭādvāita. His position, he tells us, is "equally different from the visistadvaitist view that Brahman is ultimately personal." [27] Consequently, for Hick "the Real is equally authentically thought and experienced as personal and as non-personal." [28] Hick is genuinely struggling to maintain the cognitive veracity of differing religious experiences, rather than tramelling or reducing them into a single hidden underlying religious experience.

Second, Hick safeguards his thesis against the misunderstanding that if we worship God through an image or persona and not qua God himself, would "it not follow that worship is directed to an illusion, a mere phenomenal appearance?" [29] Hick recalls Kant's statement that his (Kant's) noumenal-phenomenal distinction resulted not only in transcendental idealism but also in empirical realism. He assures critics that in his theory, as in Kant's, "the world as we perceive it is real, not illusory; but it is the appearance to us of that which exists in itself outside our experience of it." [30] People necessarily filter through and encounter the Real in concrete finite images or symbols or through specific concepts or ideas for such particularised, and therefore limited knowledge, is all that is possible for a finite mind:

> The divine presence is the presence of
> the Eternal One to our finite human
> consciousness, and the human projections
> are the culturally conditioned images and
> symbols in terms of which we concretize
> the basic concepts of deity. [31]

Finally, Hick defends himself from the criticism that if the divine noumenon is "impenetrably hidden from us" then · "any doctrine of God" is ultimately precluded. [32] Hick suggests that

---

26. 1980b p.145.
27. 1983c p.337.
28. 1983c p.337, my emphases. See also 1980b p.146, GMNUS p.53.
29. 1980b p.143.
30. 1980b p.143.
31. GMNUS p.53.
32. Hick 1980b p.146.

the opposite is in fact the case. If the Copernican suggestions are accepted, Hick argues, "then the very plurality and variety of the human experience of God provides a wider basis for theology than can the experience of any one religious tradition taken by itself." [33]

Since 1980, Hick has consistently maintained and developed this epicycle within his basic Copernican position. Therefore, over the years he has moved from Christocentricism to theocentricism to a Reality-centricism. How far does this Copernican epicycle circumvent the difficulties outlined above? At first sight it certainly seems to overcome a number of grave objections: that the "God" at the centre of the universe of faiths is definitely theistic, if not Christian, with the consequence that non-theistic religions are only finally accommodated on Hick's terms and not on their own; that the theory is inductively arrived at from an assessment of the varied phenomena rather than from within one particular religious tradition, thereby overcoming any implicit Ptolemaic imperialism.

(5.3). An assesment of Hick's epicycle.

In what follows I will explore three questions: 1. Does the noumenal "Real" overcome my objections to Hick's Copernican theocentricism? 2. Does Hick's epicycle successfully accommodate the different religions on their own terms? 3. How plausible is Hick's new inductive form of arriving at his Copernican conclusions? The answers to these questions clearly bear upon each other.

In dealing with the first question, I shall argue that Hick's Real, when closely analysed, introduces and possibly perpetuates a genuine ambiguity at the heart of the Copernican revolution. The Real turns out to be either a theistic loving God; or alternatively, reflects a transcendental agnosticism regarding the nature of the divine reality. Both these conclusions undercut Hick's Copernican intentions, his defence of the cognitive status of religious language and constitute further objections to the Copernican project in its new form.

(5.4). Hick's epicycle and an implicit theism.

The first alternative (a theistic God) presents itself when Hick's eschatological speculations are considered. If the Real is equally and legitimately manifested as personal and impersonal, will there be some clarification in the eschaton as to the nature of the Real in itself? For instance, could "Ptolemaic" Christians

---

[33]. Hick 1980b p.146. Hence his "global theology" - see 2.7 above.

(first phase) find that their beliefs were confirmed and that non-Christians were lost and mistaken? Or alternatively, would "Ptolemaic" Christians find that they were wrong? It may be that the Advaitin hierarchy was true, whereby the notion of a personal God was a provisional stage before the final realisation that Ātman is Brahman. Or may some altogether different scenario be the case?

These types of question are legitimate given that Hick defends two propositions which tend to contradict each other. The first[34] concerns the cognitive validity of religious language. Hick's defence of cognitive religious language has been a concern throughout his career. It is Hick's conviction that the cognitive veracity of religious language can only be verified in the after-life.[35] The second proposition is that "the Real is equally authentically thought and experienced as personal and as non-personal."[36] If religious beliefs actually entail cognitive claims about the nature of ultimate reality and humankind's relation to that reality, we can surely assume that on Hick's own premises his Copernican thesis should be verified in the eschaton. Even if Hick uses "neutral" terms such as a turning away from "self-centredness to Reality-centredness" to describe "salvation" or "liberation", what of the precise and particular cognitive ways in which such "liberation" or "salvation" is conceived within the different religions?

We can pursue this issue by developing an unanswered question addressed to Hick by Philip Almond who asks whether it is

> reasonable to demand a Copernican revolution...while the possibility remains that, in the final eschatological analysis, it _may_ turn out that a Ptolemaic Christian theology of some sort or other was valid?[37]

Might it eventually be the case that the Advaitin is correct in believing that there is no difference between the individual self and Brahman and that salvation constitutes the realisation that Brahman is Ātman? Such an eschatological conclusion would invalidate many theistic traditions which maintain an ultimate difference between God and the soul (although allowing for an intimate unity). Would not such a scenario thereby imply that theistic encounters with the Real were not as equally "genuine, authentic, valid perception(s) of the Eternal One" as were Advaitin encounters?[38]

---

34. PRP p.17.
35. GUF chs.2,13, PR2 pp.90-2, 1960e, FK2 ch.8; see 1.2.2 above.
36. Hick 1983c p.337.
37. Almond 1983 pp.39-40.

Hick's response to Almond is equally problematic. He argues that it is logically possible that (quoting from Acts 4:12): "there is no other name given under heaven whereby a man may be saved" and consequently a "Ptolemaic" Christian faith may turn out to be "true after all".[39] However, Hick argues that, although this is logically possible, there are overwhelming reasons for pursuing a Copernican path to avoid the paradox of a "God of universal love who has ordained that only a Christian minority...can be saved."[40]

There are a number of criticisms against this defence. Hick is certainly correct in pointing out "overwhelming reasons" against a purely "logical possibility", but his either/or dilemma is a false one for he contrasts only the first phase of "Ptolemiac" Christianity with the Copernican option, rather than the second and third phases which, I have argued, successfully overcome this paradox. Hence, if Almond's question (posed above) is not construed into a narrow "Ptolemaic" mould, it remains a legitimate question.

There is a further criticism against Hick's defence. Does his appeal to a "God of universal love" undermine the very epicycle that he is defending? His Copernican epicycle, designed to overcome the charge of theistic bias, undercuts the very basis for the Copernican revolution itself! How can Hick appeal to the reality of a God of universal love if the Real, the noumenal realm "exists independently of and outside man's perception of it?"[41] Either reality is or is not personal and loving; either the implications of reality viewed theistically are or are not true. In 1969 Hick lucidly expressed the cognitive claims of theism:

> If the word 'loving' has any meaning
> when applied to God it must bear the kind
> of positive analogy to human love that
> is indicated in so many of Jesus' sayings
> and parables. For God, the Creator and
> Lord of the universe, to be loving
> entails that evil is not ultimate and
> that infinite good will, however slowly
> and painfully, be brought out of it. And
> this in turn entails the completion of
> God's purpose for human beings beyond
> this earthly life...this purpose has
> unavoidable implications concerning the

38. GMNUS p.53, my brackets.
39. Hick 1983c p.337.
40. Hick 1983c p.338.
41. Hick 1980b p.142.

My point is this: ultimately, an authentic and genuine Advaitin could not accept the valid cognitive status of a theistic God, upon which the Copernican revolution is itself based. The converse is surely true for the theistic Christian who could not accommodate on his or her own terms, the Advaitin denial of ultimate reality as personal and distinct from humankind. Either the epicycle undercuts the very basis for the Copernican revolution in relativising or even denying the reality of a God of love; or, in accepting the reality of such a theistic God, it would entail the same problems highlighted by the implicit theism of the pre-epicyclic stage.

If Hick's initial response to Almond relied on appealing to the paradox of "Ptolemaic" theology, his next consideration concerns a "more probable 'eschatological scenario'" than apparently implied by (first stage) "Ptolemaic" theology. [43] Hick directs Almond to Death and Eternal Life, and Hick summarises the conclusions of that study:

> we move in stages towards the ultimate relationship to or union with the divine, and that as we approach nearer to that consummation our conceptions of 'how things are' will gradually become adequate. It seems likely that in this process many of the ideas embedded within each of the religious traditions will become variously modified or marginalized or superseded. [44]

Hick then argues that his own eschatological speculations suggest "the pluralist hypothesis that the great world faiths represent different conceptions and perceptions of, and correspondingly different responses to, the one ultimate divine reality." [45]

(5.4.1). An examination of Hick's eschatological defence:

However, it is precisely at the eschaton that the problem becomes magnified, for the eschaton is the place in which the veracity and cognitive import of religious language is verified. When we turn to Death and Eternal Life it becomes increasingly obvious that ultimately Hick is unable to circumvent the ontological conflict between some visions of reality as theistic and others as non-theistic.

---

42. GUF p.36.
43. Hick 1983c p.338.
44. Hick 1983c p.338.
45. Hick 1983c p.339. See also PRP pp.140ff.

In Death and Eternal Life Hick does come to conclusions about the ultimate state of things, "how things are", and they are definitely theistic! Furthermore, this theistic position concerning the eschaton is confirmed in a number of publications after the Copernican epicycle. Hence:

> I would...say that the belief in the reality of a limitlessly loving and powerful deity must incorporate some kind of eschatology according to which God holds in being the creatures whom he made for fellowship with himself, beyond bodily death, and brings them into the eternal fellowship which he has intended for them. I have tried elsewhere to argue that such an eschatology is a necessary corollary of ethical monotheism; to argue for the realistic possibility of an after-life or lives, despite the philosophical and empirical arguments against this...[47]

Admittedly, in the above quotation Hick is addressing a Christian audience. Nevertheless, it is clear that Hick himself views the thrust of the conclusions of Death and Eternal Life, even after his epicycle, as being a corollary of "ethical monotheism".[48] More significantly, Hick acknowledges in Death and Eternal Life that his eschatological conclusions require a "conception of God as personal Lord, distinct from his creation."[49] It is an eschatological situation in which there is "perfected personal community in the divine kingdom. The end-state is conceived as one in which individual egoity has been transcended in communal unity before God."[50]

---

[46]. In Hick November 1985 (private letter), Hick argued that DEL was "written ten years ago" and should not be used against him for a theologian may legitimately develop his ideas. However, it is significant that he quotes DEL in his defence against Almond in 1983 and then again in 1985 in PRP pp.96-102; see also EE pp.39-52, 63-8; PRP pp.140ff.
[47]. EE p.51, my emphases. Hick cites DEL in a footnote after this sentence.
[48]. See PRP pp.142ff (1985) in which he summarises the theism underlying DEL. Furthermore, Hick has not revised the 1985 reissue of DEL, indicating his affirmation of his original thesis.
[49]. DEL p.464.
[50]. EE p.51.

This eternal fellowship with a theistic God clearly implies, contrary to Hick's own Copernican thrust, that not all representations of the Real are as "genuine, authentic, valid" and correct. [51]   How could they be when he writes of the eschaton: "This last phase implicitly rejects the advaitist view that Atman is Brahman, the collective self being ultimately identical with God." [52]   Such a view contradicts Hick's epicyclic claim that "the Real is equally authentically thought and experienced as personal and non-personal." [53]   On the basis of Hick's own eschatological analysis, surely the Advaitin, Theravādin Buddhist and adherent of Sāṃkhya Yoga will find that their thought and experience of the Real are not as equally authentic or appropriate as perhaps the Jewish, Viśiṣṭādvaitin Hindu and Christian view of the Real?

My objection to Hick's epicycle is this: in attempting to remove a theistic God from the centre of the universe of faiths to overcome certain objections, such a God has inevitably turned up at the end of the universe of faiths thereby undercutting the effect of the epicycle. Consequently, the first question as to whether Hick's "epicycle" overcomes my objections to his Copernican theocentricism must be negatively answered. This contradictory tension is present in Hick's position for a number of reasons. I would suggest that many of Hick's theological and epistemological assumptions in his pre-Copernican days uneasily remain firmly embedded within his Copernican framework. In chapter 1, I noted that two issues preoccupied the early Hick: a defence of the cognitive value of theistic language, and theodicy. Both these concerns are carried over into his Copernican thought with some difficulty.

Since Hick is still a staunch defender of cognitive religious language, this underlying presupposition dictates a conclusion that inevitably runs counter to his Copernican proposals - i.e. that finally mutually contradictory assertions about truth, when they do properly occur, cannot be reconciled and held together with equal validity. If religious claims are judged by their cognitive adequacy, then there cannot be a genuine pluralism without self-contradiction. This may be the case when the Advaitin's view is legitimised even when it contradicts the Copernican's theological basis by which pluralism is acknowledged. Only if Hick surrenders his cognitive claims for religious language might he overcome this difficulty, but then he would run contrary to the assumptions of most religious believers in general - as he himself acknowledges [54];   and also more specifically, Christian believers. [55]

---

51. GMNUS p.53.
52. DEL p.464.
53. Hick 1983c p.337.
54. PRP p.16.

The second of Hick's preoccupations is theodicy. It is because he retains his original pre-Copernican theodicy within his Copernican framework that such eschatological difficulties remain. Running through from Evil and the God of Love to Death and Eternal Life and finally in Encountering Evil and Problems of Religious Pluralism, Hick constantly defends an Irenaean theodicy. It is also clear from Evil and the God of Love, Death and Eternal Life and Encountering Evil that theists have to deal with the theodicy issue, whereas someone who did not believe in a loving and good "God" may not even acknowledge the problem or may well conceive it differently. [56]

In answering my first question I have argued that when we turn to Hick's eschatological analysis the final conflict between genuine theism and non-theism is unresolved and it is difficult to see how it could be resolved. Such a conclusion has grave implications for my second question concerning the problem as to whether religions are accommodated on their own terms in Hick's epicycle. Hick's eschatological speculations place him on the horns of a dilemma. Either, the Advaitin is incorrect and the Christian (for example) is correct (in varying degrees) about the nature of ultimate reality, or the Advaitin is correct and the Christian incorrect. In fact, the former seems to be the obvious implication of Hick's conclusions in Death and Eternal Life and such implications do not allow for the Copernican intention of accepting each religion's claim to truth on its own terms. One could set out a whole range of beliefs regarding the different levels of truth-assertions which would logically entail some other truth-assertions being false. [57] For example, it cannot both be true that Jesus did die on the cross and that Jesus did not die on the cross. It cannot both be true that there are hundreds of reincarnations on earth of a single person working out their karma and that immediately after death there is a final judgement and no further "chances" to achieve salvation. Or again, it cannot both be true that reality is loving, personal and ultimately related to men and women in eternal joy and happiness (as is proposed in the doctrine of the Trinity and traditional Christian eschatology), and that reality is pure being, impersonal and one without a second so that ultimately only Brahman exists and that individual souls are non-existent. If one is true, then the other can only be accommodated on terms which the adherents of that other religion may not accept.

However, Hick could allow for the possibility, as he has done, that through the "para-eschaton" [58] the various religious

---

55. GUF ch.2.
56. See Bowker 1975 pp.1-2; Hebblethwaite 1976 pp.vii, 7-9.
57. See 3.2.4 above.

"traditions will become variously modified or marginalised or superseded" so that eventually the Advaitin and Christian may not ultimately find themselves in conflict. [59] Such an option lessens the tensions in accepting all religions as equally valid as they now stand. But such a solution only succeeds in raising further difficulties. First, if this option is chosen, it is questionable whether it is legitimate to claim that here and now the different religious traditions are equally legitimate, valid and authentic - as does Hick. If evolutionary development is to lead to a unity of views in the eschaton, then this very epicycle implies, correctly, that there are some irresolvable conflicts here and now. Furthermore, this option raises the question as to whether the religious traditions as we know them now will bear any resemblance to the "modified" forms in the para-eschaton. In fact, it may be suggested that an Advaitin's acceptance of Hick's eschatological scenario would render that Advaita virtually unrecognisable according to the accepted definition of Advaita. It may therefore be more legitimate to argue that in real terms the Advaitin view has been, and Hick allows for this possibility, "marginalized and superseded". [60] However, such an option runs against Hick's Copernican intentions.

To summarise: it is clear that to accommodate all religions on their own terms is not possible or coherent, even on Copernican grounds. The para-eschatological evolutionary option implicitly implies that some religions are more appropriate and valid than others. Such an option also seems to imply a covert inclusivism in acknowledging that some views could become "marginalized or superseded". In Hick's theistic eschaton, this is precisely the fate of the Advaitin.

Concerning the third question regarding the inductive starting-point of the Copernican hypothesis, I have argued above that even if the starting-point of Hick's Copernican thesis is not explicitly theistic (as it was in his pre-epicyclic days) the end-point, the eschaton, is. Consequently, even an inductive basis to the Copernican revolution would still run up against the problems of Hick's eschaton falsifying such a revolution. Even beginning on an inductive basis, once one rationally unpacked the implications of the Copernican thesis, there would inevitably be logically incompatible religious beliefs which would be magnified and accentuated in any scenario of the eschaton.

There is a further objection to Hick's inductive approach. Hick assumes that the "basic conviction that religious experience is not, as such and in toto, a realm of illusory projection"

---

58. Para-eschaton = the many stages of life in other worlds between this life and the eschaton - see DEL pp.12, 455-58.
59. Hick 1983c p.338.
60. Hick 1983c p.338.

implies that when this assumption is applied to the varied
phenomenological data, only the Copernican revolution does
satisfactory justice to the data's variety. [61] Contrary to this
I have suggested how the data may be more satisfactorily
interpreted on inclusivist lines while remaining theologically
intelligible. If this is possible than the Copernican revolution
is unnecesssary.

To summarise the argument so far: I have argued that, on
Hick's premises, religious truth claims are verified in the
eschaton and his Copernican eschaton is distinctly theistic,
thereby smuggling "God" from the <u>centre</u> to the <u>end</u> of the
universe of faiths - thereby creating the same problems prior to
the epicycle. In relation to the second of my questions, I tried
to demonstrate that the Copernican claim that all religions are
equally valid, genuine and legitimate apprehensions of the Real
is unsubstantiated. The differences within religions cannot be
accommodated on their own terms. I also argued in relation to the
third of my questions that an attempt to launch the Copernican
revolution on inductive grounds, rather than on theistic grounds,
is overcome by Hick's eschatological speculations. It should also
be noted, contrary to Loughlin's defence of Hick, that Hick <u>does</u>
use both <u>theological</u> and <u>inductive</u> arguments for his Copernican
thesis - and [62] in principle, these two approaches are not
incompatible. However, in practice, both approaches are not
without considerable difficulties, taken separately or in union -
as has been shown above.

If the implicit theism and, according to my earlier analysis,
implicit Christocentricism is still present in Hick's Copernican
revolution and its epicycle, then the inclusivist position
suggests itself as a more viable theology of religions. At the
outset of this critical section I suggested that the employment
of Hick's epicycle introduced (and possibly perpetuated) a
genuine ambiguity at the heart of the Copernican revolution. The
Real turns out to be either a <u>loving</u> <u>theistic</u> <u>God</u>, or
alternatively a <u>transcendental</u> <u>agnosticism</u> regarding the nature
of reality. This latter option is important as it seemingly
overcomes some of the difficulties posed to Hick's covert
theistic epicycle. But such an option introduces further and
substantial difficulties into Hick's Copernican project.

(5.5). <u>Hick's</u> <u>epicycle</u> <u>and</u> <u>"transcendental</u> <u>agnosticism"</u>.

An issue underlying the above criticisms concerned the criteria
for the discernment of the most appropriate phenomena of the
divine noumenon. Although Hick tried to argue that both theistic

---

[61]. Hick 1983c p.336.
[62]. Loughlin 1985a; and my response to Loughlin - D'Costa 1985c.

and non-theistic phenomena equally manifest the divine noumenon, there are good grounds within Hick's own writings to suggest that, ultimately, theistic phenomena are more appropriate - and then, I believe, we would be pushed back to the question of <u>which</u> theistic phenomena. [63] However, in Hick's writings there are comments that suggest that he would deal with the criticisms above by means of <u>yet</u> <u>another</u> <u>epicycle</u>. In response to my criticisms concerning the theistic nature of the eschaton, Hick replied in a letter dated December 1985: "the problem you point to is indeed not eliminated from my publications, although it is eliminated from my own mind and in what I am currently writing." The resolution of these difficulties is fragmentarily present in Hick's Copernican writings. I suggest that Hick may well develop this strand of thought in his Gifford lectures of 1986-1987 and I will speculate on how Hick could and may develop this position.

There are two distinctive steps in this second epicycle. The first would be to <u>press</u> the distinction between the Real <u>in</u> <u>itself</u>, and the various phenomenal manifestations in <u>relation</u> to humankind. If this distinction were pressed, then to argue that ultimately <u>either</u> the theistic, or non-theistic traditions will have more appropriate images (personae/impersonae) of the Real is inadmissible. Both are equally appropriate, for the Real cannot be known apart from the various personae and impersonae. What really is at stake is a "religious" rather than a "non-religious" (or naturalistic) view of reality. Such a position is exactly what Hick seems to put forward in 1985, in a "postscript" to his 1977 essay, "Eschatological Verification Reconsidered", which is included unaltered as chapter 8 in <u>Problems</u> <u>of</u> <u>Religious</u> <u>Pluralism</u>. [64]

The original essay concludes in a vein opposed to Hick's pluralist thesis by arguing for the validity of eschatological verification, so that if "Christian theism is true, its truth will be confirmed within future human experience to the point of cognitive conclusiveness." [65] In the postscript to this essay, added in 1985, Hick acknowledges that he has defended a "theistic, and indeed Christian" concept of reality, but he adds that a similar eschatological scenario can be posited and defended in "Jewish, in Muslim, or in theistic Hindu terms" or within non-theistic traditions by an "Advaitic Hindu or in the various schools of Buddhist thought." [66] Despite supportively referring to <u>Death</u> <u>and</u> <u>Eternal</u> <u>Life</u> in the <u>Problems</u> <u>of</u> <u>Religious</u> <u>Pluralism</u>, Hick goes on to suggest something slightly different from his argument in <u>Death</u> <u>and</u> <u>Eternal</u> <u>Life</u>. There is a suggestion that signals a possible new counter-defence of Hick's

---

63. See 3.2.5 above.
64. See the original essay - Hick 1977f.
65. <u>PRP</u> p.124.
66. <u>PRP</u> p.124.

position, which is alluded to in the private letter quoted above. Hick writes that,

> with the long span of this development (over many lives) it may well be that the final state will prove to be beyond the horizon of our present powers of imagination...(and even)...may be other than any of our earthly religious traditions anticipate...the question is not whether the truth of a Christian, or a Muslim, or a Hindu, or a Buddhist interpretation is ultimately verifiable within human experience but whether the truth of a religious as opposed to a naturalistic interpretation of the universe is capable of being verified. [67]

The fact that Hick suggests that the eschaton may be beyond the anticipations of any of our "earthly religious traditions" and possibly "beyond the horizon of our present powers of imagination" is in keeping with a solution tending towards this new epicycle. For the moment, I will call the resultant position transcendental agnosticism. "Transcendental agnosticism" affirms the transcendent divine reality over against naturalistic positions, while refusing to state that the eschaton may eventually be theistic rather than non-theistic. The "transcendental agnostic" prefers to remain agnostic on this question - and by implication, agnostic as to the ultimate nature of the transcendent reality. Such a position overcomes the objection that a theistic God emerges at the end of the universe of faiths rather than, as originally, at the centre.

This transcendental agnosticism is confirmed in another essay included in Problems of Religious Pluralism which dates back to 1983. [68] In "On Conflicting Truth Claims", originally a response to the criticisms of Hick's article "On Grading Religions" made by Griffiths and Lewis, Hick's solution to the problem of conflicting claims seems to be in line with this element of transcendental agnosticism. Regarding religious conflicts on the three different levels, [69] Hick responds similarly to all three levels of conflict with three suggestions: 1. "that we should all school ourselves to tolerate and live with such disagreements"; 2. that the partner with his or her differences "might nevertheless be closer to the divine Reality

---

[67]. PRP pp.124-5, my emphases.
[68]. Hick 1983d is included as PRP ch.6, being a response to Griffiths & Lewis 1983.
[69] Outlined above - see 3.2.4.

than I"; 3. that such ultimate beliefs are [70] "evidently not essential to our salvation or liberation". [71] Earlier I responded to the first two suggestions made by Hick, [71], and now I will argue that this third suggestion implies a transcendental agnosticism concerning the ultimate cognitive value and significance of religious beliefs. Hick, in this same essay, commends Conze's study regarding the Buddhist attitude towards a theistic God, noting that "Conze concluded that 'the Buddhists adopt an attitude of agnosticism to the question of a personal creator'." [72] He goes on to say: "Indeed it seems to me that the Buddha's doctrine of the undetermined questions, to know the answer to which is not necessary for liberation, is one (from) which non-Buddhists also could profit." [73] It would seem that as a way of circumventing the difficulties of conflicting truth claims between the theistic and non-theistic religions, Hick affirms that the "ultimate reality, beyond human picturing...is the ground of both forms of experience." [74] It would appear then, that while on one level, a belief in God may be true, on another, it is not important for salvation - as ultimate reality is beyond "human picturing". This latter emphasis leads to a transcendental agnosticism in Hick's Copernican epicycle.

This form of transcendental agnosticism has as its counterpart a pragmatic import, whereby Hick wishes to focus upon the "transformation of human existence from self-centredness to Reality-centredness" away from theological and philosophical questions that are [75] according to him, unnecessary for liberation/salvation. [75] If the initial move in Hick's theology was away from Christocentricism to theocentricism, this latter move may be termed as a move away from theocentricism to soteriocentricism. This may also be seen in an emphasis away from theory, to one on practice. It is my contention that an emphasis on soteriocentricism as a way of avoiding certain conflicting truth claims entails, as a theoretical basis, a transcendental agnosticism. [76] Hence, in a final paragraph to "On Conflicting Truth Claims" Hick writes: "Such theories and mythologies (i.e. Jesus on the cross, a personal creator God, etc.) are not however necessary for salvation/liberation, the transformation of human existence from self-centredness to reality-centredness." [77] If such a strategy apparently overcomes the criticism that a theistic God appears at the end rather than the centre of the

[70]. PRP pp.89-90.
[71]. See 3.2.4 above.
[72]. PRP p.93, citing Conze 1957 p.39.
[73]. PRP p.93, my brackets.
[74]. PRP p.94, my emphases.
[75]. PRP p.95.
[76]. Knitter also arrives at such a soteriocentricism in 1986a esp. 104-6; and Knitter 1986b.
[77]. PRP p.95, my brackets.

Copernican universe of faiths, does it, we may ask, overcome it successfully?

In discussing Hick's proposals I will pursue two related lines of criticism: first, this transcendental agnosticism at the heart of the new universe of faiths poses major philosophical, theological and epistemological difficulties - many of which run counter to the thrust of Hick's Copernican thesis. Second, the shift of attention to the soteriological _process_ or _practice_ of "self-centredness to Reality-centredness" cannot be intelligibly sustained without attention to the precise nature of the Real which informs and gives such a process meaning. In effect I shall argue that a transcendental agnostic pragmatism is ultimately self-contradictory.

(5.5.1). The _theoretical_ aspect _of_ transcendental agnosticism:

Let me develop the first criticism regarding the resultant transcendental agnosticism. Meynell's comment on Smith's thesis in the light of genuinely irresolvable conflicting religious truth claims is worth noting: "vague talk of a 'transcendent' to which all religious believers are committed conceals rather than disposes of this awkward fact."[78] Might the same be said of Hick's Real? Hick's sharp distinction between the noumenal Real and the phenomenal images framed by the human mind within particular cultures reminds one of David Hume's comment on the supposed religious object of mystics. Hume writes of mystical claims that the Reality confronted is ineffable: "Is the name, without any meaning, of such mighty importance? Or how do you MYSTICS who maintain the absolute incomprehensibility of the deity, differ from sceptics or atheists?"[79] It is precisely this "absolute incomprehensibility" regarding the nature of reality that threatens Hick's whole Copernican project by further mystifying rather than illuminating the nature of the Real through this new Copernican epicycle. One may ask with Hume whether such a position as Hick's is any different from atheism or scepticism - or indeed, as is my thesis, a transcendental agnosticism.

This kind of problem is inevitable due to Hick's adoption of a Kantian framework, for Kant's noumenon, like Hick's Real, encountered the same difficulties. How can Kant, writes Wedberg, "claim to know that there is a correspondence between phenomena and things in themselves, and that the latter act upon consciousness?"[80] Reformulating this question, one may ask how Hick can claim to know that there is a correspondence between the

---

[78]. Meynell 1985 p.154.
[79]. Hume 1970 pt.4, para.1.
[80]. Wedberg 1982 p.174.

Real and any particular personae or impersonae?

Can Hick defend himself from the type of criticisms levelled by Meynell at Smith, by Hume at mystics, and by Wedberg at Kant? Can Hick even justify the supposition that there is a noumenon "behind" the various phenomena – for it has been persuasively argued that the very existence of religious plurality and the "many incompatibilities between the claims made about the nature of the religious ultimate and the way to salvation in the world faiths" leads to a "sceptic's response, which is to deny truth to any of them" which "seems more plausible than granting truth to all."[81] One may therefore ask whether the Real's invulnerability also leads to its redundancy? There are a number of potential strategies within Hick's writings that can be utilized by him to try to circumvent these difficulties. However, all these strategies are problematic – as I shall demonstrate.

One way in which Hick could try to counter the charge of total scepticism or agnosticism would be to point out his firm and constant belief in the cognitive value of religious language. Consequently, he could maintain that the charge of transcendental agnosticism is illegitimate. Hick has always argued that in our present life we cannot show that our beliefs actually are true – in as much as they relate to reality as it is.[82] Nevertheless, consistently and up until 1985, he assumes that "the importance of religious beliefs to the believer lies ultimately in the assumption that they are substantially true references to the nature of reality."[83] Hence, on one level it would be incorrect to accuse Hick of atheism or agnosticism as it is clear that he accepts that many of the religions do make valid claims about a transcendent reality. But how does one even justify the possibility that one's religious beliefs may be true in an ambiguous universe? The answer, for Hick, lies in eschatological verification! As Hick does not accept any proofs for the existence of God and seems to accept the possibility that all religions are veridical, the only way in which he can justify such a thesis against atheists and sceptics is by his resort to eschatological verification. This is exemplified in his inclusion of his 1977 essay "Eschatological Verification Reconsidered" in Problems of Religious Pluralism (1985), while strategically arguing that the essay should be viewed in the wider context of affirming a "religious as opposed to a naturalistic interpretation of the universe".[84]

But if this is Hick's defence against the charge of scepticism or atheism (or transcendental agnosticism) then it surely

---

81. Byrne 1982 p.290.
82. FK2 pt.III.
83. PRP p.16, my emphases.
84. PRP p.125.

concedes too much.   First, it is questionable whether the contention that eschatological verification is not "directly relevant to the assessment of conflicting truth-claims" and whether Hick's subsequent use of it to counter "a naturalistic interpretation of the universe" is credible or consistent.[85] Such a bare affirmation that the universe is "religious" amounts to nothing if certain predicative descriptions are not applicable to this quality of being "religious". For instance, the naturalist may ask whether this religious reality can be described as "intelligent, personal and loving". If Hick was to reply affirmatively, then certain religious traditions would be excluded by this definition of "religious". Furthermore, if eschatological verification can apparently be used to defend Christian theism against naturalism, it is not clear why eschatological verification is not relevant to defending Christian theism over against, let us say, non-theistic Advaita. Hick seems to dismiss this type of usage by saying that eschatological verification "is probably not, however, directly relevant to the assessment of the conflicting truth-claims of the various traditions."[86]   Immediately after this sentence he adds in brackets that this "latter point is discussed briefly above, pp.99-100". However, the page references lead us to the response to Almond's article - which I have discussed and criticised above. Hence the eschatological dilemma raised earlier is still problematic and again emerges to challenge the validity of Hick's new epicycle.

If, however, Hick responded that by the term "religious" he meant only that reality is not exhaustively experienced and defined in terms of nature, then the naturalist has every right to question him as to the specific character of this "transcendence" he asserts as well as to the grounds for holding such "transcendence" to be real. My contention is this: once further predicates are employed to describe the "religious" referent, then some religious traditions will be excluded (as well as naturalist traditions - intentionally), while others will be seen to be more appropriate in terms of the Real. Alternatively, if no predicates are given, then the naturalist, a la Hume, could legitimately ask how this stance differed from atheism or scepticism.   The main point I have been driving at is this: either Hick jettisons his professed belief in the cognitive status of religious language and thereby escapes the eschatological dilemma that I have posed earlier; or alternatively, if Hick still maintains that religious language is cognitive - and this he must do to oppose naturalism - then the eschatological dilemma confounds the Copernican epicycle.

Let me draw the discussion on Hick's potential transcendental

---

85. *PRP* p.125.
86. *PRP* p.125.

agnosticism to a close. A seriously held transcendental agnosticism could be considered to imply that there were good grounds to embrace the sceptic's position, for in the light of such conflicting religious truth claims, it is perhaps more likely that religions are false.[87] Certainly such a position is encouraged if it is seriously thought that things as they really are - i.e. the contents and references of cognitive claims - bear little or no relation to "earthly religious traditions" as Hick asserts. Furthermore, such a position would hardly carry much authority in arguing against the naturalist or sceptic's position for it would lack any details of the religious referent that could then be verified in an eschatological scenario. Even the sense of conviction that religious believers do have, that their beliefs are "substantially true references to the nature of reality", is jettisoned in Hick's transcendental agnostic option.[88]

Surely the latter point itself would count against this strategy on pluralist grounds - i.e. such a hypothesis cannot accommodate the genuine religious convictions shared by most believers that their beliefs substantially relate to reality.[89] This criterion of veracity which would now be threatened is ironically one of the reasons for Hick's Copernican shift!

In conclusion there are four logical options available to Hick in this new epicycle. The first three, I would argue, all run counter to the pluralist hypothesis as it is framed, and suggest an inclusivist resolution to the problem. Given that things may turn out quite differently from what is expected, or beyond our imagination, the first three options are: 1) that some religious traditions will ultimately be deemed more appropriate than others, 2) that only one religious tradition will be deemed appropriate, 3) that no religious tradition is appropriate. The first option contravenes the pluralist principle, viz. all religions are equal; the second is the confirmation of "Ptolemaic" theology (either first, second or third stages - depending on the salvific status of those within the "appropriate" religions); the third option would be the confirmation of the sceptic's position suggested above and would be totally contrary to Hick's form of Copernican pluralism. The fourth remaining option is logically self-contradictory: that is, that all religions are equally true. I have already shown why this position cannot withstand certain irreconcilable internal contradictions.[90]

In consequence, it is difficult to see how the transcendent agnosticism within Hick's works will actually alleviate the problems his thesis faces. If eschatological verification, in

---

[87]. Byrne 1982 p.290.
[88]. PRP p.16, my emphasis.
[89]. PRP p.16.
[90]. See 5.4 and 3.2.4 above.

whatever degree, is permissible then the Copernican position is difficult to sustain in the light of Hick's own eschatological scenario, and also in the light of other possible scenarios. If, on the other hand, eschatological verification is disavowed, on Hick's premises it would be difficult for him to uphold the cognitive reference of religious language and his position would run counter to the Copernican intentions to be faithful to the genuine beliefs and convictions of most believers about religious language. Such a non-cognitive position would be difficult to distinguish from non-religious world views on an ontological level and thereby only overcomes the problem by refusing to accept it, rather than by solving it. Some critics have even suggested that Hick's[91] position eventually amounts to a non-cognitive stance.

(5.5.2). The _pragmatic_ _counterpart_ _to_ _Hick's_ _theoretical_ _transcendental_ _agnosticism_:

Having examined the theoretical aspect of this soteriological epicycle I will now pursue the related aspect of this epicycle: the emphasis on _praxis_. My criticism here concerns Hick's shift of attention to the _soteriological_ _process_ (or praxis) of turning from "self-centredness to Reality-centredness" which is apparently present in the world religions. This emphasis is in line with the Buddhist insight concerning undetermined questions such as the existence of God, "to know the answer to which is not necessary for liberation".[92] This pragmatic aspect is _intrinsically_ related to the theoretical aspect discussed immediately above. This pragmatic aspect is present within Hick's most recent Copernican writings and may be developed more fully in the Gifford Lectures of 1986-1987.

In what follows, I shall try to state what may be the strongest possible utilization of Hick's soteriological emphasis to overcome my objections to his new Copernican epicycle. Such a defence is based on clues from within Hick's own texts. The defence would have three stages. In the first, Hick argues that despite the many levels of conflicting truth claims, these differences "are not of great _religious_, i.e. soteriological, importance."[93] In effect, "Such theories and mythologies are not however necessary for salvation/liberation, the transformation of human existence from self-centredness to Reality-centredness."[94]

---

[91]. Griffiths & Lewis 1983. I have argued above that they have some grounds for such a reading, although Hick explicitly denies this - Hick 1983d.
[92]. PRP p.73.
[93]. PRP p.94.
[94]. PRP p.95.

The second step would be the confirmation of such an insight from Hick's own experience. His meeting with "Nyanaponika Mahathera, a Buddhist monk", "Kushdeva Singh, a Sikh mystic",[95] and with a Roman Catholic priest in Birmingham,[96], have impressed upon Hick the priority of the life lived, rather than on the doctrines held. His encounter with these modern saints from different religions forms the experiential basis for his affirmation. The third step can then be heuristically divided into two types of approach in developing this soteriological emphasis. I shall label these approaches "from below" and "from above". Hick utilises both approaches, while some pluralists, such as Knitter, utilise only the former. Knitter, for instance, argues that:

> For Christians, that which constitutes the basis and goal for interreligious dialogue...is not how they (non-Christian religions) are related to the church (invisibly through the "baptism of desire"), nor how they are related to Christ (Rahner's anonymously or Küng's normatively), nor even how they respond to and conceive of God, but rather, how much they are promoting Soteria (in Christian images, the basileia)---how much they are engaged in bringing about liberation with and for the poor and nonpersons.[97]

While Hick does not utilise liberation theology, as does Knitter, I believe that he would be in agreement with Knitter's approach "from below". Such an approach states that in as much as religions facilitate a turning from "self-centredness to Reality-centredness" or towards "liberation", herein lies the basis and goal of a pluralist outlook.

However, Hick also wishes to utilise an approach "from above". Hick writes: "let us" assume "the truth of the basic religious convictions and ask ourselves how the facts of religious pluralism may then be understood".[98] The approach "from above" is concerned to develop an overall systematic interpretation to explain the varieties of religious experience. Such an enterprise is discernible from some of Hick's essay titles - "Sketch for a Global Theory of Religious Knowledge", "Towards a Philosophy of Religious Pluralism".[99]

---

95. SC p.87.
96. In conversation at the Blaisdell Conference, California, March 1986.
97. Knitter 1986b p.12, my brackets; and see also 1986a.
98. GMNUS p.89.

179

There are a number of problems involved in this soteriological emphasis, both in terms of internal tensions within the Copernican epicycle and external criticisms of the project itself. If this latest of epicycles is flawed then Hick's Copernican pluralism will also be flawed - as has been the contention of this book. There are three criticisms I wish to pursue. 1) Is Hick's "from above" approach consistent with his affirmation that doctrinal beliefs (i.e. "ways of conceiving and experiencing" the divine reality) are ultimately unnecessary for salvation? If Hick's injunction concerning the ultimate irrelevance of belief is accepted, then surely he should adopt only the approach "from below" - as does Knitter. 2) If Hick accepts the criticism of (1) above, then is he not forced into a position of "transcendental agnosticism" whereby nothing specific can be said of the divine reality, thereby leading to the criticisms of 5.5.1 above? Furthermore, is the "from below" approach coherent in itself? Does it not render the notion of "soteria" hopelessly vague, undialectical and without basis? 3) If Hick does not accept (1), and therefore rejects (2), is the epicycle of any use at all? The epicycle still begs the question of the basis for the recognition of what constitutes a turning from "self-centredness to Reality-centredness" - which leads back to doctrinal formulations and their validity - and then, finally back to the eschatological dilemma? I would also contend that an inclusivist theology offers a more satisfactory explanation of the phenomena under consideration as well as accommodating the importance of praxis.

Before beginning with the first criticism, a brief clarification is necessary. From my inclusivist position, I would grant the following: that ultimately, only grace is required for salvation, so that strictly speaking one's "beliefs and mythologies" are ultimately invalid indicators of whether salvation takes place. There is no guarantee that one who holds Christian beliefs is thereby saved by virtue of formally professing such beliefs. Existential appropriation is all important, as is the priority and freedom of God's grace. On a formal level the deepest desires and promptings of a person's heart in their response to grace freely offered, is[100] hermeneutically inaccessible to us, but not to God. However, and this is all important, the analysis above is based on a set of beliefs about the nature of God's reality, based on the revelation of Jesus, hence my inclusivist position.

My first criticism of Hick concerns an internal tension within his epicycle. On the one hand, he deems that differences in belief are ultimately unimportant regarding salvation; while on

---

99
100 GMNUS chs.5,6.
. See Congar 1961 p.121; Rahner 1978 pp.101-2.

the other, he uses the notion of a common salvific process to affirm the validity of the different beliefs. (Logically, he cannot have it both ways!). This is why Hick is forced to adopt option 2 or 3.

If, like Knitter, he adopts option 2, then Küng's implicit criticism of Knitter's position is applicable to Hick's thesis:

> the Christian community may allow itself to be persuaded to replace an ecclesio-centricism with a Christo-centricism or theo-centricism (which for Christians amount to the same thing!) but they are hardly likely to be persuaded to take up some vague soteriocentricism. Practice should not be made the norm of theory undialectically and social questions be expounded as the basis and centre of the theology of religions. [101]

Although I cannot understand Küng's reason for saying that a shift from an ecclesio- to a Christo- to a theo-centric position is permissible when they "amount to the same thing", his latter comments on soteriocentricism are pertinent. If praxis, or "Reality-centredness" is made into an undialectical norm determining theory, then the transcendental agnosticism that I criticised earlier creeps back into Hick's concomitant theoretical position. [102]

The third option leads to the problem that the notion of soteria cannot be useful as a basis for pluralism if it remains "vague" and theoretically unfounded. Hick's view of "Reality-centredness" has become progressively vague and lacks a clear foundation and justification. In 1985 he defines "Reality-centredness": it "consists in a new and limitlessly better quality of existence" in that

> If one believes that God is gracious and merciful, one may imitate the divine love and compassion (e.g. a Christian). If one believes that one is, in one's deepest being, identical with the infinite and eternal Brahman, one will seek to negate the present false ego and its distorting vision in order to attain that which both transcends and underlies it (e.g. an Advaitin Hindu). If one believes that

---

101.
102. Küng 1986 p.123.
      . The same may be said of Knitter.

ultimate reality is the Buddha nature,
and that the aim of living is to become a
Buddha, one will seek to enter into the
egoless openness and infinite compassion
of the Buddha. [103]

This soteriological communality would lead to liberating "social
structures", nobility, justice and beauty. [104]

There are some major difficulties with these formulations. The
first conflates value with truth. It, perhaps too easily,
identifies a common phenomenological or psychological process and
confuses it for an ontological similarity. It mistakenly equates
a similar process with a common goal. It also assumes that there
is a neutral position or common bank of acceptable criteria which
are not ultimately founded and grounded within a specific
paradigmatic basis - and therefore acceptable to all.

Let me deal with the first of these objections. Kraemer argues
against the pragmatic tradition where value is equated with
truth, because "fictions and even lies have been extraordinarily
successful" and also because it is "philosophically superficial
to equate the psychic experience of satisfaction with the
certainty that (the experience) is therefore true in the deepest
sense, or is related to realities which are true." [105] One may
apply Kraemer's comments to Hick's soteriocentricism. There is a
danger of Hick's equating similar forms of psychological and
phenomenological behaviour with ˎ the assumption that such
behaviour must therefore participate and tend towards the same
ontological reality. Not only is there a confusion of
behavioural categories with ontological goals, but there is also
the assumption of the hermeneutical penetrability of the heart.

However, one cannot minimise the relation of categorical
expression with the inner happenings of the heart, or minimise
the importance of praxis in the acceptance of grace - as I have
shown earlier. The fundamental difficulty with Hick's thesis at
this stage is the basis of legitimately identifying and
recognising the valid activity of God's saving grace (although
Hick would phrase this differently) operative in the religious
traditions of the world. In this respect Knitter is more
sensitive to the criteriological difficulties at hand:

> as Gavin D'Costa has pointed out in his
> criticisms of my book, every theocentric
> or soteriocentric approach remains, in a

103.
104. PRP p.70, my brackets.
105. PRP p.79.
. Kraemer 1956 p.85. Interestingly, Hick acknowledges that his
criterion is "pragmatic" in PRP p.80.

> sense, inherently Christocentric...But what makes the soteriocentric approach different from Christocentricism or theocentricism is its explicit recognition that before the mystery of <u>Soteria</u>, no mediator or symbol system is absolute.[106]

However, Knitter fails to overcome my objections and his own alleged disavowal of absolutes for one sentence later he writes "the absolute, that which all else must serve and clarify, is not the Church or Christ or even God...but rather, the Kingdom and its justice."[107]   But, from where does Knitter's notion of "the Kingdom and its justice" derive, as one may ask from where does the notion of what constitutes Hick's "Reality-centredness" derive? If it is not from a secularist "modern liberal moral outlook" as Hick sometimes suggests,[108], what is it that makes the values of "acceptance, compassion, love for all humankind, or even for all life" normative?[109]

In answering this question and giving the phrases cited immediately above more precise detail, we are inevitably driven back to theory - even if theory does retain a dialogical relation to praxis. If Hick follows the transcendental agnosticism route, then he cannot answer this question - which is Knitter's predicament. If, on the other hand, one discovers that the Buddhist notion of annata, the Advaitin notion of ātman and the Christian notion of agapē have different, and possibly conflicting, ontological contexts, then we are forced back to the problems that I have posed earlier - which are inevitably highlighted in the eschatological dilemma. And Hick certainly seems to succumb to the eschatological dilemma when he writes of his "pragmatic" soteriological test of the world's religions: "They accordingly test themselves by their failure in fulfilling this soteriological function. The final verification is thus <u>eschatological</u>."[110]   Accordingly, even the adoption of option 3 is <u>unhelpful</u> as it leads to the inescapable eschatological dilemma outlined above.

(5.6). <u>Conclusion</u>.

My argument in this book is not meant to counter the possibility and probable reality of saving grace being operative in

---

[106]. Knitter 1986b p.15. Knitter refers to D'Costa 1985h and 1986b.
[107]. Knitter 1986b p.15.
[108]. <u>PRP</u> p.76.
[109]. <u>PRP</u> p.81.
[110]. <u>PRP</u> p.80.

non-Christian religions. This is a perfectly legitimate recognition within an inclusivist (or what Hick calls a "Ptolemaic" - in its second and third stages) theology of religions. Rather, my arguments are a theological critique of Hick's reflection upon this likely reality. My central objections against Hick's strategy have concerned his mischaracterisation of the "Ptolemaic" tradition in its latter stages. Against Hick, I have tried to argue that this tradition presents the resources for an intelligible and non-exclusivist theology of religions. [111]

Furthermore, I have criticised the criteria that Hick employs to affirm a non-Christocentric solution to the question of how salvation takes place and is recognised in non-Christian religions. His fundamental premise of a God of universal love requires a [112] Christocentric, and thereby ecclesiocentric, grounding. Another and related central focus for criticism concerned his attempt to sustain his theocentric shift by means of introducing the notion of "myth" to characterise the incarnation. I argued that Hick's distinction between mythic and literal language is flawed, [113] especially in the light of Hick's own Christological claims. The other arguments employed in support of the Copernican revolution are problematic in varying degrees. [114]

His later strategy to avoid even a theocentric solution to the problem of Christianity's relation to other religions is also problematic. His "epicycle" introduces what I have called an "eschatological dilemma", [115] leading back to a covert theocentricism. Alternatively, this epicycle leads to a "transcendental agnosticism", leading [116] to a form of agnosticism concerning the "divine reality". The latter option runs counter to Hick's conviction that religious language is cognitive.

My arguments are an attempt to demonstrate that Hick's Copernican theology, in either its original or epicyclic forms, does not provide an adequate theological explanation of the presence of God's grace outside Christianity. As a theology of religion representing the pluralist paradigm - and some exciting developments within that paradigm - it is deeply problematic. My arguments against Hick are not a warning against mutual co-operation by religions for justice, peace and a loving community. Rather, they question the assumption that only a Copernican basis provides the grounds for a harmonious pluralist society. While the Christian may work together with a Buddhist

---

111. See 3.1 above.
112. See 3.2 above.
113. See 4.1 above.
114. See 4.2 - 4.4 above.
115. See 3.2 and 5.4 above.
116. See 5.5 above.

and find himself or herself in deeper agreement about what "justice" or "liberation" constitutes in a particular situation, such an agreement does not mean that the normative and decisive nature of Christ's revelation is thereby called into question. Neither does it mean that such Christological criteria will not be enlarged and enriched through mutual praxis and reflection. Furthermore, neither does it mean that the Buddhist's beliefs are false. This latter judgemental aspect of dialogue can only be clarified in dialogue. Theologically, however, the Christian must necessarily admit that the grace and truth within Buddhism can only be recognised, acknowledged and embraced as the grace of God - made known definitively, but not exclusively, in Christ. Soteriocentricism cannot be divorced from theocentricism, which cannot be divorced from Christocentricism or finally from ecclesiocentricsm. Such has been the argument of my book. If much of this argument has been in a critical vein, I would justify such an analysis as necessary for "clearing the ground" and returning to and clarifying some central theological principles before a more viable theology of religions may be fully developed. Elsewhere, I have carried out a more modest but similar analysis of the theological principles underlying the exclusivist position - and also tried to develop a more viable inclusivist theology of religions.[117]   If Hick's Copernican revolution (in its gradual development and various epicycles) stands as a thoughtful, challenging and stimulating paradigm of the pluralist theology of religions which cannot be ignored in a religiously pluralist world, then the analysis of his thesis is, I hope, of some theological value.

---

[117] D'Costa 1986a chs.3,4.

GENERAL BIBLIOGRAPHY

Abe.M (1980). "The End of Religion", The Eastern Buddhist, ns.13, pp.31-45

------(1985). "A Dynamic Unity in Religious Pluralism: A Proposal from the Buddhist Point of View", in eds. Askari & Hick 1985 pp.163-90

Abeyasingha.N (1979). A Theological Evaluation of Non-Christian Rites, Theological Publications of India, Bangalore

Abhishiktananda (H. le Saux) (1969). Hindu-Christian Meeting Point, Christian Institute for the Study of Religion and Society, Bangalore

Abhishiktananda & Monchanin.J (1964). An Indian Benedictine Ashram, Times Press, Douglas

Adams.J (1961/1962). "Ernst Troeltsch as Analyst of Religion", Journal for the Scientific Study of Religion, 1, 1, pp.98-109

Almond.P (1983). "John Hick's Copernican Revolution", Theology, 86, 709, pp.36-41

Amalorpavadass.D.S (1971). Towards Indigenization in the Liturgy, National Biblical, Catechetical & Liturgical Centre, Bangalore

------(1975). ed. Research Seminar on Non-Biblical Scriptures, National Biblical, Catechetical & Liturgical Centre, Bangalore

-------(1978). Gospel and Culture, National Bibical, Catechetical & Liturgical Centre, Bangalore

Anderson.G & Stransky.T eds. (1975). Mission Trends Number 2: Evangelization, W.B.Eerdmans, Grand Rapids; Paulist Press, New York

------(1981a). Christ's Lordship and Religious Pluralism, Orbis Books, New York

------(1981b). Mission Trends Number 5: Faith Meets Faith, W.B.Eerdmans, Grand Rapids; Paulist Press, New York

Anderson.J.N (1970). Christianity: the Witness of History, Tyndale Press, London

------(1971). Christianity and Comparative Religion, Intervarsity Press, London

------(1975). ed. The World Religions, Intervarsity Press, London

------(1978). The Mystery of the Incarnation, Hodder & Stoughton, London

------(1984). Christianity and World Religions. The Challenge of Pluralism, Intervarsity Press, Leicester & Illinois (2nd ed. of 1971)

Appasamy.A.J (1942). The Gospel and India's Heritage, SPCK, London & Madras

Aquinas.T (1968). Summa Theologiae Vol 12 (ed. T.Gilby), Blackfriars & Eyre & Spottiswoode, London; McGraw-Hill, New York

------(1969). Summa Theologiae Vol 16 (ed. T.Gilby), Blackfriars & Eyre & Spottiswoode, London; McGraw-Hill, New York

------(1975). De Veritate Catholicae Fidei (ed. A.Pegis), Notre Dame University Press, Indiana

Ariarajah.W (1985). The Bible and People of Other Faiths, World Council of Churches, Geneva

Arinze.J (1985). "Prospects for Evangelization, with Reference to Areas of the non Christian Religions, Twenty Years After Vatican II", Bulletin Secretariatus pro non Christianis, 20, 2, pp.111-40

Askari.H (1982). "The Sermon on the Mount", in ed. Jathanna 1982 pp.46-56

------(1985). "Within and Beyond the Experience of Religious Diversity", in eds. Askari & Hick 1985 pp.191-218

Askari.H & Hick.J eds. (1985). The Experience of Religious Diversity, Gower, Aldershot

Augustine.St (1967). Selected Sermons of Saint Augustine (ed. Q.Howe), Victor Gollancz, London

------(1968). The Retractationis (ed. R.Defarrai), in The Fathers of the Church Vol 60, The Catholic Univerisity of America Press, Washington

------(1972). The City of God (ed. D.Knowles), Penguin, Harmondsworth

Aurobindo.Sri (1955). The Life Divine, Sri Aurobindo Ashram, Pondicherry

Bacik.J (1980). Apologetics and the Eclipse of Mystery - Mystagogy According to Karl Rahner, Notre Dame University Press,

Indiana & London

Badham.P (1976). Christian Beliefs About Life After Death, Macmillan, London

Baillie.D & Martin.H eds. Revelation, Faber & Faber, London

Baker (-Bethuene). J (1903). An Introduction to the Early History of Christian Doctrine, Methuen, London

Balthasar.H.von (1969). The Moment of Christian Witness, Newman Press, New York

Barbour.I (1974). Myths, Models and Paradigms, SCM, London

Barth.K (1959). From Rousseau to Ritschl, SCM, London

------(1969). Church Dogmatics Vol 3/2, T & T Clark, Edinburgh

------(1970). Church Dogmatics Vol 1/2, T & T Clark, Edinburgh

------(1976). Church Dogmatics Vol 4/3, T & T Clark, Edinburgh

Bartsch.H ed. (1953). Kerygma and Myth Vol 1, SCM, London

Baum.G (1966). "Christianity and Other Religions: A Catholic Problem", Cross Currents, 16, pp.461-82

Bean.W (1964). "Eschatological Verification. 'Fortress or Fairyland'?", Methodos, 17, 62, pp.91-107

Benson.E.W (1897). Cyprian. His Life. His Times. His Work., Macmillan, London

Berger.P & Luckmann.T (1971). The Social Construction of Reality, Penguin, Harmondsworth

Berkouwer.G (1958). "General and Special Divine Revelation", in ed. Henry 1958 pp.11-24

Bernstein.R (1983). Beyond Objectivism and Relativism: Science, Hermeneutics and Praxis, Basil Blackwell, Oxford

Bettenson.H ed. (1978). The Early Church Fathers, Oxford University Press, Oxford

Billot.L (1919-1923). "La Providence divine et le nombre infini d'hommes hors de la voie normale du salut", Études, 9 articles in Vols 161-176

Bloesch.D (1968). Essentials of Evangelical Theology Vol 1, Harper & Row, San Francisco

189

Bolich.G (1980). Karl Barth and Evangelicalism, Intervarsity Press, Downers Grove, Illinois

Borchsenius.P (1968). Two Ways to God: Judaism and Christianity, Vallentine Mitchell, London

Boros.L (1965). The Moment of Truth, Burns & Oates, London

Bowker.J (1975). Problems of Suffering in Religions of the World, Cambridge Univeristy Press, Cambridge

Boyd.R (1974). The Latin Captivity of the Church: The Cultural Context of the Gospel, Cambridge University Press, Cambridge

Braaten.C (1969). The Future of God, Herder & Herder, New York

------(1977). The Flaming Center: A Theology of the Christian Mission, Fortress Press, Philadelphia

Braithwaite.R (1955). An Empiricist's View of the Nature of Religious Belief, Cambridge University Press, Cambridge

Brakenheilm.C (1975). How Philosophies Shape Theories of Religion, Gleerups, Lund

Braybrooke.M (1971). Together to the Truth: Developments in Hindu and Christian Thought Since 1800, SPCK, Delhi

------(1980). Inter-Faith Organizations, 1893-1979: A Historical Directory, Edwin Mellin Press, New York

British Council of Churches (1983). Relations with People of Other Faiths. Guidelines for Dialogue in Britain, British Council of Churches, London

Brooke.C (1969). The Twelfth Century Renaissance, Thames & Hudson, London

Brown.D (1967-1970). Christianity and Islam 5 Vols, Sheldon Press, London

Brown.L.W (1956). The Indian Christians of Saint Thomas, Cambridge University Press, Cambridge

Brown.R.E (1966/1970). The Gospel According to John 2 Vols, Doubleday, New York

Bühlmann.W (1979). All Have the Same God, Saint Pauls, Slough

------(1982). The Chosen Peoples, Orbis Books, New York; St Pauls, Slough

Bullock.A (1952). Hitler: A Study in Tyranny, Odhams, Middlesex

Bultmann.R (1953). "New Testament and Mythology", in ed. Bartsch 1953 pp.1-44

------(1972). A History of the Synoptic Tradition, Basil Blackwell, Oxford (2nd ed.)

Byrne.P (1982). "John Hick's Philosophy of Religion", Scottish Journal of Theology, 35, 4, pp.289-301

Calvin.J (1961). Institutes of the Christian Religion 2 Vols (eds. J.McNeill & F.Battles), SCM, London

Camps.A (1983). Partners in Dialogue: Christianity and Other World Religions, Orbis Books, New York

Capéran.L (1934). Le Problème du Salut des Infidèles 2 Vols, Grand Séminaire, Toulouse

Carpenter.J (1921). Theism in Medieval India, William Wargate, London

Cash.W (1937). Christendom and Islam: Their Contact and Cultures Down the Centuries, SCM, London

Caspar.R (1985). "The Permanent Significance of Islamic Monotheism", Concilium, 177, 1, pp.67-78

Chadwick.H (1978). The Early Church, Penguin, Harmondsworth

Christian.W (1972). Oppositions of Religious Doctrines, Macmillan, London; Herder & Herder, New York

Chubb.J (1972). "Presupposition of Religious Dialogue", Religious Studies, 8, 4, pp.289-310

Clayton.J ed. (1976). Ernst Troeltsch and the Future of Theology, Cambridge University Press, Cambridge

Coakley.S (1979). "Theology and Cultural Relativism: What is the Problem?", Neue Zeitschrift für Systematische Theologie und Religionsphilosophie, 21, 3, pp.223-43

Cobb.J (1975). Christ in a Pluralist Age, Fortress Press, Philadelphia

------(1982). Beyond Dialogue: Towards a Mutual Transformation of Christianity and Buddhism, Fortress Press, Philadelphia

------(1985). "Christian Witness in a Plural World", in eds.

Askari & Hick 1985 pp.144-62

Congar.Y (1952). "Ecclesia ab Abel", in ed. Reading 1952 pp.79-108

------(1957). "Salvation and the non-Catholic", Blackfriars, 38, 448/449, pp.290-300

------(1961). The Wide World My Parish, Darton, Longman & Todd, London

Conze.E (1957). Buddhism: Its Essence and Development, Cassiver, Oxford (3rd ed.)

Copelston.F (1974). Religion and Philosophy, Gill & Macmillan, London

Coventry.J (1978). "The Myth and the Method", Theology, 81, 682, pp.252-61

Coward.H (1985). Pluralism: Challenge to World Religions, Orbis Books, New York

Cox.H (1965). The Secular City, SCM, London

------(1977). Turning East: The Promise and Peril of the New Orientalism, Simon Schuster, New York

Cracknell.K (1986). Towards a New Relationship. Christians and People of Other Faiths, Epworth, London

Cragg.G (1983). The Church and the Age of Reason: 1648-1789, Penguin, Harmondsworth

Cragg.K (1956). The Call of the Minaret, Oxford University Press, Oxford

------(1959). Sandals at the Mosque, SCM, London

------(1977). The Christian and Other Religions, Mowbrays, London

------(1984). Muhammad and the Christian: A Question of Response, Orbis Books, New York; Darton, Longman & Todd, London

Cullmann.O (1963). The Christology of the New Testament, SCM, London

Cupitt.D (1980). Taking Leave of God, SCM, London

------(1982). The World to Come, SCM, London

Cyprian. St (1957). The Lapsed. The Unity of the Catholic Church

192

(ed. M.Bevenot), Longman, Green & Co, London; The Newman Press, Maryland

------(1968). The Writings of Cyprian (eds. A.Roberts & J.Donaldson), Ante-Nicene Christian Library Vol 8, T & T Clark, Edinburgh

Cyriac.M (1982). Meeting of Religions, Dialogue Series no.3, no publisher, Madras

Dalton.W (1965). Christ's Proclamation to the Spirits, Pontifical Biblical Institute, Rome

Daniélou.J (1957). Holy Pagans of the Old Testament, Longman, Green & Co, London

------(1964a). The Theology of Jewish Christianity, Darton, Longman & Todd, London

------(1964b). A History of Early Christian Doctrine Before the Council of Nicaea Vol 1, Darton, Longman & Todd, London

------(1977). The Origins of Latin Christianity Vol 3, Darton, Longman & Todd, London; Westminster Press, Philadelphia

Dasgupta.S (1975a). A History of Indian Philosophy Vol 1, Motilal Banarsidass, Delhi

------(1975b). A History of Indian Philosophy Vol 2, Motilal Banarsidass, Delhi

------(1975c). A History of Indian Philosophy Vol 3, Motilal Banarsidass, Delhi

Das Gupta.K (1978). Faith Versus Humanism: A Dialogue with Professor Hick, Oriental Publishers & Distributors, New Delhi

Davies.J (1965). The Early Christian Church, Wiedenfeld & Nicolson, London

Davis.C (1970). Christ and the World Religions, Hodder & Stoughton, London

Davis.S (1975). "Theology, Verification and Falsification", International Journal for Philosophy of Religion, 6, 1, pp.1-22

D'Costa.G (1983). "A Hindu Christianity", The Tablet, 10 December, pp.1203-04

------(1984a). "Christ and Other Faiths", The Tablet, 21 July, pp.691-92

193

------(1984b). "John Hick's Copernican Revolution Ten Years After", New Blackfriars, 65, 769/770, pp.323-31

------(1985a). "Karl Rahner's Anonymous Christian: A Reappraisal", Modern Theology, 1, 2, pp.131-48

-----(1985b). "A Bibliography: Christian Attitudes Towards Other Religions", Modern Churchman, 27, 2, pp.37-44

------(1985c). "An Answer to Mr Loughlin", New Blackfriars, 66, 777, pp.135-37

------(1985d). "Elephants, Ropes and a Christian Theology of Religions", Theology, 88, 724, pp.259-68

------(1985e). Is One Religion As Good As Another?, Catholic Truth Society, London

------(1985f). "Conversations on a Tightrope", Catholic Herald, 14 June, p.5

------(1985g). "Recognising Truth and Holiness in Other Faiths", Catholic Herald, 21 June, p.7

------(1985h). Review of No Other Name? by P.Knitter, Modern Theology, 2, 1, pp.83-6

------(1986a). Theology and Religious Pluralism: The Challenge of Other Religions, Basil Blackwell, Oxford and New York

------(1986b). "The Pluralist Paradigm in a Christian Theology of Religions", Scottish Journal of Theology, 39, forthcoming

------(1986c). "Other Religions - A Reply", Theology, 89, forthcoming

------(1986d). "The Absolute and Relative Nature of the Gospel", forthcoming in ed. J.Miller, Religious Pluralism Vol 2, University of Waterloo Press, Waterloo, Ontario

------(1986e). Review of Problems of Religious Pluralism by J.Hick & The Experience of Religious Diversity eds. H.Askari & J.Hick, New Blackfriars, forthcoming

------(1986f). "A Reply to Alan Race", Theology, forthcoming

de Lubac.H (1950). Catholicism: A Study of Dogma in Relation to the Corporate Destiny of Mankind, Burns & Oates & Washbourne, London

------(1969). The Church: Paradox and Mystery, Ecclesia Press,

Shannon, Ireland

Denzinger.H (1957). The Sources of Catholic Dogma: The Church Teaches, Herder & Herder, London

Dewick.E (1953). The Christian Attitude to Other Religions, Cambridge University Press, Cambridge

Dharmasiri.G (1974). A Buddhist Critique of the Christian Concept of God, Lake House Institute, Colombo

Dhavamony.M (1971). The Love of God According to Śaiva Siddhānta, Oxford University Press, Oxford

------(1972). ed. Evangelism, Dialogue and Development, Universite Gregoriana, Rome

Dodd.C (1963). Historical Tradition and the Fourth Gospel, Cambridge University Press, Cambridge

Donovan.P (1976). Religious Language, Sheldon Press, London

Doumlin.H (1974). Christianity Meets Buddhism, Open Court, La Salle, Illinois

Drummond.R.H (1974). Gautama the Buddha: An Essay in Religious Understanding, W.B.Eerdmans, Grand Rapids

Duff-Forbes.D (1969). "Faith, Evidence, Coercion", Australasian Journal of Philosophy, 47, 2, pp.209-15

Dulles.A (1976). Models of the Church: A Critical Assessment of the Church in all its Aspects, Macmillan, London

------(1977). The Resilient Church: The Necessity and Limits of Adaption, Doubleday, New York

Dunn.J (1980). Christology in the Making, SCM, London

Dupuis.J (1966). "The Cosmic Christ in the Early Fathers", Indian Journal of Theology, 15, 3, pp.111-19

Duquoc.C (1985). "Monotheism and Unitary Ideology", Concilium, 177, 1, pp.59-66

Eminyan.M (1960). The Theology of Salvation, St Paul's, Boston

Erdmann.C (1977). The Origin of the Idea of the Crusade, Princeton University Press, New Jersey

Ernst.C (1979). Multiple Echo, Darton, Longman & Todd, London

Farias.T (1984). "Areas of Convergence of Christianity and Islam", Bulletin Secretariatus pro non Christianis, 19, 1, pp.80-90

Farmer.H (1939). "The Authority of the Faith", in ed. Paton 1939 pp.163-80

------(1952). "The Bible: Its Significance and Authority", Interpreters Bible Vol 1, Colesbury, Abingdon, pp.3-31

------(1954). Revelation and Religion: Studies in the Theological Interpretation of Religious Types, Nisbet, London

Farquhar.J (1930). The Crown of Hinduism, Oxford University Press, Oxford

Fenton.J (1944). "Extra Ecclesiam Nulla Salus", American Ecclesiastical Review, 10, pp.300-06

Flannery.A (1975). Vatican Council II. The Conciliar and Post Conciliar Documents, Dominican Publications, Dublin

Flew.A (1955). "Divine Omnipotence and Human Knowledge", in eds. Flew & MacIntyre 1955 pp.144-69

Flew.A & MacIntyre.A eds. (1955). New Essays in Philosophical Theology, SCM, London

Flew.R (1943). Jesus and His Church, Epworth Press, London

Forrester.D (1976). "Professor Hick and the Universe of Faiths", Scottish Journal of Theology, 29, 1, pp.65-72

Foster.K (1977). The Two Dantes, Darton, Longman & Todd, London

Frankfurt Declaration (1970). Christianity Today, 19 June, pp.844-46

Fransen.P (1967). "How Can Non-Christians Find Salvation in their Own Religion?", in ed. Neuner 1967 pp.67-122

Garaudy.R ed. (1967). From Anathema to Dialogue, Collins, London

Geffré.C & Jossua.J eds. (1985). Monotheism: Concilium, 177, 1, T & T Clark, Edinburgh

George.S (1939). Gandhi's Challenge to Christianity, George, Allen & Unwin, London

Gilson.E (1963). Modern Philosophers: Descartes to Kant, Random House, New York

Gispert-Sauch.G (1973). God's Word Among Men. Papers in Honour of Father Joseph Putz SJ, Vidyajyoti, Delhi

Glorieux.P (1932). "Endurcissement final et grâces denières", Nouvelle Revue Théologie, 59, pp.865-72

-------(1933). "De la nécessité des missions ou du problème du salut des infidèles", Supplement to the Union Missionaire, January, pp.88-112

Gombrich.R (1971). Precept and Practice, Oxford University Press, Oxford

Goulder.M ed. (1979). Incarnation and Myth: The Debate Continued, SCM, London

Graham.A (1963). Zen Catholicism, Harcourt Brace, New York

Green.M ed. (1977). The Truth of God Incarnate, Hodder & Stoughton, London

Griffin. D (1976). God, Power and Evil: A Process Theodicy, Westminster Press, Philadelphia

Griffiths.B (1978). Return to the Centre, Collins, London

------(1982). The Marriage of East and West, Collins, London

Griffiths.D & Lewis.D (1983). "On Grading Religions, Seeking Truth, and Being Nice to People", Religious Studies, 19, 1, pp.75-80

Grillmeier.A (1975). Christ in the Christian Tradition Vol 1, Mowbrays, London & Oxford (2nd ed.)

Gunton.C (1983). Yesterday and Today: A Study of Continuity in Christology, Darton, Longman & Todd, London

Guthrie.D (1970). New Testament Introduction, Tyndale Press, London (3rd ed.)

Gutierrez.G (1974). A Theology of Liberation: History, Politics and Salvation, SCM, London

Hacker.P (1978). Kleine Schriften, Franz Steiner Verlag, Wiesbaden

------(1980). Theological Foundations of Evangelization, Franz Steiner Verlag, St Augustin

Hahn.E (1975). Jesus in Islam: A Christian View, Christian Centre, Krishnagari

Hallencreutz.C (1966). Kraemer Towards Tambaram: A Study in Hendrik Kraemer's Missionary Approach, Gleerups, Lund

------(1970). New Approaches to Men of Other Faiths, 1938-1968: A Theological Discussion, World Council of Churches, Geneva

Harvey.A ed. (1981). God Incarnate: Story and Belief, SPCK, London

Hastings.A (1968). A Concise Guide to the Documents of the Second Vatican Council Vol 1, Darton, Longman & Todd, London

Hebblethwaite.B (1976). Evil, Suffering and Religion, Sheldon, London

------(1977). "Incarnation - the Essence of Christianity", Theology, 80, 674, pp.85-91

Hebblethwaite.B & Hick.J eds. (1980). Christianity and Other Religions, Collins, London

Henry.C ed. (1958). Revelation and the Bible, Baker Book House, Grand Rapids

Hesslegrave.D (1981). "Evangelicals and Interreligious Dialogue", in eds. Anderson & Stransky 1981b pp.123-28

Hillman.E (1966). "'Anonymous Christianity' and the Missions", Downside Review, 85, 277, pp.361-78

------(1968). The Wider Ecumenism: Anonymous Christianity and the Church, Burns & Oates, London; Herder & Herder, New York

------(1975). Polygamy Reconsidered, Orbis Books, New York

Hocking.W. (1932). Re-thinking Missions: A Laymen's Inquiry After One Hundred Years, Harper & Row, New York

------(1940). Living Religions and a World Faith, Allen & Unwin, London; Macmillan, New York

Hoekstra.H (1979). Evangelism in Eclipse, Paternoster Press, Exeter

Hogg.A (1914). "'The Crown of Hinduism' and Other Volumes", International Review of Missions, 3, 9, pp.171-74

------(1938). Towards Clarifying My Reactions to Doctor Kraemer's Book, Diocesan Press, Madras

------(1947). The Christian Message to the Hindu, SCM, London

Hogg.W (1952). Ecumenical Foundations: A History of the International Missionary Council and its Nineteenth Century Background, Harper & Row, New York

Horner.N ed. (1968). Protestant Currents in Mission: The Ecumenical-Conservative Encounter, Abingdon, Nashville

Howard.L (1981). The Expansion of God, SCM, London

Hughes.D (1984). "Christianity and Other Religions", Themelios, 9, 2, pp.15-21

Hulmes.E (1979). Commitment and Neutrality in Religious Education, Geoffrey Chapman, London

Hume.D (1970). Dialogues Concerning Natural Religion (ed. N.Pike), Bobbs-Meril, Indiana

Hunter.A (1985). Christianity and Other Faiths in Britain, SCM, London

Hunter.A.G (1951). Interpreting the New Testament 1900-1950, SCM, London

International Missionary Council Texts:

------(1910). (Edinburgh) World Missionary Council 9 Vols, Edinburgh

------(1928). The Jerusalem Series: Report of the Jerusalem Meeting of the International Missionary Council 1938 8 Vols, Cambridge University Press, Cambridge

------(1939). Tambaram Madras Series: International Missionary Council Meeting at Tambaram, Madras, 1938 7 Vols, Oxford University Press, Oxford

Jaspers.K (1953). The Origin and Goal of History, Routledge Kegan & Paul, London

Jathanna.C.D ed. (1982). Dialogue in Community: Essays in Honour of S.J.Samartha, The Karnataka Research Institute, Mangalore

Jathanna.O (1981). The Decisiveness of the Christ Event and the Universality of Christianity in a World of Religious Plurality, P.Lang, Berne

Johnston.W (1970). The Still Point: Reflections on Zen and Christian Mysticism, Fordham University Press, New York

------(1971). Christian Zen, Harper & Row, New York

------(1974). Silent Music, Harper & Row, New York; Collins,
London

Journet.C (1955). The Church of the Word Incarnate, Sheed & Ward,
London & New York

Kane.G (1975a). "Soul-Making Theodicy and Eschatology", Sophia,
14, 2, pp.24-31

------(1975b). "The Failure of Soul Making Theodicy",
International Journal for Philosophy of Religion, 6, 1, pp.1-21

Kane.J (1981). Pluralism and Truth in Religion, AAR Dissertation
Series 33, Scholars Press, California

Kant.I (1933). Critique of Pure Reason, Macmillan, London (2nd
ed.)

Kantzer.K (1975). "Unity and Diversity in Evangelical Faith", in
eds. Woodbridge & Wells 1975 pp.45-82

Kavka.G (1976). "Eschatological Falsification", Religious
Studies, 12, 2, pp.201-05

Kelly.J (1980). Early Christian Doctrines, Adam & Charles Black,
London (5th ed.)

Kerr.D (1984). "The Prophet Muhammad in Christian Theological
Perspective", International Bulletin, 8, 3, July, pp.112-16

Khodr.G (1974). "Christianity in a Pluralist World - The Economy
of the Holy Spirit" in ed. Samartha 1974b pp. 131-42

Klein.C (1978). Anti-Judaism in Christian Theology, Fortress
Press, Philadelphia; SPCK, London

Klostermaier.K (1967). Kristvidya, Christian Literature Society,
Bangalore

------(1969). Hindu and Christian in Vrindaban, SCM, London

Knitter.P (1974). Towards a Protestant Theology of Religions,
N.G.Elwart, Marburg

------(1985). No Other Name? A Critical Study of Christian
Attitudes Towards the World Religions, SCM, London

------(1986a). "Catholic Theology of Religions at the
Crossroads", Concilium, 183, pp.99-107

------(1986b). "Towards a Liberation Theology of Religions", unpublished paper delivered at the Blaisdell International Conference, California, March 1986, pp.1-27

Kraemer.H (1938). The Christian Message in a non-Christian World, Edinburgh House Press, London

------(1956). Religion and the Christian Faith, Lutterworth Press, London

Kuhn.T (1957). The Copernican Revolution, Harvard University Press, Massachusetts

------(1970). The Structure of Scientific Revolutions, Chicago University Press, Chicago

------(1974). "Second Thoughts on Paradigm", in ed. Suppe 1974 pp.459-82

Kulandran.S (1964). Grace: A Comparative Study of the Doctrine in Christianity and Hinduism, Lutterworth Press, London

Küng.H (1967). "The World Religions in God's Plan of Salvation", in ed. Neuner 1967 pp.25-66

------(1976). On Being a Christian, Doubleday, New York; Collins, London

------(1981). The Church, Search Press, London

------(1986). "Towards an Ecumenical Theology of Religions: Some Theses for Clarification", in eds. Küng & Moltmann 1986 pp.119-25

Küng.H & Moltmann.J eds. (1986). Christianity Among World Religions: Concilium, 183, T & T Clark, Edinburgh

Kunnumpuram.K (1971). Ways of Salvation. The Meaning of Non-Christian Religions According to the Teachings of Vatican II, Pontifical Athenaeum, Poona

Lamb.C (1985). Belief in a Mixed Society, Lion, London

Langley.M (1979). Ethical Dialogue with Other Religions, Grove Books, Bramcote

Lash.N (1976). Voices of Authority, Sheed & Ward, London

------(1979). Theology on Dover Beach, Darton, Longman & Todd, London

------(1986). "Considering the Trinity", Modern Theology, 2, 3, pp.183-96

Laurentin.R & Neuner.J (1966). Declaration on the Relation of the Church to Non-Christian Religions: A Commentary, Paulist Press, New York

Lausanne Committee for World Evangelization (1981). How Shall They Hear? Proceedings and Reports from the Consultation of World Evangelisation, World Wide Publications, Minneapolis

Lausanne Statement (1975). "The Lausanne Covenant", in eds. Anderson & Stransky 1975 pp.239-52

Legrand.L (1973). "The Missionary Significance of the Aeropagus Speech", in ed. Gispert-Sauch 1973 pp.59-72

Lewis.H.D (1981). Jesus in the Faith of Christians, Macmillan, London

Lindars.B (1972). The Gospel of John, Marshall, Morgan & Scott, London

Lindbeck.G (1984). The Nature of Doctrine. Religion and Theology in a Postliberal Age, SPCK, London

Lindsell.H ed. (1966). The Church's Worldwide Mission. Proceedings of the Congress on the Church's Worldwide Mission, World Books, Waco, Texas

------(1970). An Evangelical Theology of Missions, Zondervan, Grand Rapids

Ling.T (1968). A History of Religions East and West, Open University Press, Macmillan, London

Lipner.J (1975). "Christians and the Uniqueness of Christ", Scottish Journal of Theology, 22, 4, pp.359-68

------(1976). "Truth Claims and Inter-Religious Dialogue", Religious Studies, 12, 2, pp.217-30

------(1977). "Does Copernicus Help? Reflections for a Christian Theology of Religions", Religious Studies, 13, 2, pp.243-58

------(1979). "Hick's Resurrection", Sophia, 18, 1, pp.22-34

------(1986). The Face of Truth. A Study of Meaning and Metaphysics in the Vedantic Theology of Ramanuja, Macmillan, London

Lombardi.R (1956). The Salvation of the Unbeliever, Burns & Oates, London

Lonergan.B (1974). A Second Collection, Westminster Press,

Philadelphia

------(1985). A Third Collection (ed. F.Crowe), Geoffrey Chapman, London; Paulist Press, New York

Lott.E (1980). Vedantic Approaches to God, Macmillan, London; Barnes & Noble, New York

Loughlin.G (1985a). "Paradigms and Paradox: Defending the Case for a Revolution in the Theology of Religions", New Blackfriars, 66, 777, pp.127-34

------(1985b). "Persons and Replicas", Modern Theology, 1, 4, pp.303-19

Louth.A (1983). Discerning the Mystery, Clarendon Press, Oxford

Lubac. de H - see de Lubac
Macabe.H (1977). "The Myth of God Incarnate", New Blackfriars, 58, 687, pp.350-57

MacKinnon.D (1940). The Church of God, Dacre Press, London

Macquarrie.J (1963). Twentieth Century Religious Thought, SCM, London

Magee.B (1982). Men of Ideas. Dialogue with Fifteen Leading Philosophers, Oxford University Press, Oxford

Manzoor.S.P (1984). "World Order: Visions of Faith", Afkar Inquiry, 1, 2, pp.42-6

Mascall.E (1978). Theology and the Gospel of Christ: An Essay in Reorientation, SPCK, London

Mason.S. (1962). A History of the Sciences, Collier Books, New York

Mathis.T (1985). Against John Hick, University Press of America, Boston

Mattam.J (1975). Land of the Trinity: A Study of Modern Christian Approaches to Hinduism, Theological Publications of India, Bangalore

Maurice.F (1866). The Religions of the World, Boyle Lectures, Macmillan, London

Maybaum.I (1973). Trialogue Between Jew, Christian and Muslim, Routledge & Kegan Paul, London

Merton.T (1968). Zen and the Birds of Appetite, New Directions,

New York

Meynell.H (1985). "The Idea of a World Theology", Modern Theology, 1, 2, pp.149-63

Moltmann.J (1977). The Church in the Power of the Spirit, SCM, London; Harper & Row, New York

Monchanin.J (1977). In Quest of the Absolute. The Life and Works of Jules Monchanin (ed. J.Weber), Mowbray, Oxford

Mondin.B (1963). The Principle of Analogy in Catholic and Protestant Thought, Nijhoff, The Hague

Moses.D (1950). Religious Truth and the Relation Between Religions, Christian Literature Society, Madras

Moule.C (1967). The Phenomenon of the New Testament, SCM, London

------(1977). The Origin of Christology, Cambridge University Press, Cambridge

------(1981). The Birth of the New Testament, Adam & Charles Black, London (3rd ed.)

Muldoon.J (1979). Popes, Lawyers and Infidels: The Church and the non-Christian World 1250-1550, University of Pennsylvania Press, Pennsylvania

Neill.S (1960). Men of Unity, SCM, London

-------(1964). A History of the Church: Christian Missions, Penguin, Harmondsworth

------(1970). Christian Faith and Other Faiths: The Christian Dialogue with Other Religions, Oxford University Press, Oxford

------(1984a). Crises of Belief, Hodder & Stoughton, London (2nd ed. of 1970)

------(1984b). A History of Christianity in India: The Beginnings to AD 1707, Cambridge University Press, Cambridge

Neuner.J ed. (1967). Christian Revelation and World Religions, Burns & Oates, London

------(1973). "Votum Ecclesiae", in ed. Gispert-Sauch 1973 pp.147-66

Neuner.J & Dupuis.J eds. (1983). The Christian Faith in the Doctrinal Documents of the Catholic Church, Collins, London (2nd ed.)

204

Newbigin.L (1969). The Finality of Christ, SCM, London; John Knox Press, Atlanta

------(1977a). Christian Witness in a Plural Society, British Council of Churches, London

------(1977b). "The Problem, Purpose and Manner of Inter-Faith Dialogue", Scottish Journal of Theology, 30, 3, pp.253-70

------(1978). The Open Secret, W.B.Eerdmans, Grand Rapids

Newlands.G (1980). "On The Myth of God Incarnate", in ed. Sykes & Holmes, 1980, pp.181-92

Newman.J (1906). An Essay on the Development of Christian Doctrine, Longmans, Green & Co, London

Nielsen.K (1963). "Eschatological Verification", Canadian Journal of Theology, 9, 4, pp.271-81

Norman.E (1979). Christianity and World Order, Oxford University Press, Oxford

Ogden.S (1963). The Reality of God, Harper & Row, New York

Oman.J (1968). The Natural and the Supernatural, Cambridge University Press, Cambridge

Otto.R (1930). India's Religion of Grace and Christianity Compared and Contrasted, Macmillan, London

Pailin.D (1984). Attitudes to Other Religions, Manchester University Press, Manchester

Panikkar.R (1964). The Unknown Christ of Hinduism, Darton Longman & Todd, London

------(1973). The Trinity and the Religious Experience of Man, Darton Longman & Todd, London

------(1978). The Intrareligious Dialogue, Paulist Press, New York

------(1979). Myth, Faith and Hermeneutics, Fowler Wright, Leominster

------(1981). The Unknown Christ of Hinduism, Darton, Longman & Todd, London (2nd ed. of 1973)

Pannenberg.W (1967). Jesus: God and Man, Westminster Press, Philadelphia

------(1971). Basic Questions in Theology Vol 2, SCM, London

Parrinder.G (1970). Avatar and Incarnation, Faber & Faber, London

------(1976). Jesus in the Qur'an, Sheldon Press, London

Paton.W ed. (1939). The Authority of Faith, Tambaram Series 1, Humphrey Milford & Oxford University Press, London

Pedley.C (1984). "An English Bibliographical Aid to Karl Rahner", The Heythrop Journal, 25, 3, pp.319-65

Percy.E (1961). Facing the Unfinished Task: Messages Delivered at the Congress on World Mission, W.B.Eerdmans, Michigan

Phillips.D.Z (1965). The Concept of Prayer, Routledge & Kegan Paul, London

Pittenger.N (1981). Catholic Faith in a Process Perspective, Orbis Books, New York

Pollard.T (1970). Johannine Christology and the Early Church, Cambridge University Press, Cambridge

Pope John Paul II (1979). Redempter Hominis, Catholic Truth Society, London

Portalié.E (1975). A Guide to the Thought of Saint Augustine, Greenwood Press, Connecticut

Price.H (1938). Some Aspects of the Conflict Between Science and Religion, Cambridge University Press, Cambridge

------(1953a). Thinking and Experience, Hutchinson University Library, London

------(1953b). "Survival and the Idea of 'Another World'", Proceedings of the Society for Psychical Research, 50, 182, pp.1-25

Pye.M (1976). "Ernst Troeltsch and the End of the Problem about 'Other Religions'", in ed. Clayton 1976 pp.172-95

Race.A (1983). Christians and Religious Pluralism, SCM, London

------(1986a). "Christianity and Other Religions: Is Inclusivism Enough?", Theology, 89, 729, pp.178-86

------(1986b). "Report on the Blaisdell Conference", Community 41, Spring, pp.3-5

Radhakrishnan.S (1927). A Hindu View of Life, George Allen &
Unwin, London

Rahner.K Theological Investigations (All Volumes Darton, Longman
& Todd, London; Seabury Press, New York)

------(1961a). Volume 1

------(1963). Volume 2

------(1966a). Volume 4

------(1966b). Volume 5

------(1967). Volume 3

------(1969). Volume 6

------(1971a). Volume 7

------(1971b). Volume 8

------(1972). Volume 9

------(1973). Volume 10

------(1974a). Volume 11

------(1974b). Volume 12

------(1975). Volume 13

------(1976). Volume 14

------(1979). Volume 16

------(1981a). Volume 17

------(1981b). Volume 20

------(1983a). Volume 15

------(1983b). Volume 18

------(1983c). Volume 19

------(1961b). On the Theology of Death, Herder, Frieburg;
Nelson, Edinburgh-London

------(1964). On Heresy, Burns & Oates, London

--- --7 Darlap.A eds. (1968-1970). Sacramentum Mundi 6 Vols,

Herder & Herder, New York

------(1978). Foundations of Christian Faith, Darton, Longman & Todd, London

Ramm.B (1983). After Fundamentalism: The Future of Theology, Harper & Row, London

Reading.M ed. (1952). Abhandlungen uber Theologie und Kirche, Festschrift fur Karl Adam, Dusseldorf

Reardon.B ed. (1968). Liberal Protestantism, Adam & Charles Black, London

Robinson.J (1979). Truth is Two-Eyed, SCM, London

------(1985). The Priority of John, SCM, London

Rodwell.J (1979) "Relativism in Science and Theology", in ed. Goulder 1979 pp.214-23

Rouner.L ed. (1984). Religious Pluralism, Notre Dame University Press, Indiana

Rousseau.R ed. (1981). Interreligious Dialogue, Ridge Row, Montrose

Ruether.R (1972). "An Invitation to Jewish-Christian Dialogue. In What Sense can we Say that Jesus was the 'Christ'?", The Ecumenist, 10, 2, pp.17-24

------(1981). "Asking the Existential Question", in ed. Wall 1981 pp.161-68

Russell.S (1977). "The Finality of Christ and Other Religions", Epworth Review, 4, 1, pp.77-84

Sadgrove.M & Wright.T (1977). "Jesus Christ the Only Saviour", in ed. Stott 1977 pp.79-83

Sage.M (1975). Cyprian, The Philadelphia Patristic Foundation, Massachusetts

Samartha.S (1974a). The Hindu Response to the Unbound Christ, Christian Literature Society, Madras

------(1974b). ed. Living Faiths and Ultimate Goals, World Council of Churches, Geneva

------(1975). ed. Towards World Community: Resources and Responsibilities for Living Together. Colombo Papers, World Council of Churches, Geneva

------(1981). Courage for Dialogue, World Council of Churches, Geneva

Samartha.S & Taylor.J eds. (1973). Christian-Muslim Dialogue: Papers Presented at the Broumana Consultation, World Council of Churches, Geneva

Sanders.E ed. (1980). Jewish and Christian Self Definition Vol 1, SCM, London

Sanders.E et al. eds. (1981). Jewish and Christian Self Definition Vol 2, SCM, London

Sanders.E & Meyer.B eds. (1982). Jewish and Christian Self Definition Vol 3, SCM, London

Sandmel.S (1978). Anti-Semitism in the New Testament?, Fortress Press, Philadelphia

Santmire.P (1973). Critical Issues in Modern Religion, Prentice-Hall, New Jersey

Schineller.P (1976). "Christ and Church: A Spectrum of Views", Theological Studies, 37, 4, pp.545-66

Schleiermacher.F (1928). The Christian Faith (ed. H.Mackintosh & J.Stewart), T & T Clark, Edinburgh

------(1965). On Religion: Speeches to its Cultured Despisers, Harper & Row, New York

Schlette.H (1966). Towards a Theology of Religions, Burns & Oates, London

Schnackenburg.R (1974). The Church in the New Testament, Burns & Oates, London

School of World Mission (1981). "Evangelistic Outreach to the Jewish People", in eds. Anderson & Stransky 1981b pp.192-95

Schonfield.H (1965). The Passover Plot, Hutchinson, London

Schreiter.R (1985). Constructing Local Theologies, SCM, London

Schweitzer.A (1954). The Quest for the Historical Jesus, Macmillan, New York

Scott.W (1978). Karl Barth's Theology of Mission, Intervarsity Press, Illinois

------(1981). "'No Other Name' - An Evangelical Conviction", in eds. Anderson & Stransky 1981 pp.58-75, 93-6

Secretariat for non-Christian Religions (SNC) (1970). Religions: Fundamental Themes for a Dialogistic Understanding, Secretariat for non-Christian Religions, Rome

------(1984). "The Attitude of the Church towards the Followers of Other Religions", Bulletin Secratariatus pro non Christianis, 19, 2, pp.126-41

------(1985). "Prosepcts for Evangelization, with Reference to the Areas of the non Christian Religions, Twenty Years After Vatican II", Bulletin Secretariatus pro non Christianis, 20, 2, pp.111-40

Sharpe.E (1962). J.N.Farquhar: A Memoir, YMCA, Calcutta

------(1965). Not to Destroy But to Fulfil. The Contribution of J.N.Farquhar to Protestant Missionary Thought in India Before 1914, Gleerups, Swedish Institute of Missionary Research, Uppsala

------(1971). The Theology of A.G.Hogg, Christian Institute for the Study of Religion and Society, Madras

------(1975). Comparative Religion: A History, Duckworth, London

------(1977). Faith Meets Faith. Some Christian Attitudes to Hinduism in the Nineteenth and Twentieth Centuries, SCM, London

Sherbok.D (1984). "Judaism and the Universe of Faiths", New Blackfriars, 65, 763, pp.28-35

Sherbok.D & Kerr.D eds. (1985). Christians, Muslims and Jews, Centre for the Study of Islam and Christian-Muslim Relations, Birmingham

Shortner.A (1973). African Culture and the Christian Church, Geoffrey Chapman, London

Slater.T (1903). The Higher Hinduism in Relation to Christianity, E.Stock, London

Smart.N (1968). The Yogi and the Devotee: The Interplay between the Upanishads and Catholic Theology, Allen & Unwin, London

------(1981). Beyond Ideology, Collins, London

Smith.T (1986). "Other Religions", Theology, 89, 727, pp.44-5

Smith.W.C (1967). Questions of Religious Truth, Gollancz, London

-----(1972). The Faith of Other Men, Harper Torchbooks, New York

------(1978). The Meaning and End of Religion: A New Approach to the Religious Traditions of Mankind, Sheldon, London; Harper & Row, New York (2nd ed.)

------(1980). Towards a World Theology, Macmillan, London

------(1985). Scriptures from a Comparative Religionist Point of View, Claremont Graduate School, Claremont

Solomon.N (1986). "Judaism and World Religions", World Faiths Insight, ns.12, pp.11-25, 53-6

Speer.R (1933). 'Re-thinking Missions' Examined, Revel & Oliphants, London

Stead.C (1977). Divine Substance, Clarendon Press, Oxford

Stott.J (1975). "The Biblical Basis of Evangelism", in eds. Anderson & Stransky 1975 pp.4-23

------(1977). ed. Obeying Christ in a Changing World Vol 1, Fontana, London

------(1981). "Dialogue, Encounter, Even Confrontation", in eds. Anderson & Stransky 1981b pp.156-72

Straelen.H van (1966). The Catholic Encounter with World Religions, Burns & Oates, London; Newman Press, New York

Suppe.F ed. (1974). The Structure of Scientific Theories, University of Illinois Press, Urbanna

Swinburne.R (1979). The Existence of God, Clarendon Press, Oxford

Sykes.S (1971). Fredrich Schleiermacher, Lutterworth Press, London

------(1984). The Identity of Christianity: Theologians and the Essence of Christianity from Schleiermacher to Barth, SPCK, London

Sykes.S & Clayton.J eds. (1978). Christ, Faith and History, Cambridge University Press, Cambridge

Sykes.S & Holmes.D eds. (1980). New Studies in Theology, Duckworth, London

Taylor.A (1964). The Origins of the Second World War, Penguin, Harmondsworth

Thomas.M (1969). The Acknowledged Christ of the Indian Renaissance, SCM, London

Thomas.O ed. (1969). Attitudes Towards Other Religions, SCM, London

Thurston.H (1935). "Memory and Imminent Death", The Month, January, pp.49-60

Tillich.P (1963). Christianity and the Encounter of the World Religions, Columbia University Press, New York

Tooley.M (1976). "John Hick and the Concept of Eschatological Verification", Religious Studies, 2, 2, pp.179-99

Toon.P (1978). Jesus Christ is Lord, Marshall, Morgan & Scott, London

Toynbee.A (1957). Christianity Among the Religions of the World, Scribners, New York

------(1965). An Historian's Approach to Religion, Oxford University Press, Oxford

------(1968). et al. Man's Concern with Death, Hodder & Stoughton, London

Trethowan.I (1967). "Dr Hick and the Problem of Evil", The Journal of Theological Studies, 18, 2, pp.407-16

Trigg.R (1983). "Religion and the Threat of Relativism", Religious Studies, 19, 3, pp.297-310

Troeltsch.E (1923). Christian Thought: Its History and Application, University of London Press, London

------(1972). The Absoluteness of Christianity and the History of Religions, SCM, London

Turner.H (1976). Jesus the Christ, Mowbrays, London & Oxford

Vandana.Sr (1982). Social Justice and Ashrams, Asian Trading Coporation, Bangalore

Vatican II Documents (in ed. A.Flannery 1975):

------(1964). Dogmatic Constitution on the Church

------(1965a). Declaration on the Relation of the Church to Non-Christian Religions

------(1965b). Decree on the Church's Missionary Activity

------(1965c). <u>Declaration</u> <u>on</u> <u>Religious</u> <u>Liberty</u>

-----(1965d). <u>Pastoral</u> <u>Constitution</u> <u>on</u> <u>the</u> <u>Church</u> <u>in</u> <u>the</u> <u>Modern</u> <u>World</u>

------(1965e). <u>Dogmatic</u> <u>Constitution</u> <u>on</u> <u>Divine</u> <u>Revelation</u>

Verghese.P (1974). "Christ and All Men", in ed. Samartha 1974b pp.159-64

Visser't Hooft.W (1963). <u>No</u> <u>Other</u> <u>Name:</u> <u>The</u> <u>Choice</u> <u>Between</u> <u>Syncretism</u> <u>and</u> <u>Universalism,</u> SCM, London

Vorgrimler.H ed. (1969). <u>Commentary</u> <u>on</u> <u>the</u> <u>Documents</u> <u>of</u> <u>Vatican</u> <u>Two,</u> Burns & Oates, London; Herder & Herder, New York

Wainwright.W (1984). "Wilfred Cantwell Smith and Faith and Belief", <u>Religious</u> Studies, 20, 3, pp.353-67

Walker.G (1968). <u>The</u> <u>Churchmanship</u> <u>of</u> <u>St.</u> <u>Cyprian,</u> Lutterworth Press, London

Wall.J ed. (1981). <u>Theologians</u> <u>in</u> <u>Transition,</u> Crossroads, New York

Ward.K (1969). "Freedom and Irenaean Theodicy", <u>The</u> <u>Journal</u> <u>of</u> <u>Theological</u> Studies, 20, 1, pp.249-54

Warren.M (1967). <u>Social</u> <u>History</u> <u>and</u> <u>Christian</u> <u>Mission,</u> SCM, London

------(1976). <u>I</u> <u>Believe</u> <u>in</u> <u>the</u> <u>Great</u> <u>Commission,</u> Hodder & Stoughton, London

Weber.J ed. (1977). <u>In</u> <u>Quest</u> <u>of</u> <u>the</u> <u>Absolute.</u> <u>The</u> <u>Life</u> <u>and</u> <u>Works</u> <u>of</u> <u>Jules</u> <u>Monchanin,</u> Mowbray, Oxford

Wedberg.A (1982). <u>A</u> <u>History</u> <u>of</u> <u>Philosophy</u> Vol 2, Oxford University Press, Oxford

Whaling.F ed. (1984). <u>The</u> <u>World's</u> <u>Religious</u> <u>Traditions:</u> <u>Essays</u> <u>in</u> <u>Honour</u> <u>of</u> <u>Wilfred</u> <u>Cantwell</u> <u>Smith,</u> T & T Clark, Edinburgh

Wickremesinghe.L (1979). <u>Togetherness</u> <u>and</u> <u>Uniqueness</u> <u>-</u> <u>Living</u> <u>Faiths</u> <u>in</u> <u>Inter-Relation,</u> Second Lambeth Interfaith Lecture (published in <u>Crucible,</u> October-December, 1979, pp.7-11)

Wiles.M (1978). "Does Christology Rest on a Mistake?", in eds. Sykes & Clayton 1978 pp.3-12

Williams.R (1977). "Myth and Faith: Some Reflections on <u>The</u> <u>Myth</u>

of God Incarnate", Theoria to Theory, 11, 3, pp.203-12

Willmer.H (1977). "A Comment by Haddon Willmer" (pp.159-61) and "The Distinctiveness of Christ: Further Comment by C.F.D.Moule and Haddon Willmer" (pp.164-71), in Moule 1977

Wittgenstein.L (1922) Tractatus Logico-Philosophicus, Routledge & Kegan Paul, London

------(1968). Philosophical Investigations, Basil Blackwell, Oxford (2nd ed.)

Wood.H (1960). Jesus in the Twentieth Century, Lutterworth Press, London

Wood.J ed. (1971). Jewish-Christian Relations in Today's World, Markham Press Fund of Baylor University, Waco, Texas

Woodbridge.J & Wells.A (1975). The Evangelicals: What They Believe, Who They Are, Where They Are Changing, Abingdon, Nashville

World Council of Churches (1979). Guidelines on Dialogue with People of Living Faiths and Ideologies, World Council of Churches, Geneva

Zaehner.R (1958). At Sundry Times, Faber & Faber, London

------(1970). The Concordant Discord, Oxford University Press, Oxford

BIBLIOGRAPHY OF JOHN HICK'S WORKS

1952

(a) "The Will to Believe: William James' Theory of Faith", _The London Quarterly and Holborn Review_, 127, pp.290-95

1953

(a) "The Nature of Religious Faith", _Proceedings of the XIth International Congress of Philosophy_, North Holland, Amsterdam, 11, pp.57-62

1954

(a) "The Structure of the War Problem", in _Studies in Christian Social Commitment_, ed. J.Ferguson, Independent Press, London, pp.19-36

1956

(a) Review of _A Modern Philosophy of Religion_ by S.Thompson, _The Philosophical Review_, 65, 375, pp.427-29

1957

(a) _Faith and Knowledge. A Modern Introduction to the Problem of Religious Knowledge_, Cornell University Press, New York

(b) Review of _The Modern Predicament_ by H.Paton, _The Philosophical Review_, 66, 378, pp.271-74

(c) "Love", _The Inner Disciplines_ (Series of Sermons preached in the Sage Chapel, Cornell University), pp.16-8

(d) "The Engineer: his need for education as well as training", _The Cornell Engineer_, 22, 6, pp.29-36

1958

(a) "The Christology of D.M.Baillie", _Scottish Journal of Theology_, 11, 1, pp.1-12

215

(b) Review of Words and Images by E.Mascall, Scottish Journal of Theology, 11, 1, pp.83-6

(c) "Design and the Designer", Saturday Review, 41, 39, pp.4-6

1959

(a) "A Non-Substance Christology?", Colgate Rochester Divinity School Bulletin, May, pp.41-54

(b) Review of The Self as Agent by J.Macmurray, Scottish Journal of Theology, 12, 2, pp.193-95

(c) Review of An Analytical Philosophy of Religion by W.Zurdeeg, Ethics, 69, 4, pp.297-99

(d) Article review of Systematic Theology Vols 1 & 2 by P.Tillich, Scottish Journal of Theology, 12, 3, pp.286-97

(e) Review of The Reality of Faith by F.Gogarten, Theology Today, 16, 3, pp.412-14

(f) "Belief and Life: The Fundamental Nature of the Christian Ethic", Encounter, 20, 4, pp.494-516

(g) Review of Christ and the Christian by N.Ferré, Scottish Journal of Theology, 12, 4, pp.414-17

1960

(a) Review of The Role of Knowledge in Western Religion by J.H.Randall, Theology Today, 16, 4, pp.543-45

(b) Review of Revelation Through Reason by E.Harris, Theology Today, 16, 4, pp.554-55

(c) Review of Religion and Culture ed. by W.Leibrecht, Scottish Journal of Theology, 13, 1, pp.83-5

(d) Review of The Gospel of the Incarnation by G.Hendry, Scottish Journal of Theology, 13, 1, pp.86-9

(e) "Theology and Verification", Theology Today, 17, 1, pp.12-31

(f) Review of The Freedom of the Will by A.Farrer, Theology Today, 17, 2, pp.268-70

(g) Review of The Word Incarnate by N.Pittenger, Princeton Seminary Bulletin, July, pp.76-7

(h) Review of Introduction to Religious Philosophy by
G.MacGregor, Princeton Seminary Bulletin, July, pp.77-8

(i) Review of An Analytical Philosophy of Religion by W.Zurdeeg,
Scottish Journal of Theology, 13, 3, pp.312-15

(j) "The Idea of Necessary Being", Princeton Seminary Bulletin,
November pp.11-21

(k) "God as Necessary Being", The Journal of Philosophy, 57,
22/23, pp.725-34

1961

(a) "Is Religion an American Heresy?", Theology Today, 18, 1,
pp.1-9

(b) "Meaning and Truth in Theology", in Religious Experience and
Faith, ed. S.Hook, New York University Press, New York, pp.203-10

(c) "Necessary Being", Scottish Journal of Theology, 14, 4,
pp.353-69

(d) Introduction to Grace and Personality by J.Oman, Association
Press, New York, pp.5-10

(e) Review of Ethical Naturalism and the Modern World-View by
E.Adams, Theology Today, 18, 2, pp.242-44

(f) Review of Language, Logic and God by F.Ferré, Theology Today,
18, 2, pp.247-50

(g) Review of Relativism, Knowledge and Faith by G.Kaufman,
Interpretation, 15, 3, p.368

(h) Review of The Transcendence of God by E.Farley, Religion in
Life, 30, 4, pp.630-31

(i) Review of Religious Knowledge by P.Schmidt, Religious
Education, 56, 6, p.464

1962

(a) "Courteous Query for Bennett and Ramsey", Theology Today, 18,
4, pp.503-05

(b) "Theological Table-Talk", Theology Today, 19, 3, pp.402-11

(c) "A Philosopher Criticises Theology", The London Quarterly,

217

187, 2, pp.103-10

(d) "What Does It Mean to Believe in God?", Princeton Seminary Bulletin, 55, 3, pp.53-7

(e) "What Characterises Religious Language? - A Comment", Journal for the Scientific Study of Religion, 2, 1, pp.22-4

(f) Review of Philosophy and Religion by J.Wilson, The Christian Century, 89, 6, p.166

(g) Review of The Teachings of the Mystics ed. by W.Stace, The Journal of Philosophy, 59, 5, pp.135-36

(h) Review of The Faith of a Heretic by W.Kaufmann, Theology Today, 19, 1, pp.120-22

(i) Review of Prospect for Metaphysics ed. by I.Ramsey, Theology Today, 19, 3, pp.451-53

(j) "Existence Question", Christian Century, 79, 166, pp.12-4

1963

(a) Philosophy of Religion, Prentice Hall, New Jersey

(b) "A Comment on Professor Binkley's Reply", Journal for the Scientific Study of Religion, 2, 2, pp.231-32

(c) Review of Exploring the Logic of Faith by F.Ferré & K.Bendall, Princeton Seminary Bulletin, 56, 2, pp.61-2

(d) Review of The Logic of Perfection by C.Hartshorne, Theology Today, 20, 2, pp.295-98

1964

(a) ed. Classical and Contemporary Readings in the Philosophy of Religion, Prentice Hall, New Jersey

(b) ed. Faith and the Philosophers, Macmillan, London; St Martin's Press, New York

(c) The Existence of God, Macmillan, New York

(d) Review of Reason in Religion by N.Ferré, Religion in Life, 33, 4, pp.632-34

(e) Review of Meaning and Truth in Religion by W.Christian, Religious Education, 59, 6, pp.519-20

218

1965

(a) <u>Filosofia</u> <u>de</u> <u>la</u> <u>Religion</u> (Spanish Translation of <u>Philosophy</u> <u>of</u> <u>Religion</u>), Union Tipografica Editorial Hispano Americana, Mexico

(b) "The Purpose of Evil", <u>The</u> <u>Listener</u>, August 12, pp.231-32

(c) "Evil and the God of Love", John <u>O'Gaunt</u>, (Independent Paper of the University of Lancaster) 5, May, pp.5-6

(d) Review of <u>Metaphysics</u> <u>and</u> <u>Religious</u> <u>Language</u> by F.Dilley, <u>Theology</u> <u>Today</u>, 22, 2, pp.285-86

(e) "To Believe or Not to Believe", <u>Saturday</u> <u>Review</u>, 48, 63, pp.39-40

1966

(a) <u>Evil</u> <u>and</u> <u>the</u> <u>God</u> <u>of</u> <u>Love</u> (2nd ed.) Macmillan, London; Harper & Row, New York; Collins-Fontana, London

(b) <u>Faith</u> <u>and</u> <u>Knowledge</u> (2nd ed.), Cornell University Press, New York; Macmillan, London

(c) "Vapor Theologicum", <u>Theology</u> <u>Today</u>, 22, 4, pp.528-29

(d) Review of <u>Christian</u> <u>Ethics</u> <u>and</u> <u>Contemporary</u> <u>Philosophy</u> ed. by I.Ramsey, <u>Theology</u>, 69, 555, pp.417-1

(e) "Christology at the Crossroads", in <u>Prospects</u> <u>for</u> <u>Theology</u>, ed. F.Healey, James Nesbit, London, pp.137-66

1967

(a) "Faith and Coercion", <u>Philosophy</u>, 42, 161, pp.272-73

(b) Review of <u>God,</u> <u>Pain</u> <u>and</u> <u>Evil</u> by G.Buttrick, <u>Theology</u> <u>Today</u>, 23, 4, pp.583-84

(c) Review of <u>Signs</u> <u>and</u> <u>Wonders</u> by L.Monden, <u>Journal</u> <u>of</u> <u>Ecumenical</u> <u>Studies</u>, 4, 1, pp.157-58

(d) Review of <u>The</u> <u>Concept</u> <u>of</u> <u>Prayer</u> by D.Z.Phillips, <u>Journal</u> <u>of</u> <u>Ecumenical</u> <u>Studies</u>, 4, 2, pp.320-21

(e) ed. with A.McGill, <u>The</u> <u>Many</u> <u>Faced</u> <u>Argument.</u> <u>Recent</u> <u>Studies</u> <u>on</u> <u>the</u> <u>Ontological</u> <u>Argument</u> <u>for</u> <u>the</u> <u>Existence</u> <u>of</u> <u>God</u>, Macmillan, New

219

York & London

(f) Review of <u>New Studies in Berkeley's Philosophy</u> ed. by
W.Steinkraus, <u>Journal of Theological Studies</u>, ns. 18, 2,
pp.535-37

(g) Review of <u>Faith and Philosophy</u> by J.Richmond, <u>Journal of
Theological Studies</u>, ns. 18, 2, pp.550-52

(h) Review of <u>Faith and Speculation</u> by A. Farrer, <u>Theology</u>, 70,
570, pp.557-58

(i) Review of <u>God and Philosophy</u> by A.Flew, <u>Theology Today</u>, 24,
1, pp.85-7

(j) Articles in <u>The Encyclopedia of Philosophy</u>, ed. P.Edwards,
Macmillan & The Free Press, New York. Articles: "Christianity";
"Evil, the Problem of"; "Oman, John"; "Ontological Arguments for
the Existence of God"; "Revelation"; "Tennant, Fredrick Robert".

<u>1968</u>

(a) <u>Christianity at the Centre</u>, SCM, London; Herder & Herder,
New York

(b) "Theology's Central Problem", Inaugural Lecture, University
of Birmingham

(c) "On Being Mortal", in <u>Sermons From Great St Mary's</u>, ed.
H.Montefiore, Collins-Fontana, London, pp.100-07

(d) "The Justification of Religious Belief", <u>Theology</u>, 71, 573,
pp.100-07

(e) "God, Evil and Mystery", <u>Religious Studies</u>, 3, 2, pp.539-46

(f) "Comment on <u>War and the New Morality</u>" by D.Hoitenga, <u>The
Reformed Journal</u>, 18, 2, pp.24-5

(g) Review of <u>The Symbolism of Evil</u> by P.Ricoeur, <u>Theology Today</u>,
24, 4, pp.521-22

(h) Review of <u>God Talk</u> by J.Macquarrie, <u>Journal of Theological
Studies</u>, 19, 1, pp.395-96

(i) Review of <u>A Question of Conscience</u> by C.Davis, <u>Outlook</u>,
(Journal of the Presbyterian Church of England), May, p.18

(j) "The Problem of Evil in the First and Last Things", <u>Journal
of Theological Studies</u>, ns. 19, 2, pp.591-602

(k) Review of Theological Ethics Vol I by H.Thielicke, The Expository Times, 80, 1, p.23

(l) Review of Man's Concern with Death by A.Toynbee et al., Birmingham Post, November 30, p.12

(m) Philosophy of Religion (Japanese translation), Prentice Hall of Japan, Tokyo

1969

(a) "Religious Faith as Experiencing As", in Talk of God, ed. N.Vesey, Macmillan, London; St Martin's Press, New York, pp. 20-35

(b) "Theology's Central Problem" (Abbreviated version of Inaugural Lecture), The Expository Times, 80, 8, pp.228-32

(c) "A Plea for Systematic Theology", Regina (The Magazine of the Queen's College, Birmingham), 3, pp.15-7

(d) Review of Origins of Pragmatism by A.J.Ayer, The Expository Times, 80, 6, pp.172-73

(e) Review of Adam by A.Cunningham, The Church Quarterly, 1, 4, p.344

(f) Review of Evil and the Concept of God by E.Madden & P.Hare, Philosophy, 44, 168, pp.160-61

(g) Review of Theological Science by T.F.Torrance, The Expository Times, 81, 2, pp.57-8

(h) Review of Death and Immortality by J.Pieper, Birmingham Post, November 15, p.14

(i) Uskonnon Filosofia (Finnish translation of Philosophy of Religion) Helsinki

1970

(a) ed. Classical and Contemporary Readings in the Philosophy of Religion, (2nd ed.), Prentice Hall, New Jersey

(b) "Towards a Christian Theology of Death", in Dying, Death and Disposal, ed. G.Cope, SPCK, London, pp.8-25

(c) "A New Form of Theistic Argument", Proceedings of the XIVth International Congress of Philosophy, Vienna, Vol 5, pp.336-41

(d) "The Reconstruction of Christian Belief for Today and Tomorrow: I", Theology 73, 602, pp.339-45

(e) "The Reconstruction of Christian Belief for Today and Tomorrow: II", Theology, 73, 603, pp.399-405

(f) Review of Experience of God by J.Smith, Philosophy, 45, 171, p.74

(g) Review of The Moment of Truth by L.Boros, Scottish Journal of Theology, 23, 1, pp.107-08

(h) Review of The Foundations of Belief by L.Dewart, Theology Today, 27, 1, pp.111-13

(i) Review of Do Religious Claims Make Sense? by S.Brown, Philosophical Books, 11, 2, pp.3-4

(j) Review of The Five Ways by A.Kenny, Mind, 79, 315, pp.467-69

(k) "Freedom and the Irenaean Theodicy Again", The Journal of Theological Studies, ns 21, 2, pp.419-22

(l) Review of The Elusive Mind by H.D.Lewis, The Expository Times, 81, 11, p.335

(m) Review of The Mind/Brain Identity Theory ed. by C.Borsch, The Expository Times, 82, 2, pp.56-7

(n) Review of The Theology of Death by K.Rahner, The Journal of Religious Studies (Punjabi University), 2, 1, pp.161-63

(o) Filosofia de Religiao (Portugese translation of Philosophy of Religion) Zahar Editores, Rio de Janeiro

1971

(a) Arguments for the Existence of God, Macmillan, London; Herder & Herder, New York

(b) "Faith, Evidence, Coercion Again", Australasian Journal of Philosophy, 49, 1, pp.78-81

(c) "Religious Language - Cognitive or Non-Cognitive?", Anviksiki (Banares Hindu University), 3, 3 & 4, pp.131-46

(d) "Reincarnation: A Critical Examination of One Form of Reincarnation Theory", The Journal of Religious Studies (Punjabi University), 3, 1, pp.56-69

(e) "The Idea of Rebirth - A Western Approach", Indian

222

Philosophical Annual (University of Madras), pp.89-101

(f) "Towards a Global Theology" (Pamphlet), All Faiths For One Race, Birmingham (reprint of 1970e), pp.1-7

(g) Review of Theism and Empiricism by A.Gibson, Philosophy, 46, 178, p.365

(h) Review of Grace and Common Life by D.Harned, The Journal of Religious Studies (Punjabi University), 3, 4, pp.186-88

(i) "Some Recapitulation Theories of Immortality", The Visva-Bharati Journal of Philosophy, 7, 2, pp.60-7

1972

(a) Biology and the Soul, Eddington Memorial Lecture, Cambridge University Press, Cambridge

(b) "Comment" on "Hick, Necessary Being, and the Cosmological Argument" by D.Duff-Forbes, Canadian Journal of Philosophy, 1, 4, pp.485-87

(c) "The Christian View of Other Faiths", The Expository Times, 84, 2, pp.36-9

(d) "Mr Clarke's Resurrection Also", Sophia, 11, 3, pp.1-3

(e) Foreword to Reflective Faith by A.Farrer, SPCK, London, pp.xiii-xv

(f) Review of Clement of Alexandria's Treatment of the Problem of Evil by W.Floyd, Religious Studies, 8, 2, pp.175-76

(g) Review of Meaning and Method by A.Nygren, The Times Literary Supplement, November 24, p.1434

(h) Religionsfilosofi (Swedish translation of Philosophy of Religion) Almquist & Wiksell, Stockholm

1973

(a) God and the Universe of Faiths, Macmillan, London

(b) Philosophy of Religion (2nd ed.), Prentice Hall, New Jersey

(c) "Resurrection Worlds and Bodies", Mind, 82, 327, pp.409-12

(d) "Coherence and the God of Love Again", Journal of Theological Studies, 24, 2, pp.522-8

223

(e) "Christianity and Reincarnation", in Sri Aurobindo: A Garland of Tributes, ed. A.Basu, Sri Aurobindo Research Academy, Pondicherry, pp.65-9

(f) Review of Science and Sentiment in America by M.White, Theology Today, 30, 1, pp.88-92

(g) Review of Essays in the Philosophy of Religion by H.H.Price, Religious Studies, 9, 2, pp.238-41

(h) Review of The Edges of Language by P.van Buren, Journal of Theological Studies, 24, 2, pp.633-35

(i) Review of Reality and Value by A.Ewing, Times Literary Supplement, December 28, p.1594

(j) "Christians and Colour", Birmingham Council for Christian Education, New Initiative Papers, 1

1974

(a) ed. Truth and Dialogue, Sheldon Press, London; Westminster Press, Philadelphia

(b) Preface to Faith and Knowledge, reprint in Fontana, London edition

(c) "Christ's Uniqueness", Reform, October, pp.18-9

1975

(a) "John Hick Replies", Reform, January, p.5

(b) "Whatever Path Men Choose is Mine", The Modern Churchman, 18, 1 & 2, pp.8-17

(c) "The Lordship of Christ", Carr's Lane Journal, April, pp.8-17

(d) "Christians and Other Faiths", New Initiative Papers, 3, Birmingham Council of Christian Churches

(e) "On Multi-Religious Birmingham", One World, June, pp.7-9

(f) "Philosophy, Religions, and Human Unity", in Philosophy - Theory and Practice (University of Madras), pp.462-71, and "Comments", pp.12-21, 162-63, 344-46

(g) Review of Positivism and Christianity by K.Klein, Philosophical Books, 16, 3, pp.27-9

(h) "The Christian church and people of other religions", The Times, October 4, p.16

(i) "Changing Views on the Uniqueness of Christ", The Times, October 11, p.14

(j) "Seeing the pattern in a puzzle picture", Times Educational Supplement, December 12, p.30

(k) Review of Evil, Karma and Reincarnation by G.C.Nayak, Religion, 5, Autumn, pp.175-76

(l) Review of Why Does Evil Exist? by C.Connelan, Religious Studies, 11, 4, pp.494-95

(m) "Christians and the Uniqueness of Christ - A Reply", unpublished manuscript, pp.1-7

1976

(a) Death and Eternal Life, Collins, London; Harper & Row, New York

(b) "Is There a God?", Radio Times, April 17-23, p.17

(c) "Education and the Law in Birmingham - a Comment", Learning for Living, Summer, pp.135-36

(d) Review of The Forgotten Dream by P.Baelz, Reconciliation, June, pp.53-4

(e) Review of The Resurrection of Man by M.Perry, The Christian Parapsychologist, 1, 4, p.59

(f) Review of The Transcendent Unity of Religions by F.Schuon, The Ecumenical Review, 28, 3, pp.369-70

(g) Review of Reason and Belief by B.Blanshard, The Journal of Religion, 56, 4, pp.400-03

1977

(a) Evil and the God of Love (2nd ed.), Macmillan, London; Harper & Row, New York

(b) The Centre of Christianity (2nd ed. of Christianity at the Centre), SCM, London

(c) ed. The Myth of God Incarnate, SCM, London; Westminster Press, Philadelphia

225

(d) "Mystical Experience as Cognition", in Mystics and Scholars, eds. H.Coward & T.Penelhum, Alfred Laurier University Press, Waterloo, pp.41-56, 61

(e) "Incarnation", letter, Theology, 80, 675, pp.204-06

(f) "Eschatological Verification Reconsidered", Religious Studies, 13, 2, pp.189-92

(g) "Christian Theology and Inter-Religious Dialogue", World Faiths, 103, pp.2-19

(h) "The New Nazism of the National Front and National Party", pamphlet, All Faiths for One Race, Birmingham

(i) "Remarks" on the problem of evil, in Reason and Religion, ed. S.Brown, Cornell University Press, New Jersey and London, pp.122-28

(j) New preface to reissue God and the Universe of Faiths, Collins, Fount, London

(k) Review of Evil, Suffering and Religion by B.Hebblethwaite, Learning for Living, Summer, pp.187-88

(l) Review of The Truth of God Incarnate ed. by M.Green, Reform, November, p.25

(m) Review of Believe it or Not by G.Moore, Faith and Unity, 21, 3, pp.60-1

1978

(a) "Christian Theology and Interfaith Dialogue", in The Frontiers of Human Knowledge, ed. T.Segerstedt, Almquist & Wicksell, Stockholm, pp.1-14

(b) "Living in a Multi-Cultural Society: Practical Reflections of a Theologian", Expository Times, 89, 4, pp.100-04

(c) "The Challenge to the Churches", in The Chosen Race: Christians and the Rise of the New Fascism, SCM, London, pp.22-4

(d) Foreword to The Meaning and End of Religion by W.Cantwell Smith, SPCK, London; Harper & Row, New York, pp.ix-xviii

(e) "Racism - the Church's Responsibility", Regina, 48, 3, pp.8-9

(f) "Not troubled by more orthodox", Religion and Freedom, July, p.16

(g) "The Bible and Race", pamphlet, All Faiths for One Race, Birmingham

(h) Chairman's Report, All Faiths For One Race News, October

(i) Review of God, Freedom and Evil by A.Plantinga, Religious Studies, 14, 3, pp.407-09

(j) "Christ and the Universe of Faiths", The Seeker, Autumn, pp.14-23

(k) "Present and Future Life", Harvard Theological Review, 71, 1/2, pp.1-15

(l) Dood en Eewwig Leven (Dutch translation of Death and Eternal Life), Uitgeverij Jelmond, Helmond; Uitgeverij Orion, Bruges

(m) "Ernst Troeltsch and the 'Copernican Revolution' in the theology of religions", unpublished manuscript, December 1, pp.1-6

(n) Faith and Knowledge (2nd ed.), Collins, Fount Paperback, London (reprint of 1966 issue)

1979

(a) Foreword to An Introduction to Buddhist Psychology by P.de Silva, Macmillan, London; Barnes & Noble, New York, pp.ix-x

(b) Foreword to The Problem of Self in Buddhism and Christianity, by L. de Silva, Macmillan, London; Barnes & Noble, New York, pp.ix-x

(c) "Christianity and Race in Britain Today", pamphlet, All Faiths for One Race, Birmingham

(d) "Pilgrimage in Theology", Epworth Review, 6, 2, pp.73-8

(e) "Is there a Doctrine of the Incarnation?" (pp.47-50); "Evil and Incarnation" (pp.77-84); and "A Response to Hebblethwaite" (pp.192-94), in Incarnation and Myth: the Debate Continued, ed. M.Goulder, SCM, London

(f) "Black and white as well as green and pleasant" (book reviews), Reform, July/August, pp.7-8

(g) New Year Messages, Reconciliation Quarterly, 9, pp.23-4

(h) Review of Religious Encounters with Death ed. by F.Reynolds & E.Waugh, The Journal of Religion, 59, 4, pp.495-96

(i) <u>Evil</u> <u>and</u> <u>the</u> <u>God</u> <u>of</u> <u>Love</u>, Collins, Fount Paperbacks, London (reprint of 1977 issue)

1980

(a) ed. with B.Hebblethwaite, <u>Christianity</u> <u>and</u> <u>Other</u> <u>Religions</u>, Fount, Collins, London

(b) "Towards a Philosophy of Religious Pluralism", <u>Neue</u> <u>Zeitschrift</u> <u>für</u> <u>Systematische</u> <u>Theologie</u> <u>und</u> <u>Religionsphilosophie</u>, 22, 2, pp.131-49

(c) <u>God</u> <u>Has</u> <u>Many</u> <u>Names</u>, Macmillan, London

(d) "Apartheid Observed", pamphlet, All Faiths For One Race, Birmingham

(e) "Life after Death", <u>Epworth</u> <u>Review</u>, 7, 1, pp.58-63

1981

(a) "Sketch for a Global Theory of Religious Knowledge" in <u>Verdag</u> <u>Och</u> <u>Evighet:</u> <u>Festkrift</u> <u>till</u> <u>Hampus</u> <u>Lyttkens</u>, eds. B.Hanson, J.Hemberg & C.Stenquist, Doxa, Lund, pp.101-07.

(b) "Pluralism and the Reality of the Transcendent", <u>The</u> <u>Christian</u> <u>Century</u>, January 21, pp.45-8

(c) "On Grading Religions", <u>Religious</u> <u>Studies</u>, 17, 4, pp.451-67

(d) "Christology in an Age of Religious Pluralism" (pp.4-9) & "Response to James Moulder" (pp.24-6), <u>Journal</u> <u>of</u> <u>Theology</u> <u>for</u> <u>Southern</u> <u>Africa</u>, June, 35

(e) "An Irenaean Theodicy", in <u>Encountering</u> <u>Evil</u>, ed. S.Davis, T & T Clark, Edinburgh

1982

(a) <u>God</u> <u>Has</u> <u>Many</u> <u>Names</u> (US ed.), Westminster Press, Philadelphia

(c) "Is there Only One Way to God", <u>Theology</u>, 85, 703, pp.4-7

1983

(a) <u>The</u> <u>Second</u> <u>Christianity</u> (3rd ed. of <u>Christianity</u> <u>at</u> <u>the</u> <u>Centre</u>), SCM, London

(b) The Philosophy of Religion (3rd ed.), Prentice Hall, New Jersey

(c) "The Theology of Pluralism", Theology, 86, 713, pp.335-40

(d) "On Conflicting Religious Truth-Claims", Religious Studies, 19, 4, pp. 458-92

(e) with M.Goulder, Why Believe in God?, SCM, London

(f) Articles in A New Dictionary of Christian Theology, eds. J.Bowden & A.Richardson, SCM, London. Articles: "Arguments for the Existence of God", "Life After Death", "Reincarnation", "Theocentricity".

1984

(a) "Religious Pluralism and Absolute Claims", in Religious Pluralism, ed. L.Rouner, Notre Dame University Press, Indiana, pp.193-213

(b) Foreword to Gandhi's Religious Thought by M.Chatterjee, Macmillan, London; University of Notre Dame Press, Indiana

(c) "Seeing-As and Religious Experience", in Proceedings of the 8th International Wittgenstein Symposium, 15 to 21 August, 1983, Part 2, Holder-Pichley-Tempsky, Wien, pp.45-52

(d) "A Recent Development within Christian Monotheism", in Christians, Muslims and Jews, eds. D.Kerr & D.Cohn-Sherbok, Centre for the Study of Islam and Christian-Muslim Relations, Birmingham, pp.1-20

(e) "Jesus and Mohammed", in Christians, Muslims and Jews, eds. D.Kerr & D.Cohn-Sherbok, Centre for the Study of Islam and Christian-Muslim Relations, pp.222-28

(f) "The Foundation of Christianity: Jesus or the Apostolic Message?", a review article of The Point of Christology by S.Ogden, The Journal of Religion, 64, 3, pp.363-69

(g) "The Philosophy of World Religions", Scottish Journal of Theology, 37, 2, pp.229-36

(h) Review of Immortality or Extinction? by P. & L. Badham, The Journal of Religion, 64, 3, p.410

(i) Review of A History of the Future: A Study of the Four Major Eschatologies by C.Hong, Journal of Ecumenical Studies, 21, 2, p.369

(j) "A Philosophy of Religious Pluralism", in The World's Religious Traditions: Current Perspectives in Religious Studies. Essays in Honour of Wilfred Cantwell Smith, ed. F.Whaling, T & T Clark, Edinburgh, pp.147-64

1985

(a) Problems of Religious Pluralism, Macmillan, London; St Martin's Press, New York

(b) Foreword to Scripture from a Comparative Religionist Point of View by W.C.Smith, Claremont Graduate School, Claremont

(c) ed. with H.Askari, The Experience of Religious Diversity, Gower, Aldershot

(d) Gott und seine vielen Namen (German translation of God Has Many Names), Akademische Bibliothek, Altenberge

1986

(a) "The Absoluteness of Christianity", unpublished manuscript, pp.1-39

(b) Review of Faith and Rationality, eds. A.Plantinga & N.Wolterstoff, Journal of Religion, 66, 1, pp.84-5

Unpublished letters from John Hick to the author cited in text:

May 1984

July 1984

October 1985

November 1985

December 1985

Note on Unpublished Manuscripts:

1975m: A Reply to Lipner 1975. Submitted to and rejected by the Scottish Journal of Theology

1978m: A report written for W.Tomm, undertaking post-graduate studies with Hick at Birmingham University.

1986a: to form part of a collection edited by J.Hick & P.Knitter, forthcoming. Originally a paper presented at the Blaisdell International Conference, California, March 1986

INDEX

ABOUT THE AUTHOR

Dr Gavin D'Costa is an Indian Roman Catholic theologian. He did his first degree at Birmingham University and studied with Professor John Hick. He then went on to Cambridge Univeristy where he undertook his Ph.D in the Divinity School under the supervision of Dr Julius Lipner. He has lectured in India, the United States and Canada and is currently lecturer at the West London Institute of Higher Education. He has written numerous articles and contributed to a number of books. His first book, Theology and Religious Pluralism was published by Basil Blackwell, Oxford/New York, 1986. He is secretary to the British Council of Churches Committee for Relations with People of Other Faiths (Theological Issues Consultative Group) and a member of the Roman Catholic Committee for Other Faiths (England and Wales). Dr D'Costa is now researching a book on the theology of Jewish-Christian relations.

239